AMERICAN ECONOMIC HISTORY

AMERICAN ECONOMIC HISTORY

FROM ABUNDANCE TO CONSTRAINT

JOHN O'SULLIVAN
Florida Atlantic University

EDWARD F. KEUCHEL
Florida State University

A GROLIER COMPANY

FRANKLIN WATTS
New York / London / Toronto / Sydney

Library of Congress Cataloging in Publication Data

O'Sullivan, John, 1939–
 American economic history.

 Bibliography: p.
 Includes index.
 1. United States—Economic conditions.
I. Keuchel, Edward F., joint author.   II. Title.
HC103.083   330.973   80-25339

ISBN   0-531-05630-9 (pbk.)

Franklin Watts
730 Fifth Avenue
New York, New York 10019

TO MARJORIE AND MARY

PREFACE

American Economic History: From Abundance to Constraint is a relatively short text which embodies historian Carl Becker's call to "search for a usable past." The principle of selection in choosing which aspects of American economic growth to emphasize consists of focusing on those lines of development that most directly converge in the economy of the 1970s and 1980s. With those considerations we have devoted one-half of the text to twentieth-century American economic history.

The interpretive theme lies in tracing the historical emergence of an economy of abundance which, in recent years, has encountered a variety of constraints. From their historical beginnings, the American people have been, in David Potter's phrase, a "people of plenty," laying claim to enormous lands rich in resources. Three-and-a-half centuries of economic growth and industrialization have transformed that plentiful environment into the most productive economic system in the world. In the past decade, however, widespread doubts and anxieties have emerged concerning the future pathway of the American economy. The long-standing focus on abundance is giving way to a concern about scarcity of resources and a growing awareness of global ecology.

American Economic History: From Abundance to Constraint seeks to provide students with an insight into the historical process of American economic development. Certain key components, e.g., energy and technology, are explored in each time period. Every chapter contains a profile (Samuel Gompers, Andrew Mellon, etc.) that presents a more detailed portrait of significant figures. The text covers the entirety of the 1970s, examining recent economic trends such as the energy crisis, affirmative action programs, difficulties in key industries (steel and automobiles) at some length. Our goal, in short, is to encourage college students to develop an historical awareness of the economic dimension of American life and to gain an essential background to weigh current economic issues.

ACKNOWLEDGMENTS

I would like to thank William E. Leuchtenburg, whose teaching and guidance during my years as a graduate student provided me with a sense of the craft of history. My colleagues in the History Department at Florida Atlantic University have been a continuing source of intellectual stimulation, and the departmental secretary, Thelma Spangler, once again retained her title as the world's fastest and most meticulous typist. Finally, my deepest debt of gratitude is owed to my wife Marjorie. Her keen editorial eye and unflagging support made the rough ways smooth.

J. O'S.

I am grateful to my former teachers, James C. Malin and Paul W. Gates, and to my colleague, John Hebron Moore, for his suggestions and encouragement.

E. F. K.

We would also like to thank Will Davison, executive editor of the college division of Franklin Watts, who initially recommended we do this book and whose gentle prodding helped bring it to completion.

CONTENTS

ONE / EARLY BEGINNINGS TO 1740   **1**

THE "FIRST AMERICANS"   1
    Agricultural Contributions   2

EUROPEAN COLONIZATION   3

ENGLISH MERCHANTS AND COLONIZATION   5

MERCANTILISM   6

THE ESTABLISHMENT OF ENGLISH COLONIES IN AMERICA   7

PROFILE: Two Early Colonists—John Smith and   7
           John Winthrop

RESOURCES OF THE ENGLISH COLONIES   9

LABOR IN COLONIAL AMERICA   10

COLONIAL AGRICULTURE   12
    New England   13
    Middle Colonies   13
    Southern Colonies   14

HOUSEHOLD MANUFACTURING   15

COMMERCIAL INDUSTRIES   16

AMERICAN CAPITALISM   17

TWO / REVOLUTION AND INDEPENDENCE: 1740–1783   19

MERCANTILISM AND THE AMERICAN REVOLUTION   20
    The Old Colonial System   20
    The New Colonial System   22
    The Proclamation of 1763   23
    Revenue Acts   23
    The Intolerable Acts   25

PROFILE: Adam Smith and The Wealth of Nations   26

DID THE BRITISH EXPLOIT THE AMERICAN COLONIES?   28

THE AMERICAN ECONOMY DURING THE REVOLUTION   29
    Financing the War   30
    Economic Effects of the Revolution   31

THREE / BEGINNINGS OF A NATIONAL ECONOMY: 1783–1815   33

FOREIGN AND DOMESTIC TRADE   33

SHAYS' REBELLION   35

LAND ISSUES AND WESTWARD EXPANSION   36
    The Northwest Ordinance   37

A NEW GOVERNMENT UNDER THE CONSTITUTION   38
    Charles A. Beard and the Economic Interpretation   39
    of the Constitution

THE FEDERALIST ECONOMIC PROGRAM   40

PROFILE: American Technology—   42
    Oliver Evans and Eli Whitney

JEFFERSONIAN AGRARIANISM   45

FEDERALISM AND THE JUDICIARY   47

FOREIGN RELATIONS   49

FOUR / A DEVELOPING NATIONAL ECONOMY: 1815–1840   51

AGRICULTURE   51
    Southern Agriculture   52

MANUFACTURING   53

PROFILE: Alexis de Tocqueville's America   56

TARIFFS   57

TRANSPORTATION 59
   Canals 60
   Turnpikes 62
   Railroads 63
   Ocean Transportation 63

GOVERNMENT LAND POLICIES 64

GOVERNMENT AND BANKING 66

LABOR 68

PANIC OF 1837 69

FIVE / AN ACCELERATING ECONOMY: 1840–1865 71

THE TAKE-OFF STAGE IN ECONOMIC GROWTH 72

AGRICULTURAL TECHNOLOGY 72
   The Northeast 73

PROFILE: Cyrus Hall McCormick 74

   The West 75
   The South 76

SLAVERY 76

INDUSTRIAL GROWTH 78
   Internal Transportation 78
   Railroads 79
   Coal 80
   Bessemer Steel 81

TRANSCONTINENTAL RAILROADS 82

LABOR 84

IMMIGRATION 85

MECHANIZATION 86

THE CIVIL WAR 87
   Economic Comparison of the Union and the Confederacy 87
   King Cotton 88
   The Wartime Economy 89
   Financing the War 90
   The National Banking System 91
   Costs of the War 92

SIX / AMERICA'S RISE TO INDUSTRIAL POWER: 1865–1900 95

AGRICULTURE 97

TECHNOLOGY AND AGRICULTURE 97

REGIONAL SPECIALIZATION 98

RURAL UNREST 102
Farmers' Political Movements 104
Greenbackers 104
Farmers' Alliance 105
Populism 106
Free Silver 106

THE COMING OF BIG BUSINESS 108

THE INDUSTRIAL PROCESS 109

DISTRIBUTION AND MARKETING 110
Prototypes of Big Business: Steel and Oil 111

PROFILE: Andrew Carnegie and John D. Rockefeller— 111
Robber Barons or Industrial Statesmen?

IMMIGRATION AND URBANIZATION 115

LABOR 117

GOVERNMENT AND THE ECONOMY 119

SHERMAN ANTI-TRUST ACT 120

AMERICA AT THE END OF THE NINETEENTH CENTURY 120

SEVEN / AN EXPANDING INDUSTRIAL POWER: 1900–1913 123

AMERICA IN 1900 123

THE PROGRESSIVE MOVEMENT 124
Scientific Management 129
Labor 130

PROFILE: Samuel Gompers 131

THE PERFORMANCE OF THE AMERICAN ECONOMY: 1900–1913 134

TECHNOLOGY 135

EIGHT / REFORM AND WAR: 1913–1920 139

OVERVIEW 139

WILSON'S NEW FREEDOM AND TARIFF REFORM 140

BANKING REFORM 141

ANTI-TRUST 143

WORLD WAR I AND THE AMERICAN ECONOMY 144

PROFILE: Henry Ford 148

THE ECONOMIC AFTERMATH OF WORLD WAR I   **150**
    Labor   **151**

NINE / PROSPERITY AND COLLAPSE: 1920–1932   **155**

THE AMERICAN ECONOMY IN 1920   **157**

AGRICULTURE IN THE 1920s   **157**

GOVERNMENT AND BUSINESS   **159**

PROFILE: Andrew Mellon   **159**

ORGANIZED LABOR IN THE 1920s   **161**

THE PERFORMANCE OF THE ECONOMY IN THE 1920s   **163**

THE STOCK MARKET IN THE 1920s   **165**

THE SLIDE INTO THE GREAT DEPRESSION   **167**

GOVERNMENTAL RESPONSE TO THE ECONOMIC CRISIS   **169**

TEN / DEPRESSION AND WAR: 1933–1945   **173**

PROFILE: The Unemployed   **175**

LEGISLATION DURING THE HUNDRED DAYS   **177**
    Tennessee Valley Authority   **178**
    National Recovery Administration   **178**
    Agricultural Adjustment Act   **180**
    Bank and Stock Exchange Regulations   **181**
    Legislation Affecting Farmers   **184**
    Social Security Legislation   **185**

ECONOMIC RECOVERY   **186**

ORGANIZED LABOR   **188**

PERSPECTIVE ON THE NEW DEAL   **190**

THE IMPACT OF WAR   **191**

**ELEVEN / RECONVERSION AND THE RISE OF
A CONSUMER CULTURE: 1945–1960**   **197**

POSTWAR AMERICA   **197**
    Housing   **198**
    Automobiles   **199**

RECONVERSION   **199**

ECONOMY AND THE GOVERNMENT   **200**

TAFT-HARTLEY ACT   **202**

DEFENSE SPENDING   **202**

THE CONSUMER CULTURE   **204**

THE TECHNETRONIC ERA   **205**

THE WORK FORCE   **206**

ENERGY   **208**

PROFILE: The Automobile Industry in the 1950s   **209**

AGRICULTURE   **211**

THE PERFORMANCE OF THE AMERICAN ECONOMY: 1945–1960   **213**

TWELVE / FROM AFFLUENCE TO CONSTRAINT: 1960–1980s   **217**

POPULATION   **218**

ECONOMIC GROWTH   **219**

MANAGING THE ECONOMY   **219**

FEDERAL SPENDING   **225**

DEFENSE SPENDING   **225**

SOCIAL WELFARE EXPENDITURES   **227**

ENERGY   **231**
   Oil   **231**
   Coal   **233**
   Nuclear Energy   **235**
   Other Energy Sources   **239**

THE AUTOMOBILE INDUSTRY   **240**

THE STEEL INDUSTRY   **242**

GOVERNMENT REGULATION   **243**

PRODUCTIVITY   **244**

AGRICULTURE   **245**

LABOR   **246**

PROFILE: Women Workers   **246**

OVERVIEW   **250**

REFERENCES AND SUGGESTED READINGS   **253**

INDEX   **263**

LIST OF TABLES

Table 1:1	Estimated Total Population and Black Population of Colonial America	11
Table 5:1	Immigration to the United States: 1820–1859	85
Table 6:1	Immigration to the United States: 1865–1914	116
Table 7:1	Value of Exports: 1900–1913	135
Table 7:2	Growth of the Automotive Industry: 1900–1913	136
Table 8:1	Federal Government Finances: 1916–1919	147
Table 8:2	Economic Performance: 1913–1920	147
Table 10:1	Unemployment: 1929–1945	176
Table 10:2	Gross National Product, Federal Government Expenditures, and National Debt: 1940–1945	195
Table 11:1	National Defense and Veterans Benefit Outlays as Percentages of Total Federal Spending and GNP: 1945–1960	203
Table 11:2	Labor Union Membership as Percentage of Total Labor Force and Nonagricultural Employment: 1945–1960	207
Table 11:3	Energy Consumption by Major Source: 1940–1960	209
Table 11:4	Passenger Car Factory Sales and Wholesale Value: 1950–1960	210
Table 11:5	GNP in Current and Constant Dollars and Real Growth Rate, 1945–1960	213
Table 11:6	Federal Budget Receipts and Outlays, Fiscal Years 1950–1960	215
Table 12:1	Consumer Price Index: 1967–1979	220
Table 12:2	Federal Spending and Surpluses or Deficits: 1960–1979	223
Table 12:3	National Defense Expenditures as Percentages of Total Federal Spending and GNP: 1960–1979	224
Table 12:4	Energy Consumption by Major Source: 1960–1977	232
Table 12:5	Women in the Civilian Labor Force: 1960–1979	247

LIST OF ILLUSTRATIONS

OLIVER EVANS'S MECHANIZED MILL.   44

CENTRAL PACIFIC RAILROAD AND UNION PACIFIC RAILROAD JOIN
LINES AT PROMONTORY POINT, UTAH, MAY 10, 1869.   83

BREAKER BOYS AT A MINE IN PENNSYLVANIA, 1911.   125

SAMUEL GOMPERS, 1904.   132

MCCORMICK REAPER STILL IN USE IN 1916.   156

MACHINERY BURIED BY DUST STORM, 1936.   182

SAN JOAQUIN VALLEY, CALIFORNIA, 1940.   183

GIANT GEARS FOR AMERICAN WARSHIPS.   192

WOMEN WORKERS AT CALIFORNIA AIRCRAFT PLANT.   193

THREE MILE ISLAND NUCLEAR POWER PLANT.   236

PRESIDENT JIMMY CARTER EXAMINING THREE MILE ISLAND
CONTROL ROOM, APRIL 1, 1979.   237

AMERICAN ECONOMIC HISTORY

ONE

EARLY BEGINNINGS TO 1740

THE "FIRST AMERICANS"

Although Europeans looked upon the world Columbus discovered as new, it was already the home of native peoples they came to call Indians. A Spanish missionary, Fray José de Acosta, speculated in 1590 that the Indians had originated in Asia and had traveled to North America by means of a northern land route some 1,000 years before Columbus. In 1876 geologist C. C. Abbott uncovered some stone artifacts, which he estimated to be 20,000 to 30,000 years old, in a glacial moraine in the Delaware River Valley. A few years later these artifacts were found to be the remains of recent Indians, and scholars returned to the older view that Indians had occupied North America only some 1,000 years prior to Columbus. In 1927 these assumptions came under challenge when human stone tools were found with the bones of an extinct bison near Folsom, New Mexico. This evidence received reinforcement a few years later when, in an excavation near Clovis, New Mexico, a stone spear point was discovered among the bones of a mammoth known to have been extinct since the last ice age. Recent radioactive-carbon dating now places the age of the Folsom discovery around 10,500 years ago and the Clovis materials around 11,500 years ago. Currently scholars are divided, with one group claiming that North America was not peopled prior to some 12,000 years ago, whereas the opposing group contends that the continent had human inhabitants at least 50,000 or even 100,000 years ago.

Whatever conclusion this scientific controversy ultimately arrives at, it serves to remind us that the area of the present United States had a history of human occupancy long before European settlement. Moreover, these early peoples had an influence upon the economic activities of later European settlers, particularly in the realm of agriculture where corn, white potatoes, beans, pumpkins and squashes, tomatoes, and other important foods were all "gifts" of the New World.

Agricultural Contributions

Corn has played a substantial role in American economic history. The Indians cultivated it in areas that are presently parts of Peru, Mexico, and the eastern half of the United States. Corn required less labor to raise than many of the other basic cereal grains. Frequently the first crop of the American pioneer, it soon became the most important grain for human and animal food. Corn is used today primarily as a livestock feed, but may take on increased importance as a source of alcohol for fuel in the future.

The white potato quickly achieved an impact on the world's economy and has been credited as the single most important factor in the population boom of Europe in the eighteenth century. Native to the Andes Mountains of South America, it was introduced into Spain in the mid-sixteenth century. Potato cultivation spread throughout Europe, and plant disease among the crop in the 1840s prompted large-scale migration of Germans and Irish to the United States. The potato continues to be an important human food and stock feed.

The common string bean and kidney bean, variations of the same original species, are probably the oldest plant native to the United States. Early explorers to the New World found them cultivated in all areas. Brought back by the Spanish to Europe, they became an important vegetable food.

The Indians grew squashes and pumpkins over large geographical areas of the New World, and Columbus made mention of them on his voyage of 1492. De Soto in Florida and Cartier in Canada both noted the large crops of pumpkins, squashes, and cucumbers grown by the Indians.

The tomato, widely cultivated by the Aztecs, met with suspicion on its introduction into Europe by the Spanish as the plant resembled the poisonous mandragora, or mandrake. Although the Spanish soon accepted the fruit, many northern Europeans treated it as an ornamental. From the late sixteenth century on, the tomato increasingly became part of the culinary art of Spain, Italy, France, and the rest of Europe. It eventually was one of the first agricultural products processed by the commercial canning industry of the United States during the nineteenth century.

Along with these foods, tobacco and cotton emerged as economically important farm products of the New World. Columbus found tobacco cultivated in the West Indies on his voyage of 1492, and other explorers found extensive crops of the plant from Brazil to the St. Lawrence. By the mid-sixteenth century tobacco had become established as an expensive luxury item in Europe. Promoters of smoking tobacco listed it as a cure for almost every known disease, while opponents condemned it as unhealthy. The Portuguese in Brazil cultivated tobacco as early as 1534, and by 1548 some sixteen settlements in Brazil were growing tobacco destined for Europe, China, and Japan. John Rolfe is credited with introducing tobacco cultivation in the Jamestown settlement in 1612. The first crop was marketed in England in 1614, and by 1627 the exportation of Virginia tobacco topped 500,000 pounds. Cotton, eventually to become a major staple of American agriculture, had been cultivated as early as the 1540s by the Indians of the Southwest, according to Coronado. English settlers in Virginia grew it from the late seventeenth century onward, but cotton did not become a major commercial crop until after the invention of the cotton gin by Eli Whitney in 1793.

EUROPEAN COLONIZATION

As important as these agricultural gifts of the New World became, they were not the primary goal of the early explorers and colonists.

Columbus came in search of the "gold roofs of Cipango" (Japan), and precious metals proved the lure for the Spanish, French, Portuguese, English, and other colonial nations. The gold of the Incas and the Aztecs provided much of the capital for the large-scale economic expansion of Western Europe in the sixteenth century. In addition to gold and silver, the European nations looked upon colonies as a source of raw materials not found in the home country and as a market for manufactures. The European settlements in North America during the sixteenth and seventeenth centuries were a part of the general European competition for colonies. In the sixteenth century the Spanish established settlements in Mexico, the West Indies, the southwestern part of the present United States, and Florida. St. Augustine, Florida, was settled in 1565, well before the English settlement at Jamestown in 1607 or the French settlement at Quebec in 1609.

Spanish control of the gold and silver mines of the New World gave Spain a considerable economic advantage in the sixteenth century. Mercantilism, the name later given to the economic philosophy of this period, stressed that the true measure of a nation's wealth and economic power lay in the amount of gold and silver it possessed. Spain, however, relied so heavily upon her gold and silver mines in the New World that a strong system of international trade, comparable to that of other European nations, never developed.

The French sought their empire to the north and established settlements along the St. Lawrence River and into the region of the Great Lakes. The economic base of New France differed substantially from that of New Spain. The French never found gold, but earned a measure of wealth in the fur trade. At its height, the French empire of North America covered half of present Canada plus the Mississippi Valley.

England came late into the European competition for colonies, and indeed, prior to about 1350, England played a minor role in the economy of Europe. Although England had a population only about half as large as that of Spain and about one-fourth as large as that of France, it experienced, during the Elizabethan era, a serious problem of overpopulation. The breakdown of the manorial system in Europe produced significant economic changes in England. As industry and trade expanded in the developing towns of Europe, a demand grew for fine quality woolen garments. England was well-suited for sheep-raising, and English landowners met the demand for more wool by "enclosing" (fencing in agricultural land) in order to raise more sheep.

Unemployment rose in agricultural areas. The Crown tried to check the enclosure movement, but met resistance from landowners profiting from high rents and merchants benefiting from the wool trade. As England shifted to exporting woolen cloth rather than raw wool, the developing textile industry absorbed some of the surplus population. Colonization offered the possibility of further alleviating the problem.

ENGLISH MERCHANTS AND COLONIZATION

The sale of woolens brought gold and silver to England, which in turn supported additional manufacturing and trade. Both the merchant classes and royal officials saw that colonies would provide markets for English goods as well as an outlet for surplus population. English merchants became actively involved in commercial expansion through colonization.

Before the development of the woolen industry the principal merchants of England, called the Merchants of the Staple, exported raw wool. As woolen cloth replaced raw wool, the merchants handling this trade formed an organization called the Company of Merchant Adventurers. In this association the merchants owned their own ships, but agreed to abide by the trade regulations imposed by the company. From about 1550 on, these merchant adventurers were increasingly supplemented by joint-stock companies operating under royal charter and possessing monopolistic trading privileges within particular regions. The Russia or Moscovy Company received a charter in 1555, the Levant or Turkey Company in 1558, and the East India Company, one of the largest, in 1600.

The joint-stock company operated on the principle of opening membership to all investors who purchased shares, rather than limiting it to ship-owning merchants. This arrangement proved well-suited for the promotion of foreign trade as such ventures were extremely hazardous in an age of sailing ships and uncharted seas. If a merchant risked his entire fortune on a voyage and it failed, he suffered ruin. A joint-stock venture enabled a large number of investors to share this risk, and the relatively small minimum share purchases widened the potential investor pool. Joint-stock companies offered an excellent inducement to foreign trade investment and enabled England to take a leadership position, not in the older established trade in Europe, but in the development of commerce with the New World.

MERCANTILISM

The transition from a medieval to a modern economy produced an economic philosophy labeled "mercantilism" by eighteenth century economists. Mercantilism represented both a system of economic thought and an exercise in statecraft, a program of economic warfare for national gain. It reflected the values of an age of emerging nation-states and proved dominant during the years of England's rise to world power. Mercantilist thought focused on the central importance of a favorable balance of trade. It perceived the foreign trade of a nation in terms of an individual shopkeeper who profited when his sales exceeded his purchases. A nation, it taught, should likewise export more than it imported, with the profits serving to accumulate gold. Manufacturing lay at the heart of mercantilist thinking because it provided the main products for export. The tasks assigned to agriculture were to lessen imports by making the nation self-sufficient in food and to provide some of the raw materials for manufacturing.

Under the mercantilist system Parliament placed high tariff duties on foreign manufactures, thereby encouraging domestic production. Similar protection was accorded English agriculture through duties called "corn laws" designed to restrict the importation of foreign grains and wool. This program also fostered the development of a merchant marine so that English money would not have to go to foreign shipowners and merchants.

Colonies played a special role in mercantilist thought. Colonies might contain deposits of gold and silver. They also provided secure sources for raw materials and markets for manufactured goods. In addition, for a nation concerned about excessive population, colonies could siphon off the surplus. For a wide range of social classes colonial migration looked appealing. Paupers, vagabonds, and criminals could escape the disgrace of the old life in a new setting. Unemployed farm laborers and artisans saw opportunities for work. Small landowners and merchants, at a disadvantage in competing with larger operators in England, looked favorably on the possibilities in the New World.

Established English merchants anticipated new markets, and even the landowning gentry could establish estates for their younger sons who would not inherit the family lands.

THE ESTABLISHMENT OF ENGLISH COLONIES IN AMERICA

The first permanent English settlements in America were organized by joint-stock companies. Under a charter granted by King James I in 1606, the London Company received authority to settle in the southern tier, between the 34th and 38th parallels, and the Plymouth Company received access to the northern tier, between the 41st and 45th parallels. These grants resulted in the Jamestown settlement in 1607 and the Plymouth colony in 1620.

Many subsequent settlements came as the result of proprietary grants of large tracts of land to individuals such as William Penn and Lord Baltimore. Pennsylvania, Maryland, New Jersey, New Hampshire, and the Carolinas began as proprietary colonies.

The seizure of what had been New Sweden and New Netherland, subsequently named Delaware and New York, allowed an unbroken line of English settlement along the Atlantic coast from New England to the Carolinas. The founding of the last English colony in America, Georgia, in 1732 pushed the line farther south.

PROFILE:

Two Early Colonists—
John Smith
and John Winthrop

John Smith (1580–1631) pursued a range of occupations in his lifetime: soldier of fortune, explorer, author, and businessman. After serving as a mercenary against the Turks, he returned to England (c. 1604) and participated in the formation of the Virginia Company of London (1606). The over 700 original investors who joined Smith in this venture included knights, members of the landed gentry, peers of the realm, and assorted merchants, sea captains, professionals, and gentlemen. The royal charter granted the company approximately 10,000 square miles and included lucrative tax and tariff exemptions. The company was obligated to remit to the Crown a fifth of all gold and silver deposits it might find.

In December, 1606, under company sponsorship, 120 settlers set sail from England to establish a colony. Smith was one of the 104 survivors of the voyage who landed at Jamestown in May, 1607. He became a member of the governing council and provided valuable services securing food from the local Indians. Smith is best remembered because of his own, possibly apocryphal, account of being seized by the Indians and condemned to death, and then saved by Pocahontas, daughter of the chief, Powhatan. Smith realized earlier than most that the quest for gold in that region was illusory. Rather than the goldsmiths and refiners who had arrived, Smith preferred "a plaine soldier that can use a pickaxe and a spade." Smith was elected president by the council in 1608 but ran into political difficulties and returned to England a year later. In 1614 he sailed with an expedition along the New England coast and returned with a profitable cargo of fish and furs.

Smith proved one of the fortunate early colonists of Virginia—he survived. Of the 300 settlers who came during the first year and a half, only 80 were alive by the summer of 1609. That year a group of 600 arrived, including women and children for the first time. A year later only 60 survived. Indeed, during the first seventeen years of Jamestown's existence, about 10,000 Englishmen sailed to the colony, but only 1,275 were still alive in 1624. Indians, starvation, and disease posed constant threats to the settlers, with disease taking the greatest toll.

Virginia presented various levels of opportunities to the English. To the king, it was an area vast in wealth with a potential for future empire. To the stockholders of the company, it promised a windfall return on their investments. For potential colonists it was a chance for land and a better life. To the first generation of settlers, however, Jamestown was more than a dream unfulfilled; it proved a nightmare.

John Winthrop (1588–1649) shared the role of colonist with John Smith, but their experiences differed markedly in other respects. Born in the year of England's defeat of the Spanish Armada, Winthrop's life was significantly shaped by the changes affecting his country. His grandfather, Adam, had left farming during the enclosure movement and joined the cloth workers' guild as an apprentice. Eventually attaining the status of master clothier, he acquired a significant fortune and became part of the landed gentry. His grandson John, far from being an adventurer like John Smith, attended Cambridge, practiced law, and lived the life of a country squire. His Puritan religious convictions, however, prompted him to take an interest in the Massachusetts Bay Company, which planned to establish a colony in New England. Winthrop was elected governor of the company and sailed with 700 colonists in 1630, eventually settling at the present site of Boston. In his diary of the journey Winthrop remarked that his religious convictions were paramount in his decision to go to America, but he also mentioned that he looked upon the new land as holding great opportunity for his future.

Although the colony experienced problems and lost about 200 settlers during the first winter, it did not suffer the abject misery that plagued Jamestown. By the end of the second winter ample food was available and the Indian danger had been reduced by the Puritan army. The Bay colony quickly developed its commercial opportunities. Winthrop launched Massachusetts' first fishing boat in 1631, and cod soon became a staple trade item. Fur trade with the Indians proved lucrative as well. Increasingly New Englanders engaged in trade with their own ships, instead of depending on English merchants and ships. By the late eighteenth century New England merchants were shipping furs, cod, and other products to Europe and the West Indies, carrying slaves to the West Indies and Virginia, and manufacturing rum from molasses. John Winthrop might have been disappointed at the erosion of spiritual enthusiasm, but he probably would have been most impressed by the evidence of a thriving economic community.

RESOURCES OF THE ENGLISH COLONIES

For the land-hungry settlers of the English colonies the greatest treasure lay in the almost unlimited expanse of good land. The southern colonies (Virginia, Maryland, Georgia, and the Carolinas) proved ideal for tobacco, which found excellent market acceptance in Europe, while the middle area, the "bread colonies" (New York, New Jersey, and Pennsylvania), was suited for wheat and general agriculture. New England's soil could not measure up to that of the middle colonies except for limited sections such as the Connecticut Valley, but it could raise livestock, and the bountiful harvest of the sea offset the deficiencies of the land.

To seventeenth century Englishmen already witnessing a depletion of their nation's forests, the great forests of the New World looked inexhaustible. Wood was needed for construction, for fuel, and for the myriad manufactured goods of colonial society. Sailing ships required large amounts of wood, and America had the great oaks for hull structures and tall pines for masts. The pines, in addition, provided tar and pitch for sealing ships, as well as turpentine. Tar, pitch, and turpentine production (naval stores) proved valuable to the colonies, and the Carolina designation "tarheel" emerged from these activities. Shipbuilding became a major industry in New England.

Fur-bearing animals roamed the forests of the New World, and fur trapping achieved economic importance in New York and New England. Indeed, competition between fur traders and settlers became an issue in the settlement of the Northeast and on into the Great Lakes region. Merchants and others connected with the fur trade favored restriction of settlement to keep the forested regions in a natural state and suitable for fur-bearing animals. Land speculators, farmers, and others interested in settling an area posed a threat to the fur trade. Competition between the two groups caused strife throughout the colonial period.

The New World offered an abundant range of other natural resources. Almost all of the colonies contained deposits of iron ore, with no shortage of wood for charcoal to process it. Later generations would discover and develop the large quantities of coal, natural gas, and petroleum. Many of the resources, however, could be exploited with the available technology of the colonial era.

Numerous rivers and streams flowed into the Atlantic, offering harbors to sailing ships and water routes into the interior. In New England the "fall line," the change in elevation between the coastal plateau and the upland regions, lay near the coast presenting a range of water-power sites that became important in the early industrial development of the area. In the southern colonies the fall line ran as far as 150 miles inland, resulting in a large, relatively level tidewater area excellent for a plantation economy, with gentle rivers flowing to the coast providing access for the tobacco and other plantation crops to the shipping ports.

LABOR IN COLONIAL AMERICA

John Smith noted, in the first years of English settlement in America, that the country was long on land and short on men. Because, as

Richard Hofstadter remarked, "Never at any time in the colonial period was there a sufficient supply of voluntary labor, paying its own transportation and arriving masterless and free of debt, to meet the insatiable demands of the colonial economy," other solutions were sought. The resolution of the labor shortage problem came through the use of indentured servants and the development of slavery.

Close to one-half of all white immigrants to the colonies came as indentured servants. The indenture system allowed a prospective settler who lacked the means to immigrate to the colonies to pay for his transportation by contracting for a fixed period of labor. This term of service usually ran three or four years, but in some cases extended as long as seven. Upon completion of their service, indentured servants were frequently given a "headright" of land, generally fifty acres.

Not all settlers came to America voluntarily. There were cases of unscrupulous contract agents kidnapping children for the indentured servant system. In addition, convicts were often sentenced to servitude in the colonies, and many remained afterward. The estimated number of convicts shipped to all of England's New World colonies runs as high as 50,000, and approximately two-thirds of those arrived in Virginia and Maryland.

Slavery, however, provided the greatest number of involuntary laborers. The early development of slavery in the American colonies remains somewhat unclear: the first blacks arrived in Jamestown in 1619, but no slavery law appeared in the Virginia statute books until

TABLE 1:1
Estimated Total Population and Black Population of Colonial America

Year	Total Population	Black Population
1640	26,634	597
1660	75,058	2,920
1680	151,507	6,971
1700	250,888	27,817
1720	466,185	68,839
1740	905,563	150,024

Source: U.S. Department of Commerce, *Historical Statistics of the United States, Colonial Times to 1970.*

1661. Some of the early blacks to arrive in the colonies clearly came as indentured servants, but the evidence from court records and wills indicates that the condition of slavery had developed well before the enactment of the Virginia and Maryland slave laws of the early 1660s. The logic of the indenture system had been pushed to its dehumanizing limit. In indentured servitude, the master owned a fixed period of labor. In slavery, he owned the person.

In 1672 the Crown chartered the Royal African Company, granting it a monopoly of the English slave trade. Slavery developed more rapidly and intensively in the Caribbean colonies. Of the total of 9 to 10 million Africans transported to the New World, less than 500,000 came to the American colonies and states. Slavery existed in all the colonies until the Revolutionary period, but it took deepest root in the South where it became intimately tied to the agricultural system.

COLONIAL AGRICULTURE

During the seventeenth century, upwards of 95 percent of the settlers in the colonies engaged in farming. Indeed, agriculture remained the most important economic activity in America from the colonial beginnings until late in the nineteenth century. Agriculture not only furnished a basic livelihood for Americans, but also, through the philosophy of agrarianism, provided a central cultural theme in the nation's history. Agrarianism, which saw farming as the pivotal economic activity around which the good society could be organized, found its fullest expression in the democratic philosophy of Thomas Jefferson.

New England and the middle colonies developed diversified, and somewhat self-sufficient, economies centering on agriculture (corn, wheat, rye, oats, barley, buckwheat, livestock) and household manufacturers. Although New England offered the poorest soil region of the colonies, most residents still drew their living from the land. New England, however, did not develop agricultural surpluses and so its settlers turned to household manufacturing, lumbering, shipbuilding, and fishing for purposes of trade. The middle colonies, blessed with better soil, produced wheat, flour, beef, and pork for export.

Maryland and Virginia proved better suited for agriculture than New England, but generated no sizable surpluses of food items. Tobacco, however, grew readily, and this great staple of the colonial era became the primary export of those colonies. Tobacco was of lesser importance in North Carolina, while South Carolina did not develop a specialty export until the rice crops of the 1690s.

New England

Corn served as the primary grain crop of New England throughout the colonial period. About 1660 the wheat crop of Massachusetts was destroyed by black-stem rust, and only the Connecticut Valley remained as a New England wheat-producing region. Some rye, oats, barley, and buckwheat were also cultivated in New England. Buckwheat became an excellent crop in the northern areas because of its short growing season. New England farmers grew considerable quantitites of vegetables such as cabbages, turnips, onions, peas, beans, pumpkins, and squashes. Of the fruits, apples proved the most popular, with considerable quantities made into cider.

Most New England farms had some livestock, although few specialized in either meat or dairy production. Most milk went to produce cheese and butter, but the yield was low from the cows of that period. Sheep-raising depended upon protection from wolves and stray dogs, and, initially, only protected areas such as the islands in Narragansett Bay or Martha's Vineyard were used. By the middle of the eighteenth century Rhode Island emerged as the primary sheep-raising region of New England. Most farms raised hogs, but the numbers were small since the hogs were usually left to fend for themselves in the woods and feed crops were not raised for them. Corn and other cereal grains proved too valuable to use for animal feed, except in the case of dairy cows. Chickens had to search for their food, and often fell prey to foxes, weasels, and other predators. Oxen were preferred over horses for draft purposes throughout the colonial era.

Middle Colonies

Small farms, ranging in size from 10 to 200 acres, were common throughout the settled areas of New York, New Jersey, and Pennsylvania. The middle colonies possessed better soil than New England, with the richest region being central Pennsylvania where German farmers from the Rhineland had settled. The areas along the Hudson and Mohawk rivers in New York where Dutch and French Huguenot farmers had settled also proved fruitful agricultural areas.

Wheat constituted the primary crop of the middle colonies, and in the colonial era its cultivation required considerable labor. The land generally had to be plowed three times before the seed was planted, broadcast by hand, usually in September. The wheat, harvested with sickles in July, lay stored in barns until threshed with hand flails. Corn planting came in April or May with harvesting in early fall. The corn would then be shelled by farm children during the fall months. Corn, not a cash crop, ranked second behind wheat in the middle colonies. Rye, oats, buckwheat, barley, and various vegetables made up the rest of agricultural production. The German farmers of Pennsylvania particularly liked rye bread. The grain found an additional use in distilling whiskey, and much barley went into brewing beer. The abundance of food available on the farms and in the towns of New York, New Jersey, and Pennsylvania caused contemporary observers to marvel.

The middle colonies engaged in more extensive livestock farming than in New England, but by today's standards output was low. The best milk cows averaged about four quarts a day when pasturage was good, and little or none during the winter months. Sheep on the farms of New York and Pennsylvania yielded only about a third of the wool of their English counterparts. Here, as in New England, hogs were forced to forage in the woods, but a diet of acorns and forest plants did not produce high-quality meat. Many horses were bred in Pennsylvania and New York, but they were primarily used for riding, not as draft animals.

Southern Colonies

The raising of tobacco distinguished the agriculture of the South from that of the middle colonies and New England, and it became the most valuable commercial crop produced in colonial America. As early as 1627 Virginia growers raised one-half million pounds, and by 1700 Maryland and Virginia exported some 35 million pounds of tobacco.

Tobacco, a labor-intensive crop, achieved its economic importance in the South through large-scale units of production and extensive use of slave labor. Indentured servants provided the bulk of labor on the tobacco plantations of Maryland and Virginia until about 1680 when they were displaced by slaves. By the mid-eighteenth century slaves constituted approximately 40 percent of the population of Virginia and 30 percent of the population of Maryland. Although tobacco had a ready market in Europe, and the plantation system encouraged large-scale production, it was not without its drawbacks. Boom production periods, with producers selling for little or no profit, alternated with other years when tobacco growers reaped large returns. Tobacco also quickly depleted the soil after several consecutive plantings, and tobacco farming required a continuing search for new land. Although it lent itself to plantation operations, tobacco could be grown as well on small family-type farms; it became a standard crop of frontiersmen moving into the hilly regions of Virginia and North Carolina.

Tobacco remained the dominant commercial crop in the colonial South, but rice and indigo proved quite important in the more limited areas of their cultivation. Before 1740 most American rice came from South Carolina, but rice growing had begun in Georgia. The primary market for American rice lay in the West Indies, although some was shipped to Portugal as well. Indigo, a significant cash crop grown mainly in the Carolinas, was used for dyes in the English woolen industry, and Parliament offered subsidies for its production. Both rice and indigo developed as plantation crops suitable for indentured-servant or slave labor.

Although commercial agriculture characterized southern farming, noncommercial crops were also important in the area's economy. Corn was cultivated on plantations for both human and animal food. Virginia produced some wheat, especially after 1730 when many lands were no longer suitable for tobacco. The southern colonies produced smaller quantities of oats, barley, rye, and some vegetables and fruits. These, however, were consumed on the farms, with tobacco, rice, and indigo serving as the cash crops.

HOUSEHOLD MANUFACTURING

Two types of manufactures existed in the colonial era: household manufacturing, which consisted of family-produced articles consumed primarily by the producing family, and commercialized items produced by the family for sale.

Colonial families had to provide themselves with a wide variety of items now commonly prepared in commercial establishments—cheese, sausage, ham, bacon, beer, wine, and other prepared foods. Moreover, the household had to manufacture its own linen and woolen cloth, although in the southern colonies, the sale of tobacco frequently allowed the purchase of such items. In the northern and middle colonies cloth production (spinning and weaving) proved a time-consuming task that involved all members of the family. In the case of wool, men sheared the sheep and prepared the wool for spinning, while the women operated the spinning wheel, which twisted the wool into yarn. The men then wove the yarn into cloth on a hand loom. Linen from flax involved a considerable amount of work as well. Indeed, the whole process of manufacturing cloth and making clothing required so much effort that it ensured that clothes would rarely be discarded until they were completely worn out. Individual households also produced their own candles from tallow, and soap from lye and fats.

COMMERCIAL INDUSTRIES

The principal products of the commercial industries of colonial America consisted of fish, flour, ships, and iron. New England waters teemed with halibut, haddock, mackerel, and most important, cod. Gloucester, Marblehead, and Salem, Massachusetts, became the main fishing ports. The best fish were shipped to Europe, while the poorer specimens, called "refuse," went to feed the slaves in the West Indies.

Shipbuilding in New England received early encouragement from Parliament. England lacked sufficient ships to maintain trade with the colonies after it excluded the Dutch from British trade in 1651, so a shipbuilding industry in America was established. By 1700 over a thousand ships had been built in New England, about half of them in Boston.

Iron production and flour milling were lesser colonial enterprises. Iron works lay scattered throughout the colonies, but most of the iron was utilized locally, and it did not become a major export item. Flour mills, driven primarily by water power, took advantage of the numerous small rivers and streams. Most mills produced less than twenty-five barrels of flour meal a week.

AMERICAN CAPITALISM

By 1740 the English colonies in America had developed from the scattered settlements on the edge of the continent into thriving economic societies. Rural capitalism prevailed among the southern planters who used indentured servants and slaves for their labor force and produced tobacco, rice, and indigo for commercial markets. To the north similar growth was evident on the great landed estates of the Hudson and Mohawk River valleys of New York where the labor force consisted of tenants who produced a surplus for the landlord in the form of rental payments of grain and livestock. Lesser rural capitalists could be found on the larger farms of the middle and northern areas where additional labor was required beyond that provided by the family.

Merchant capitalists conducted business in the towns. Shipowners hired sailors and received returns on their investments in the form of freight payments. Fur merchants employed trappers and profited from the sale of the pelts. Other entrepreneurs engaged in the slave trade. Far more numerous were the town merchants who traded with the farmers in the adjacent rural areas. These merchants provided long-term credit that enabled the farmers to buy land, buildings, and livestock, and short-term credit for tools, cooking utensils, and other store goods. The merchant in turn became the marketing agent for the surplus products of the farm. Additional colonial capitalists developed various industries that hired laborers—shipbuilding, lumbering, fishing, flour milling, naval stores, iron, and other manufacturing.

By 1740 these colonial businessmen had not reached a high degree of specialization, and it was quite common for town merchants and southern planters alike to invest in land, manufacturing, money-lending, and other activities. The capitalistic system had sufficiently developed, however, so the colonial economy was moving into increasing conflict with the economy of the mother country, England. This situation would intensify over the next three decades, culminating in war and independence.

TWO

REVOLUTION AND INDEPENDENCE:
1740–1783

Growth, the "American multiplication table," proved the most striking feature of colonial life in the eighteenth century. Between 1700 and 1760 the population of England and Wales increased 23 percent. Over that same time period, the number of residents in the American colonies jumped 600 percent. In 1700 the colonies, as Richard Hofstadter described them, were "small outposts of Western civilization, an advance guard on the fringe of the raw continent numbering about 250,000 souls." By mid-century the population had passed the one million mark, and Philadelphia had become one of the largest cities in the British Empire.

The dynamism of American life reflected more than mere numerical growth. As Carl Degler noted, "Paradoxically enough, Europe's colonizing experience in the New World was doomed by its success; in the act of flourishing, the English colonies were also ceasing to be European." The political, economic, and cultural changes experienced in the New World had a profound psychological consequence as well. The colonists perceived of themselves less and less as transplanted Englishmen and came more readily to accept their new identity, Americans. This psychological revolution prepared the way for the subsequent American Revolution. John Adams, reflecting upon those years, wrote, "The Revolution was effected before the war commenced. The Revolution was in the minds and hearts of the people. . . . This radical change in the principles, opinions, sentiments, and affections of the people, was the real American Revolution."

This new American consciousness that had emerged by the 1760s responded with increasing sharpness to those points of friction between its interests and British imperial policy. Economic issues by themselves do not explain the revolution, but they lay at the core of many of the colonists' grievances against England. An understanding of the American Revolution necessarily begins with an analysis of the economic relationship between the American colonies and the mother country.

MERCANTILISM AND THE AMERICAN REVOLUTION

England's economic administration of her American colonies fell into two distinct phases. The "old colonial system" took form with the Navigation Acts of the 1660s and continued with regulatory measures until 1763. In that year, with the British Empire at its zenith, the "new colonial system" emerged, marking an attempt by England to administer her colonies more efficiently and advantageously.

In analyzing the role of mercantilism in the economic development of the colonies, it is important to keep in mind, as Curtis Nettles notes, that no important industry or trade in colonial America owed its birth to English law. For the most part the role of government in the mercantilistic structure lay in regulating some particular industry or trade once it had been started by private citizens. The production of indigo, which received a direct government subsidy, constituted the only exception to this policy. In Virginia, for example, the government did not initiate tobacco development and did not regulate it until it had become an established industry.

The Old Colonial System

The Navigation Act of 1660 restricted British trade entirely to English and colonial shipping. All trade between England and the colonies had to employ English or colonial ships, and three-fourths of the crew had to be English or colonial. Tobacco, sugar, raw cotton, indigo, and ginger were "enumerated" items, which had to be passed through English ports before they could be sold elsewhere. Tobacco, for example, had to go from the colonies to England before it could be sold in Europe. This meant that the colonial producer received a smaller share of the world price than would have been the case if the tobacco had gone directly to the markets of Europe. The enumerated list grew during the eighteenth century to include naval stores (1704), molasses and rice (1706), and furs (1722). The Staple Act of 1663 required planters to purchase most of their manufactured goods from England and their slaves from English slave traders. Planters were also obligated to use English sources for credit and capital.

In addition to the Navigation Acts, the British devised other measures to produce revenue or to respond to specific problems. The Molasses Act of 1733, for example, imposed a high tax on molasses imported from the foreign West Indies into the colonies. Molasses, a by-product of sugar refining, served as the basis of the New England rum industry. The New Englanders purchased their molasses from the foreign West Indies, finding it cheaper than that produced in the British islands. The act of 1733 sought to end this trade and force the purchase of British molasses. In practice, however, the act proved difficult to enforce, and the sale of rum, based upon cheap foreign molasses, remained an important part of the trade of New England.

Acts designed to deal with other specific industries included the Wool Act (1699), the Hat Act (1732), and the Iron Acts (1750 and 1757). The Wool Act was passed to prevent any American competition with the English woolen industry. It prohibited the exportation of wool products from any American colony either overseas or in intercolonial trade. The Hat Act was intended to protect London hatmakers by preventing the exportation of hats from one colony to another, and by requiring a seven-year apprenticeship for all colonial hatmakers. Moreover, colonial hat shops could not employ more than two apprentices, and no black could serve as an apprentice. The Iron Acts of 1750 and 1757 protected the English iron industry by prohibiting the colonial manufacture of finished iron products, but American pig and bar iron were admitted duty free to England.

These mercantilist regulations affected the colonies in different ways. They proved relatively easy to enforce in the tobacco colonies, where British warships could monitor trade going in and out of Chesapeake Bay, lessening the chances of evasion through smuggling. Colonial tobacco planters were required to employ British shipping, British merchants, and British sources of credit, capital, and slaves. Nettles maintains that even though considerable economic development occurred in the tobacco colonies, the operation of the British mercantilist system was restrictive, fostered discontent, and goaded the planters into resistance and revolt.

The policies that touched upon New England and the middle colonies were markedly different in character from those applied to the South. Under the Navigation Act of 1660 colonial shipbuilders received the same privileges as those of the mother country. As a result, shipbuilding flourished in New England. Moreover, unlike southern products, northern goods (fish, livestock, lumber, and wheat) could be sold directly to foreign markets. This allowance came because these products, if exported directly to England, would compete with English fishing and agricultural interests. The most serious restrictions for the northern colonies lay in the attempts to control colonial manufacturing. Colonial entrepreneurs wishing to engage in manufacturing faced major obstacles. The imperial government was hostile and the colonial governments were prohibited from offering assistance. New industries in developing areas had particular need of support in order to overcome the advantages of tariffs, bounties, and other aid given to the industries of the mother country. The colonists, moreover, could not coin money, nor could they establish commercial banks or other agencies necessary for the development of a manufacturing industry. Fortunately, some capital for expansion came in the form of military expenditures in the colonies by the Crown during the period of the wars with France prior to 1763.

The New Colonial System

The year 1763 marked an end to the old colonial system and the beginning of a new stage in the economic relationship between England and the American colonies. From 1689 to 1763 Great Britain had been intermittently at war. The final conflict, the French and Indian War, concluded in 1763. Great Britain had won Canada, and its competition with France in North America had ended successfully.

After 1763 the colonies no longer received money from the Crown for military purposes, and instead they were now called upon to finance through taxes the maintenance of British forces in the colonies. From the British standpoint this was not unreasonable; their national debt had doubled during the war period, and the sentiment was that the colonists should pay their share of the cost of administering this expanded empire. In 1763 the Tory ministry under the new prime minister, George Grenville, decided to end the policy of "salutary neglect" and tighten the screws of colonial administration.

The Proclamation of 1763

One of the first manifestations of the new direction in colonial administration came with the issuance by King George III of the Proclamation of 1763, closing off settlement in the trans-Appalachian West. The intent of the proclamation was to minimize confrontations between colonists and Indians, but it also reflected a concern that movement away from the Atlantic coastline would reduce the colonial involvement in the British economy. Colonists who had already settled in the region were ordered to return to the East, and even fur traders could not operate in the area—regarded as an Indian reservation—without a royal license. The policy particularly antagonized those colonists—tobacco planters and others—who looked upon the area of the upper Ohio as prime territory for land speculation.

Revenue Acts

Grenville proposed to station 10,000 troops in the colonies to enforce the Proclamation of 1763. To finance this occupation force Parliament passed the Sugar Act of 1764 and the Stamp Act of 1765. The Sugar Act extended the Molasses Act of 1733, but reduced the prohibitive duties from sixpence a gallon to threepence. Duties were increased on a wide range of imported goods, and iron, hides, whale fins, raw silk, and potash were added to the enumerated list of products that could be exported only to England. This act struck hard at the profitable colonial trade with the foreign West Indies, increasing antagonism among the merchants of New England toward the British mercantile system. The Currency Act of 1764 required that the sugar tax be paid in specie (gold and silver). Its principal target was Virginia, which had issued legal-tender paper money during the French and Indian War, but because it was a general act, it applied to all of the colonies.

The second major revenue measure was the Stamp Act of 1765. Although similar laws had been in effect in Britain for years, this was the first internal tax ever imposed on the colonies by Parliament. It required that a tax stamp be affixed to mortgages, bonds, deeds, other legal documents, occupational licenses, and newspapers. The law affected the most articulate elements in the colonies, lawyers and newspapermen, who helped organize general protests. James Otis, who raised the issue of "no taxation without representation," led the Masaachusetts Assembly's call for an intercolonial congress to be held in New York City in October, 1765. The Stamp Act Congress, attended by delegates from nine of the colonies, denied Parliament's authority to enact such taxation. Merchant groups made plans to boycott English goods until the repeal of the Stamp Act. Business throughout the colonies was generally suspended when the Stamp Act went into effect on November 1, 1765. Although business soon resumed, the law was resisted, often by violent mobs. Parliament, faced with a rather effective American boycott of British goods, and a wholesale refusal to purchase the stamps, acquiesced in the face of the pressure and repealed the Stamp Act on March 18, 1766. That same day, however, Parliament passed the Declaratory Act, which asserted its full authority over the American colonists "in all cases whatsoever."

A new attempt to produce revenue in the colonies came in June, 1767, when Acting Prime Minister Charles Townshend revealed plans to impose import duties on glass, lead, paints, paper, and tea. Since these duties were external and had been used before on other items, the colonists could not claim they were the direct taxes they had successfully defeated. Nevertheless, opposition developed and once again a boycott of British goods proved the principal tactic. This second boycott had considerable effect in New England and the middle colonies, but trade between Great Britain and the South actually increased. Overall, however, colonial imports from Britain declined about 40 percent, and the new prime minister, Lord Frederick North, called for the repeal of the Townshend Acts in January, 1770. North proposed to withdraw all of the Townshend duties except for those on tea and pledged no new taxes upon the colonists. The duties were repealed in March, 1770, and a period of relative tranquillity and prosperity developed over the next three years.

The next serious disturbance took place in 1773 when Parliament, to bolster the finances of the failing East India Company, granted it a monopoly on the sale of tea to the colonies. The company, with seventeen million pounds of tea in its warehouses, also received a rebate on export taxes and was allowed to bypass the ordinary auction process and sell the tea directly through its agents in the colonies. This measure threatened the economic status of the colonial tea merchants; others feared that this marked the beginning of new monopolistic controls by Parliament. Shipments of the tea landed at Charleston, but were refused at New York and Philadelphia. At Boston on December 16, 1773, a group of colonists disguised as Indians boarded the ships and dumped the tea into the harbor.

The Intolerable Acts

Parliament, outraged by this defiance, passed a series of measures during the spring of 1774 branded "the Intolerable Acts" by the colonists. The port of Boston was closed until restitution was made to the East India Company; town meetings could be held in Massachusetts only with the permission of the governor; the governor was to appoint and remove judges, and defendants accused of capital crimes could be tried in England or another colony; the quartering of British troops in occupied dwellings was legalized throughout the colonies. At the same time, the Quebec Act extended the boundaries of that Canadian province to include lands north of the Ohio River claimed by Virginia, Massachusetts, and Connecticut. For land speculators from these colonies the Quebec Act proved more detrimental to their interests than the hated Proclamation of 1763, because future land grants in this vast area would be made by the government of Quebec rather than the colonial governments over which they had some influence. American colonists also resented the act's designation of Catholicism as the official religion in Quebec.

Parliament's assumption that its strong response would tamp down radicalism and isolate Massachusetts proved erroneous. In the fall of 1774 the first Continental Congress met in Philadelphia, with representatives from all the colonies except Georgia. A Declaration of American Rights was adopted. Merchants formed a Continental Association and imposed a new nonimportation agreement against British goods. Parliament retaliated with additional restrictive acts against the colonies. Rhetoric yielded to violence when fighting began at Lexington and Concord in April, 1775. The following month, the Second Continental Congress convened and made preparations to forcefully resist the British. The formal severance of ties with England finally came on July 4, 1776, when Congress approved the Declaration of Independence.

PROFILE:
Adam Smith and
The Wealth of Nations

"The rulers of Great Britain have, for more than a century past, amused the people with the imagination that they possessed a great empire on the west side of the Atlantic. This empire, however, has hitherto existed in imagination only. It has hitherto been, not an empire, but the project of an empire; not a gold mine, but the project of a gold mine; a project which has cost, which continues to cost, and which, if pursued in the same way it has been hitherto, is likely to cost, immense expense, without being likely to bring any profit; for the effects of the monopoly of the colony trade, it has been shown, are, to the great body of the people, mere loss instead of profit."

These words, published in 1776, are not the reflections of an American political pamphleteer. They came from the pen of political economist Adam Smith, contained in his *Inquiry into the Nature and Causes of the Wealth of Nations*. In that fateful year, 1776, as Robert Heilbroner has written, a "political democracy was born on one side of the ocean; an economic blueprint was unfolded on the other."

Adam Smith (1723–1790) was born in Kirkcaldy, County Fife, Scotland, a town with a population of 1,500. At the age of seventeen he received a scholarship to Oxford where he remained for six years. At twenty-eight he became professor of moral philosophy at Glasgow University, a leading intellectual center. In 1764 Smith left Glasgow to accept a more remunerative position as tutor for the stepson of Charles Townshend. He traveled in France with his charge for two years, meeting Voltaire at one point, and toward the end of this period began working on a manuscript that became *The Wealth of Nations*. Smith finished his term as tutor in 1766 and returned to his home in Kirkcaldy to work for the next decade on his economic treatise. Ironically, his pension from Townshend, one of the architects of the new colonial system, allowed him to complete work on his critique of mercantilism.

Smith rejected the mercantilist philosophy, with its reliance on governmental regulation. In its place he put forward the classic statement of laissez-faire capitalism, arguing that the forces of the marketplace should be allowed to provide a balance as each individual pursued his own self-interest. Instead of regulating business, the proper role of government, according to Smith, lay simply in maintaining law and order and providing a legal structure for the protection of private property and personal liberty, and for the enforcement of contracts. In a climate of economic freedom, each individual could increase his own wealth to a maximum and, since the wealth of a nation represented the sum total of the individual wealth of its citizens, the nation as a whole would prosper. Moreover, Smith contended that the forces of self-interest would not lead to destructive ends because of the "invisible hand" of competition. Competition, not government, would provide a system of regulation resulting in maximum benefit to the individual and the nation. Governed by the rules of competition and self-interest, the economic world would function with the same harmony and precision as the physical universe.

Smith understood human nature and was aware of the dark side of the marketplace. Regarding merchants and manufacturers, Smith noted that they "complain much of the bad effects of high wages in raising prices . . . [but] say nothing concerning the bad effects of high profits." He mentioned the irresponsibility of corporate directors toward stockholders' money and the tendency of lawyers paid by the length of their brief "to multiply words beyond all necessity." Dealers in any trade or manufacturing, Smith stated, act "to widen the market and narrow the competition. . . ." In one of his most famous passages he remarked, "People of the same trade seldom meet together, even for merriment and diversion, but the conversation ends in a conspiracy against the public, or in some contrivance to raise prices." Despite his awareness of these dangers, Smith still strongly believed that competition and not government assured the best control.

In an appraisal of *The Wealth of Nations*, economist Paul A. Samuelson concludes that the work had so dramatic an impact because it provided the rising bourgeois class with an ideology that served its purpose. It offered, as well, an economic philosophy in harmony with American optimism. Indeed, Smith looked upon the English colonies in North America as the best example of a progressive society, predicting that one day America would surpass Britain in both wealth and population. He wrote prophetically about the American future: "From shopkeepers, tradesmen and attorneys they become statesmen and legislators and are employed in contriving a new form of government for an extensive empire which, they flatter themselves, will become and indeed seems very likely to become, one of the greatest and most formidable that ever was in the world."

DID THE BRITISH EXPLOIT THE AMERICAN COLONIES?

In a pioneering study of the Navigation Acts' influence on the economic development of the American colonies, Lawrence A. Harper compiled statistics on American trade within the British mercantile system. He analyzed these statistics in terms of "burdens" and "benefits." In terms of benefit to the mother country, Harper concluded, the Navigation Acts helped eliminate Dutch competition, stimulated shipbuilding and seamen's training useful for both a merchant marine and a navy, and generally assisted British economic growth. For the American colonies, however, Harper determined that the acts imposed a net annual burden of between $2.5 million and $7 million. That, Harper's calculations showed, was the extent to which the British mercantile system "exploited" the colonies.

More recently Douglass C. North, Robert P. Thomas, and others have challenged Harper's methodology and reached substantially different conclusions. In their analyses of the burdens and benefits of British mercantilism, both North and Thomas also considered what the Americans stood to lose by independence. Harper had not included a factor for the costs of British military protection, estimated by North to be worth some $2 million yearly. North also questioned Harper's calculation that American rice growers received 2 to 3 cents less per pound than the world price. North determined the deficit to be between ½ and 1½ cents per pound. Thomas's assessment of the overall benefits and burdens of British mercantilism concluded that while there was a net loss to the colonies, for the period 1763–1772 that loss amounted to a per capita burden of only 26 cents—a rather small sum even in an age when the per capita annual income of the colonists stood around $100.

Although Curtis Nettles did not utilize a burden-and-benefits analysis, he also concluded that British policies after 1763 proved destructive to the economic interests of the colonists. The colonies no longer received the money the British had previously spent for military expenditures and, indeed, the British expected the colonists to foot part of that bill in the future. Britain abandoned its older, more liberal policies relating to land and immigration, replacing them with increasingly restrictive measures. Moreover, the Crown proceeded to enforce existing trade regulations with greater vigor and to add new additional controls. For the colonists this change of policy aggravated the problem of paying for the manufactured goods they had to purchase from England. At the same time, the colonists, according to Nettles, were committed to the mercantilist system and, since the British imperium would not allow them to grow and expand sufficiently, their only option lay in creating their own mercantilist state on this side of the Atlantic. The colonists' commitment to an independent American mercantilist state, moreover, was in harmony with the general evolution of an "American" consciousness. As Clinton Rossiter remarked in his *Seedtime of the Republic,* "Despite all the shouting about English rights and ways, the colonial mind was growing steadily less English and more American."

THE AMERICAN ECONOMY DURING THE REVOLUTION

The outbreak of war between the American colonies and England had immediate economic consequences. All of the various products that had previously been imported from Great Britain now had to be acquired from other sources. The fishing industry of New England suffered from British naval control of the Atlantic fishing areas during the war. The lucrative trade that had developed with the West Indies was quickly brought to a halt, depriving the northern areas of a major outlet for their lumber, livestock, and agricultural products. The New England rum industry declined with the curtailment of molasses and sugar supplies from the West Indies.

There was some compensation, however, when new trade areas, previously closed to the Americans, were opened. Those American merchants who could evade the British navy were able to ship their goods directly to the European continent. Some traders maintained their economic ties with the British West Indies, but now as smugglers rather than under the protection of British rule. Others outfitted their merchant ships with cannon and became privateers preying on British commerce. Elias Derby of Salem, Massachusetts, was reported to have made some 400 captures during the war, becoming one of the wealthiest merchants of New England.

Household manufacturing and many local industries were largely unaffected by the war. Farmers in areas where military supplies were purchased frequently prospered, although not always because of sales to the patriots. One reason why the Americans at Valley Forge suffered so severely was that the farmers and merchants of the area preferred to sell to the British who paid in gold or silver.

Financing the War

The inability of Washington's army at Valley Forge to purchase supplies reflected only one of the many financial problems that plagued the war effort. There was a severe shortage of specie (gold and silver) in the new nation, with even less in the hands of the new government. The Continental Congress tried to obtain financing through borrowing, taxation, and paper money issuances. By the end of 1779 close to $250 million in paper currency (Continentals) had been issued by Congress. The states added $200 million in paper notes to this deluge. A severe inflation resulted because specie and goods stood in short supply whereas paper money was plentiful. To check the inflation Congress recommended that the states impose price controls, but to little avail. Congress also attempted to force the states to accept Continental currency from taxpayers at the rate of $40 paper to $1 silver. By 1778 it took $100 paper to purchase $1 silver, and that ratio soon worsened. The expression "not worth a Continental" became a common phrase of Americans trying to cope with the new nation's first experiment with inflated currency.

By the end of the war the financial situation had improved. Some specie was obtained from foreign trade and more from foreign loans.

Robert Morris, the able financier of the new nation, obtained $11.5 million (specie value) in domestic borrowing; John Adams, Benjamin Franklin, and John Jay solicited European financial support while pursuing their diplomatic responsibilities. France was the major benefactor, providing $6.4 million in loans and nearly $62 million in military supplies and support services. A private loan from Dutch bankers added $1.3 million, and the government of Spain assisted with a loan of $174,000. War's end found the new nation facing a federal debt of $42 million (specie value), while the states had debts of $18 million. These financial difficulties would prove one of the more unsettling elements in the postwar period.

Economic Effects of the Revolution

The Treaty of Paris (September 3, 1783) concluded the hostilities on terms very favorable to the American cause. The vast territory of the new nation stretched from the Great Lakes in the north to the Mississippi River in the west, and south to the 31st parallel. Although the separation of the American economic system from the British mercantile structure posed some immediate disadvantages, the long-term situation looked promising. Northern merchants, kept now from trade with the British West Indies, looked to the Far East for new opportunities. Southern indigo planters had lost their subsidized market, but now began to move into cotton.

Historian Clarence L. Ver Steeg looked beyond these shifts in trade and production to consider the broader question: "How significant was the American Revolution generally upon the rise of capitalism in America?" He found important economic implications in the area of natural resources and land transfer. Under colonial rule, when the Crown granted land to a proprietor or joint-stock company, it always retained the right to a fifth of the gold or other minerals that might eventually be discovered. Since little gold or silver was ever mined in the English colonies, the Crown gained nothing from this right. Ver Steeg regarded it as significant that the new American government did not continue the policy of the state's retaining a share of mineral rights. Land ownership thus conveyed with it the right to command the natural resources—coal, oil, gas, iron ore, copper, and so forth—it might contain.

The revolution affected land holding as well. During the war period Congress recommended that the states confiscate and sell the properties of the pro-British Loyalists. These included the 22 million acres of Lord Granville in North Carolina, the 1 million acres of Lord Fairfax in Virginia, and 18 million acres of the proprietary holdings of William Penn in Pennsylvania. Maryland seized the estate of Lord Baltimore, while New York forfeited 2.5 million acres belonging to 59 Tories, including the Johnson, DeLancey, and Morris families. At the end of the war, 2,560 Loyalists claimed losses of 10 million pounds through forfeitures and sought compensation from the Crown. The Granville, Penn, and Baltimore estates became the public domain of the states in which they were located and subsequently were granted or sold by them. In New York the large manorial estates along the Hudson and Mohawk rivers passed intact to favored government officials and other insiders. Consequently there was not as much land reform there as in other states where large tracts were broken up and sold or granted in smaller units.

Quitrents, a legacy of feudalism, were eliminated during the revolution. These hated obligations served as a tax on land and were particularly resented by the small landowners of Maryland and the Carolinas. Primogeniture, another vestige of feudalism, was also abolished during this period. Primogeniture, the right of the firstborn son to inherit the family estate intact, had little meaning in land-rich America. Its elimination strengthened the generally liberalizing aspects of land acquisition in America.

The development of foreign investments in the United States marks a final effect of the revolution. Non-British foreign investment started during the war and continued afterward. Some of the French capital moved into the new commercial houses of New York and helped begin that city's rise toward becoming the nation's economic center.

These significant economic changes associated with the revolution would soon be surpassed by even more fundamental economic modifications shaped by the new Constitution. The nation's political, economic, and moral fiber, however, would be severely tested in the short years before that new framework of government was adopted.

THREE

BEGINNINGS OF A NATIONAL ECONOMY:
1783–1815

Winning independence from Great Britain in 1783 marked only a first step toward securing a stable nation. Serious foreign and domestic problems confronted the new nation, and before long the United States would fight the British again in a "second war for independence" in 1812. On a more positive note the period witnessed some important thrusts in manufacturing and trade, as well as the basic formation of a settlement policy for public lands with the Land Ordinance of 1785 and the Northwest Ordinance of 1787. Most important, a stable government conducive to economic development was established under the Constitution.

FOREIGN AND DOMESTIC TRADE

The British were in no mood to reward rebellion and understandably allowed only such trade with the United States as suited their interests. The balance of trade, therefore, stood heavily against the United

States. The British sold their goods cheaply in America, a policy welcomed by consumers who had been deprived of many products during the war, but this made it difficult for the new American manufacturers to compete. England, morever, would not allow the Americans to trade with the British West Indies, an area that had consumed considerable quantities of American fish, lumber, and agricultural products before the war. In 1784 British exports to the United States totaled 3.6 million pounds sterling whereas imports from the United States amounted to only .75 million pounds.

Other difficulties made for a troubled relationship with the former mother country. The British, in violation of the peace treaty, continued to occupy frontier posts along the Great Lakes within the United States, thereby depriving Americans of the valuable fur trade in this region. The British maintained that they would hold these posts until all prewar debts had been paid to English creditors and until Loyalists were compensated for their confiscated property. The Confederation government lacked the power to force either individuals or states to resolve these issues. At the diplomatic level, John Adams negotiated with the British from 1786 to 1788, but his efforts proved fruitless.

America sought to improve her economic situation by developing ties with other nations. France allowed trade with her West Indies, but that market could not absorb sufficient quantities of American products to appreciably offset the trade deficit. Spain and Portugal operated within the strict confines of mercantilism and essentially allowed no foreign trade within their empires. John Jay negotiated with Spain for nearly a year in 1785, but Spanish control of the lower Mississippi River complicated the issue and a satisfactory commercial treaty could not be worked out. Minor commercial treaties were negotiated with the Netherlands, Sweden, and Prussia. Congress also authorized the payment of protection money ($10,000) to the sultan of Morocco so that American merchant ships could trade in the Mediterranean without pirate interference.

America's internal trade had its own problems. The inability of the Confederation government to deal with trade disputes between the states produced a chaotic situation destructive to internal commerce. States erected tariff barriers against each other as well as against foreign products. The massive depreciation of Continental and state paper money resulted in a situation where only foreign gold and silver coins functioned as circulating currency. Only the Bank of

North America in Philadelphia, the Bank of New York in New York City, and the Bank of Massachusetts in Boston were sufficiently sound to issue paper money, and their notes did not circulate much beyond their immediate area.

SHAYS' REBELLION

Internal issues reached crisis proportions when a violent protest developed among some Massachusetts farmers led by Revolutionary War veteran Daniel Shays. Farmers were in a particularly difficult situation in this period. Farm product prices had dropped (they were about 20 percent less in 1785 than in 1780), while taxes on land, the primary source of revenue for local government, rose. Debt-ridden farmers petitioned their state governments for such devices as stay laws and tender laws. Stay laws authorized moratoriums during which no debts could be collected, and tender laws authorized that depreciated paper currency had to be accepted at face value for repayment of debts and taxes.

When the Massachusetts legislature adjourned in July, 1786, without enacting any stay or tender laws, farm protest groups met in many of the small farm communities throughout the eastern part of the state. Several incidents of mob action took place in late August and early September, and Governor Bowdoin assembled a militia force of 600 to protect the state supreme court meeting in Springfield. Against this force a group of some 500 farmers led by a destitute farmer, Daniel Shays, assembled, but the confrontation was averted when the court adjourned. In late December, 1786, a force of some 1,200 men under Shays marched on Springfield to join forces with other insurgent groups. A militia force of 4,400 men led by General Benjamin Lincoln routed Shays' forces in a series of skirmishes in late January and early February, 1787. By the end of February the rebellion had ended.

The uprising, although serious in itself, had not posed a grave threat to the government. Reports, however, described it as a conspiracy of alarming dimensions. Shays and his followers were said to favor a radical division of property, along with the abolition of all debts and taxes. The Shaysites were accused of seeking to overthrow the government of Massachusetts and, ultimately, the central government. In actuality the rebels had no intentions beyond the immediate task of preventing the seizure of their farms for nonpayment of debts and taxes. Their course of action primarily consisted of going in armed bands to prevent court seizures and sheriffs' sales. Shays' Rebellion failed as military venture, yet it had important consequences for the nation. The uprising confirmed the judgment of George Washington and other leaders that the federal Republic under the Articles of Confederation could not deal with such problems and that a stronger government was needed. Washington, alluding to Shays' Rebellion, wrote: "Let us have a government by which our lives, liberties and properties will be secured; or let us know the worst at once."

LAND ISSUES AND WESTWARD EXPANSION

When the Revolutionary War started, only a few thousand settlers lived west of the Appalachians; by 1790 their numbers had reached 120,000. Some settlement had gotten underway before the revolution when the British opened the region south and east of the Ohio River to settlement in 1768. While the Pennsylvania frontier was filling, other settlers moved into the river valley regions of eastern Tennessee. James Robertson took a group of North Carolinians to the Watauga settlement in 1771, and by 1779 a group of settlers led by John Donelson arrived in the Nashville area. Explorers and hunters had started to travel through the Cumberland Gap into Kentucky in the late 1760s. In early 1775 Daniel Boone and thirty axmen cut a trail to the Kentucky River where his employer, North Carolina land developer Richard Henderson, planned a settlement. This settlement was to be a part of Henderson's grandiose Transylvania Company, which intended to buy Kentucky from the Indians and establish a new proprietary colony in the heart of America. Numerous land disputes plagued the company and the venture failed, but it did serve to stimulate the growth of Kentucky.

The problems of the Transylvania Company serve as one example of the many difficulties pioneers and land speculators faced in the settlement of western lands. Jurisdiction over these new areas was a matter of concern since Virginia, New York, Massachusetts, Connecticut, North Carolina, South Carolina, and Georgia all had claims to lands as far west as the Mississippi River, and in some cases the claims overlapped. Sections of the present states of Ohio, Indiana,

Illinois, Michigan, and Wisconsin were claimed by Virginia, Massachusetts, and Connecticut. The western part of what is now New York State was claimed by both New York and Massachusetts.

In 1781 Virginia ceded her western territory north of the Ohio River to the United States, but imposed certain conditions to cloud the issue. In 1782 New York ceded its claims to western land to the United States, and in 1784 Virginia ceded all of its lands, except Kentucky. Massachusetts yielded its position on western lands in 1785, and the stage was now set for a national land policy.

Congress passed the Land Ordinance of 1785, which provided for a system of survey and sale of public lands. The land north of the Ohio River would be surveyed following the New England pattern of rectangular township grids. Each township was to consist of 36 sections of land, with each section containing 640 acres. In each township 4 sections would be reserved for the United States, and one for public schools. The remaining 31 sections would be sold at auction at a minimum price of one dollar an acre, with no sale or settlement allowed prior to survey. The southeastern part of Ohio became the first area surveyed under the ordinance.

This arrangement provided for orderly settlement, but the minimum price of a dollar an acre and the minimum unit of 640 acres required a sum of money beyond the means of many farmers. Also, many of the lands of Ohio did not fall available to settlers under the auction system. Virginia and Connecticut had already reserved millions of acres as bounty lands for their Revolutionary War veterans, whereas Congress favored land companies, such as the Ohio and Scioto, with several million acres at only a few cents an acre.

The Northwest Ordinance

Congress moved now in the direction of establishing a governmental policy for this area, enacting the Northwest Ordinance of 1787, the greatest achievement of the Confederation government. The act applied only to the region north of the Ohio River, bounded by Pennsylvania to the east and the Mississippi River to the west, but it established fundamental principles that were subsequently applied to other areas of the public domain. The basic concept of the Northwest Ordinance lay in organizing the region into territories that would be subject to congressional jurisdiction until their admission as states. These new states, which prohibited slavery, would be admitted on an equal footing with the original states.

Congress provided for a division of the Northwest Territory into at least three and no more than five smaller territories. Each of these territories would go through a step-by-step process before being admitted as a state. In the first stage, Congress would appoint a territorial governor and other officials. Then, when a territory reached a population of 5,000 adult males, it could elect a territorial legislature that would share power with the appointed officials. Finally, after the territory had gained 60,000 inhabitants, the citizens could petition Congress for admission as a state. Ohio became the first public-land state to be admitted, entering the Union on March 1, 1803.

A NEW GOVERNMENT UNDER THE CONSTITUTION

On February 21, 1787, with Shays' Rebellion still fresh in the public mind, Congress endorsed the plan, drafted by Alexander Hamilton, for a convention to be held in Philadelphia in May for the purpose of revising the Articles of Confederation. The weakness of the Confederation government in dealing with the multiplicity of foreign and domestic problems had convinced Congress that a major governmental revision was needed.

Fifty-five men, representing all of the states except Rhode Island, assembled for the Constitutional Convention. Although they were in general agreement about the need for a stronger central government, the delegates differed as to the degree of such strength and the specific powers that should be granted. Debate over competing plans favoring the large states and smaller states divided the convention for close to two months. Finally, a compromise settlement was arrived at, producing a Constitution that created a legislature consisting of a House with proportional representation and a Senate in which each state had an equal voice. An executive branch, headed by a President, and a judicial branch, capped by a Supreme Court, were designed to balance powers with the legislature. Pennsylvania delegate Benjamin Franklin expressed the spirit of compromise exhibited in the convention when he remarked: "Thus I consent, Sir, to this Constitution, because I expect no better, and because I am not sure that it is not the best."

Charles A. Beard and the
Economic Interpretation of the Constitution

In 1913 historian Charles A. Beard published a provocative study entitled An Economic Interpretation of the Constitution of the United States. Beard's thesis stressed that the Founding Fathers were influenced by economic motives at the Constitutional Convention. Beard described the Constitution as "an economic document drawn with superb skill by men whose property interests were immediately at stake...."

In his analysis Beard found several areas of economic influence. He maintained that the movement for the Constitution originated and was carried through by special economic interest groups who had been adversely affected under the Articles of Confederation: those representing money, public securities, manufactures, and trade and shipping. He concluded that the process was less than democratic in that no popular vote had been taken directly or indirectly on the proposition to call a Constitutional Convention and that those without property had been excluded from participation (through representatives) because of the prevailing voting qualifications. He judged the various property qualifications for voting in the states as responsible for the fact that about three-fourths of the adult males failed to vote on the question of ratification of the Constitution. In conclusion, Beard stated that "The members of the Philadelphia Convention which drafted the Constitution were, with few exceptions, immediately, directly, and personally interested in, and derived economic advantages from, the establishment of the new system."

Although Beard's study evoked considerable controversy, it became an accepted interpretation and did not face challenge until the 1950s with the publication of works by Robert E. Brown and Forrest McDonald. In his study, Charles Beard and the Constitution, Brown argued that the Constitution had wider popular support than Beard assumed. He maintained that most adult white men within the states were qualified to vote and that the Constitution was adopted by an essentially democratic society of middle-class land and personal property owners.

In his work, We the People, Forrest McDonald found that the most common and important property holdings of the delegates lay not in money, public securities, manufactures, and trade and shipping, but rather in agricultural lands. McDonald claimed that Beard had oversimplified the issues and that the delegates had not acted as a consolidated special economic interest group. He pointed out that about one-fourth of the delegates had voted for paper money and stay and tender laws in their state legislatures and, moreover, that some of the opponents of the Constitution held more than twice as much property as some of its staunchest supporters. McDonald stressed the need for a pluralistic understanding of the process of drafting the Constitution: "Economic interpretation renders intelligible many of the forces at work in making the Constitution. It is far from adequate to explain it in its entirety, however; this would require that countless noneconomic factors be taken into consideration."

It should be kept in mind that the delegates who gathered in Philadelphia had behind them over ten years of experience in governing a new nation. They knew the strengths and weaknesses of the Articles of Confederation and had a good sense of what would be likely to work in a future government. The Constitution they produced was pragmatic, incorporating a flexibility that has enabled it to function as the basis of government for the United States down to the present.

THE FEDERALIST ECONOMIC PROGRAM

The men who took the reins of the new government in 1789 faced serious problems relating to public finance and diplomatic relations. Alexander Hamilton, the first secretary of the treasury, emerged as the primary architect of the Federalist economic program. His goal lay in developing, with governmental assistance, a strong and diversified economy. Hamilton had read Adam Smith's *Wealth of Nations* and accepted much of his critique of mercantilism, but he remained more impressed with the role the British government had played in promoting that nation's manufacturing. He looked to the Washington administration to do the same in the United States. He essentially agreed with Smith in looking to production as the key to national wealth, and self-interest as man's primary motivation.

Hamilton put forth his blueprint for the nation's economy in a series of reports. The first, his "Report on Public Credit," was issued in January, 1790. The new nation stood more than $50 million in debt when the Washington administration took office. Hamilton looked upon this debt as providing an opportunity to implement some of his programs. Hamilton believed that the economic survival of new government depended on the support of the wealthy classes. He accordingly planned a financial program that would commit the wealthy, propertied classes to the federal government through profitable investments and protection of their interests.

To establish confidence in the new government, Hamilton realized its debts and credit had to be placed on a sound basis. He proposed that the existing national debt be "funded," that is, that all the paper money, depreciated certificates of indebtedness, and other devices which Congress under the old government had issued be called in and exchanged for interest-bearing bonds of the new government. He next proposed that the new government "assume" the $21.5 million of state revolutionary debts by exchanging these obligations for the new federal securities. Hamilton's plan had both federal and state bondholders looking to the central government for payment. They would profit if the new government succeeded and the interest on the bonds was paid regularly, and they would lose if the government failed. They had a clear stake in the prospering of the new government. Moreover, as J. C. Miller points out in his biography of Hamilton, the funding system stimulated economic development: "Every three months, almost a million dollars was pumped into the national economy; and this money, drawn from the taxpayers of the United States, made possible capitalistic enterprise on a scale hitherto unknown in the republic."

In addition to funding the federal debt and assuming the state debts, Hamilton sent a second report to Congress in December of 1790 calling for the establishment of a national bank. The Bank of the United States received a federal charter in 1791 but 80 percent of its $10 million stock issue was privately held. The bank assisted businesses by making loans and issuing currency in the form of bank notes. These notes were secured by the bank's capital, 60 percent of which could consist of government securities with the rest in specie. The bank and its branches served the government by acting as a depository and disbursement agency for federal funds. The supporters of Thomas Jefferson, now emerging as the major critics of the Federalist economic program, particularly opposed the Bank of the United States on the grounds that the Constitution did not give Congress the express authority to create such an agency. The bank's charter ran for a period of twenty years and during its lifetime the bank increased and stabilized the money supply and generally assisted economic development. It proved, as well, a financial success for its stockholders.

Along with the bank, Hamilton promoted the creation of a mint, which Congress established in 1792. Hamilton recommended a bi-metallic coinage of gold and silver. The ratio was set at 15 to 1, with 371¼ grains of pure silver or 24¾ grains of pure gold in a dollar. The mint coined gold in ten-dollar and one-dollar pieces, and silver in one-dollar and ten-cent pieces. Copper was used for one-cent and one-half-cent pieces.

Hamilton's most notable economic statement came in his "Report on Manufactures." Hamilton regarded the nation's preponderance of agriculture as a weakness. He favored the growth of industry in the United States, arguing that it would make the nation more self-sufficient in time of war. Hamilton recommended governmental assistance for manufacturing in the form of bounties, awards, and other financial aids, and through protective tariffs. Tariffs could fill a dual role of protecting infant American industries while providing revenue to fund the various Hamiltonian economic programs. Hamilton thought the nation could quickly become self-sufficient in the manufacture of firearms, iron products, distilled spirits, and malt liquors. A woolen and cotton textile industry—the foundation of British industry—could come later. In 1792 Congress established two federal armories at Springfield, Massachusetts, and Harpers Ferry, Virginia. The early foundation of an American textile industry had commenced with the arrival in 1789 of a young Englishman, Samuel Slater, who brought with him the memorized plans of a British textile mill. The United States was getting ready for its own industrial revolution.

PROFILE:

**American Technology—
Oliver Evans and
Eli Whitney**

During the nineteenth century the United States developed a level of technology that equaled and in some areas surpassed that of Great Britain. Conditions encouraged technological advancement: a need existed for labor-saving devices and the United States benefited from the inventive genius of men such as Oliver Evans and Eli Whitney.

Oliver Evans (1755–1819) grew up on a farm in New Castle County, Delaware. He served an apprenticeship as a wheelwright (one who makes and repairs wagon and carriage wheels), which gave him experience in practical mechanical operations. Although he had little formal technical or scientific training, he read widely in popular textbooks on mechanics. Evans invented a card-making machine, made improvements upon steam engines, and wrote America's first textbook of mechanical engineering, The Young Mill-Wright's and Miller's Guide (1795). His most remarkable achievement, however, was the construction of an automated flour mill.

Historian of technology Siegfried Giedion has noted that, while Richard Arkwright and other late-eighteenth-century British inventors mechanized relatively simple crafts such as spinning and weaving, the American Oliver Evans mechanized the complex process of milling. A typical flour mill at that time employed men to carry bags of wheat to an upper loft where they dumped the wheat into a hopper. The hopper fed the wheat through turning millstones, which cracked and ground it. The workers then carried the meal in tubs back upstairs where it was spread and dried. After hand-sifting, it was placed in barrels for marketing.

Evans's mill, constructed in 1784–1785 in Redclay Valley near Philadelphia, was powered by water and could take on grain from either boats or wagons. Screw and bucket conveyers carried the grain to the top level of the mill and a continuous-belt conveyer moved it through the various stages of milling. It required only two workers: one at the beginning of the process to open the bags of wheat and the other at the end to close and roll away the barrels of flour. The mill could process 200 bushels of wheat an hour. Evans's mill was completely automatic and was one of the earliest, if not the first, continuous-process production lines incorporating the principles of the assembly line and automation so typical of modern American industry.

Eli Whitney (1765–1825) became acquainted with mechanical crafts in his father's metalworking shop in Westboro, Massachusetts. He is said to have developed a mechanical apple parer when only thirteen years old. After graduating from Yale in 1792 he traveled south to begin his law studies on the Georgia plantation of the widow of General Nathanael Greene. Noticing the tedious and costly process of removing the green seeds from cotton, Whitney designed and built a cotton gin (short for engine) in 1793.

OLIVER EVANS'S MECHANIZED MILL.
Smithsonian Institution

Whitney's gin used a toothed roller that intermeshed with a wire grate. The cotton fibers were pulled through the grate, leaving the seeds behind. His idea was easily copied, and he profited little from the invention, but it had enormous repercussions in southern agriculture, slavery, and territorial expansion. Prior to the invention of the cotton gin it was economically feasible to process only long-staple or "sea-island" cotton, which could be grown successfully only along the coast or on the offshore islands of Georgia and South Carolina. The cotton gin enabled short-staple or "upland" cotton to be processed profitably, and it could be grown throughout the South. Cotton cultivation spread throughout the South, and slavery, which had become a dying institution with the decline of tobacco, now revived and expanded.

Eli Whitney has also been credited with the concept of making large numbers of identical parts that could be used interchangeably in devices or machines—the so-called American system. Robert Woodbury, in his article "The Legend of Eli Whitney and Interchangeable Parts," offers evidence that claims about Whitney's role in this process have been exaggerated. Working along these lines were a number of innovators, several of whom made contributions more substantial than Whitney's. The small-arms industry became the spawning ground of the American system, especially at the national armories at Springfield, Massachusetts, and Harpers Ferry, Virginia, where water-powered machines performed various steps in the manufacture of standardized firearms. By the 1830s the concept had spread from the firearms industry to other areas of manufacturing, such as clocks and locks. By the 1850s the American system had become the marvel of the industrialized world.

JEFFERSONIAN AGRARIANISM

Hamilton's economic programs had won enactment, but not without evoking opposition that coalesced around James Madison and Thomas Jefferson. Madison had opposed Hamilton's funding proposal, convinced that many speculators who had purchased depreciated federal securities would receive an improper windfall profit. He proposed instead that the original purchasers receive half of the value when the new securities were issued. Madison also objected to the assumption plan, annoyed, in part, because his state (Virginia) had been paying off its debt and he saw no reason why the new government should bail out those states that had been lax in fulfilling their obligations.

Madison's dissent was shared by Secretary of State Thomas Jefferson. The followers of Jefferson and Madison were mainly small farmers and debtors. Some had opposed the Constitution on the grounds that it favored a powerful federal government at the expense of states' rights. This opposition group adopted the name Democratic-Republicans, or Republicans, while the supporters of Hamilton (merchants, bankers, speculators) began to call themselves Federalists. Jefferson resigned as secretary of state in late December, 1793. The immediate issue concerned the question of maintaining friendship with France in the midst of the international tensions arising from the French Revolution, but the basic philosophical and political differences between Hamilton and Jefferson proved important as well.

Jefferson's economic views derived from his conviction that the farmer stood as the most productive member of society and that the family-owned and operated farm offered the ideal form of economic activity. The fact that colonial America was primarily rural and agricultural blended readily with eighteenth century philosophical thought about a mythical state of nature. Jefferson voiced a widely held sentiment when he wrote that "our governments will remain chiefly virtuous . . . as long as they are chiefly agricultural; and this will be as long as there shall be vacant lands in any part of America." He warned that when Americans "get piled upon one another in large cities, as in Europe, they will become corrupt as in Europe." On another occasion he stated, "Those who labor in the earth are the chosen people of God. . . ." Jefferson's democratic theory was essentially grounded upon a society of largely self-subsistent farmers, yeomen, whose autonomy enabled them to properly exercise political freedom.

In more practical terms Jefferson recognized the need for domestic trade in order to provide a market for agricultural surpluses. He looked upon foreign trade, however, as potentially dangerous because it could easily lead to American involvement in European wars. In contrast to Hamilton's view that the government should actively promote industry, finance, commerce, and shipping, Jefferson would limit the government's role in such activities, and essentially allow only that which developed through self-interest in a free market centering around agriculture.

Agriculture grew steadily during this period. The growth of cities expanded the market of farmers along the Atlantic seaboard, while wheat and other cereal grains from New England and the Middle Atlantic states continued to be an important American export product. Prior to the coming of the steamboat, commerce in the interior regions remained restricted, but an important trade did develop along the Ohio River valley with farm products of the region going down the Ohio and Mississippi by barge and raft to New Orleans. Douglass North noted that the value of goods arriving at New Orleans increased from $1 million in 1799 to over $5 million by 1807.

In the South Eli Whitney's cotton gin revolutionized agriculture. Cotton cultivation spread initially from the sea-island cotton regions of Georgia and South Carolina into the backcountry areas of those states. It then spread north into North Carolina and Virginia and west into Tennessee and Kentucky. By 1800 Kentucky had a population of 220,000 and Tennessee had 105,000. After the War of 1812 the cotton-growing region spread into Alabama, Mississippi, and Louisiana. By 1825 the newer areas were outproducing Georgia and South Carolina, and cotton had come to determine the direction of southern agriculture.

FEDERALISM AND THE JUDICIARY

The election of Jefferson as President in 1800 signaled a change of direction for the nation in the executive and legislative branches of the government, but Federalism continued its influence long afterward in the judicial branch of the government. Outgoing President John Adams made appointments to the newly created system of circuit courts of appeal and, in his most important act, named John Marshall as chief justice of the Supreme Court, a position he was to hold for thirty-four years.

Marshall, a leading Virginia Federalist, had strong convictions about the supremacy of the national government and the need for that government to protect private property. Many of the most important decisions of the Marshall Court centered on those issues, including such leading cases as *Marbury v. Madison* (1803), *Fletcher v. Peck* (1810), *Dartmouth College v. Woodward* (1819), *McCulloch v. Maryland* (1819), and *Gibbon v. Ogden* (1824).

Marbury v. *Madison* involved one of the late ("midnight") appointments of President John Adams. William Marbury had been named justice of the peace for the District of Columbia, but the new secretary of state, James Madison, refused to grant him his commission. In 1803 the case reached the Supreme Court, where Marshall and his colleagues ruled that although Marbury was entitled to his commission, an order could not be issued by the Court because the act that created the judgeships—the Judiciary Act of 1789—was unconstitutional. Marshall thus had laid out the principle of judicial review: that the Supreme Court could rule on the constitutionality of acts of Congress.

The case of *Fletcher* v. *Peck* dealt with a controversy between private property and public interests. At issue was the sale of large tracts of land along the Yazoo River (in present Alabama and Mississippi) by the Georgia legislature to land companies in 1795. Because so much fraud and bribery had been involved, a new legislature later voided the sale. When the case reached the Marshall Court in 1810, the Court ruled that the sale of 1795, even though marked by corruption, was valid and the next legislature could not violate the contract.

The sanctity of contract received further reinforcement in 1819 in the Dartmouth College decision. In 1816 the Republican-dominated New Hampshire legislature modified the royal charter (1769) of Dartmouth College and created a new board of trustees. The old board of trustees asserted that the legislative act was unconstitutional because it violated the original charter, which they viewed as a contract. The Supreme Court agreed and effectively established a principle that placed the charters of existing corporations beyond the scope of control by the states that had chartered them. As such it encouraged business growth, but it also led to abuses of corporate privileges.

State authority was further weakened in the McCulloch case (1819), which involved a Maryland tax upon the Second Bank of the United States. Marshall declared that the bank was constitutional and that a state could not legislate against it. "The power to tax," he stated, "involves the power to destroy," and the state could not have that power over federal acts.

The Gibbon decision (1824) gave broad meaning to the commerce clause of the Constitution. The case involved a monopoly granted by the New York legislature in 1808 to Robert Fulton for steamboat commerce on the Hudson River. Marshall ruled that commerce, according to the Constitution, embraced "every species of commercial intercourse," and the Constitution gave to Congress, not the states, the power to regulate interstate commerce. The developing steamboat, canal, and later railroad companies were left largely free of state restraint in their growth.

FOREIGN RELATIONS

The United States sought to avoid entanglement in the war that enmeshed Great Britain and France almost continuously from 1793 to 1814, but that eventually proved impossible. During the period 1793 to 1807 the war had a positive impact on the American economy. Both the French and the British relied upon neutral nations such as the United States to provide shipping services to their colonies, and American shipbuilding, shipping, and agriculture experienced significant growth. American exports rose during these years from $24 million to $49 million. Re-exports (goods shipped first to the United States and then to a third party) increased even more dramatically, jumping from $2 million in 1793 to $60 million in 1807.

Although the European nations at war needed American shipping, each also sought to deny such transportation to its enemy. Gradually, the English and the French increased their attacks on American ships, with the English adding to the crisis by impressing some 5,000 American seamen. Between 1805 and 1807 the British seized about a thousand American ships, and the French captured about 500. Graphic evidence of America's powerlessness came in 1807 when the British warship *Leopard* fired upon the American frigate *Chesapeake* off Norfolk, Virginia, killing three and wounding eighteen American sailors.

President Jefferson, hoping to avoid war, asked Congress for an Embargo Act that would prohibit Americans from exporting any products to foreign countries. Jefferson believed that the French and British would cease their attacks on American vessels once they were deprived of American products and shipping services. The embargo harmed American agricultural and shipping interests more than it hurt the French and the British. In 1809 James Madison, Jefferson's successor, discontinued the embargo and substituted the Non-Intercourse Act, which allowed trade with all nations except Britain and

France. The Madison administration experimented with various forms of trade restrictions for three years, but interference with American shipping continued and acted as a primary cause of the War of 1812 with Great Britain.

The embargo and other trade restrictions seriously curtailed American trade. New England fell into a severe state of depression, and some seaport towns such as Salem and Plymouth never recovered. American manufacturing received some stimulation as new factories were established to meet domestic needs. It was not until the trade embargo that cotton textile manufacturing in New England began in earnest. The domestic consumption of cotton increased from 500 bales in 1805 to 90,000 in 1815. The woolen industry also benefited but to a lesser degree. These industries, however, found it difficult to meet British competition once the war had ended. The major thrust in American economic development as of 1815 still lay in agriculture and foreign commerce.

FOUR

A DEVELOPING NATIONAL ECONOMY:
1815–1840

After the War of 1812 American attention shifted away from external difficulties and toward internal development. During the next twenty-five years, the nation's economy would diversify and grow more productive. Agriculture would continue as the dominant sector of the economy, but manufacturing would exhibit significant growth during these years. Most important, a transportation revolution involving turnpikes, canals, and railroads would get under way during this period. It would link the regions of the nation, provide a stimulus to the economy, and create a necessary infrastructure to allow for rapid industrialization in the years to come.

AGRICULTURE

Agriculture continued to be the primary economic occupation of Americans in this period. Indeed, historian Paul W. Gates has characterized the whole period from 1815 to the Civil War as the "Farmer's

Age." In both the North and South new territories opened to settlement, resulting in a large expansion of land for agricultural purposes.

Northern farmers relied upon cereal grains, particularly corn and wheat. The rich prairie soil of the Old Northwest proved well-suited for corn production. Corn, which could be planted and harvested with a minimum of work, was a major food source for both humans and animals and was also distilled into liquor. Pork and whiskey were among the leading products shipped down the Ohio and Mississippi rivers to New Orleans.

Wheat, the major cash crop for northern farmers, grew well in New York, Pennsylvania, and Ohio. Even before the completion of the Erie Canal in 1825, some New York wheat traveled down the Chenango, Chemung, and Susquehanna rivers to the mills of Harrisburg and Baltimore. Excellent wheat yields were produced by "Dutch" farmers in southeastern Pennsylvania and then either shipped down the Susquehanna to the mills of Baltimore or hauled overland to Philadelphia.

After 1815, as construction of the Erie Canal proceeded, wheat cultivation developed in the agricultural areas along that route. Rochester and Buffalo emerged as milling centers. After the completion of the canal in 1825, Buffalo became the milling center for much of the wheat from northern Ohio. Ohio wheat could be taken by boat across Lake Erie to the mills of Buffalo, and then the flour in turn could be transported down the Erie Canal to New York City.

By the 1830s wheat cultivation in New York State declined as new production got under way in areas west of Ohio. As corn and wheat moved westward, northeastern farmers increasingly turned to vegetables, dairy products, wool, and meat to satisfy demands from the developing urban centers.

Southern Agriculture

Although the South produced a significant amount of corn and some wheat, the area received its agricultural identity from its cash crops— tobacco, sugar, rice, and especially cotton. With the English textile industry becoming more technologically advanced in the years after 1815 and with increasing production in American mills, the South had little difficulty in marketing its cotton. By the early 1840s cotton constituted about one-half of the value of America's exports. This demand for cotton inflated land prices as settlers poured into Alabama and Mississippi. By 1840 these new areas were outproducing the older cotton-growing regions to the east.

The cultivation of tobacco, the staple of the colonial period, did not witness much expansion during the early nineteenth century. American tobacco still played an important role in the world tobacco market, but the demand had slowed. Domestic consumption of manufactured tobacco lagged far behind population growth until the 1870s. In the East tobacco cultivation had shifted from the tidewater region of Virginia to the Piedmont region of Virginia and North Carolina, while in the west Kentucky and Tennessee were becoming the important tobacco states, producing about half of the nation's tobacco leaf by 1840.

Cotton and tobacco could be grown on small family farms as well as on larger plantations. Rice and sugar, however, required heavy expenditures of capital. Rice growing in this period was confined to some 500 plantation in the coastal swampy regions of Georgia, South Carolina, and North Carolina. Considerable investment went for the construction of levees, bridges, and ditches, as well as for slaves to work the operation. Most of the rice produced was exported to Europe and the West Indies. Sugar cultivation necessitated large investment, as well, in levees, bridges, processing machinery, and slaves. The center of sugar production lay in the southern sections of Louisiana along the rivers and bayous. The rice and sugar areas of the South contained some of the largest slave-worked plantations, with a number having in excess of a thousand slaves.

The expansion of southern agriculture increased the demand for slave laborers. Cotton required extensive hand labor, and good field hands were scarce in the developing areas. The average price of a field-hand slave increased from around $700 in 1815 to close to $1,000 by 1840. Many planters in the older agricultural regions of Maryland and Virginia adjusted to the decline of agriculture in their areas by profiting from the sale of slaves to the newer regions of the South.

MANUFACTURING

The restrictions on imported goods during the Embargo Act and later during the War of 1812 demonstrated the need for expanded manufacturing in America. As of 1815 most domestic manufactured goods were produced in household-handicraft operations. Blacksmiths, tin-smiths, cobblers, weavers, tailors, and other craftsmen worked out of these household operations and essentially produced for local markets.

Most communities had water-powered gristmills and sawmills. In the older, established communities other common neighborhood industries were iron works, paper mills, wool carding and fulling mills, brickyards, tanneries, and breweries, all essentially marketing their goods locally. Some flour mills in Baltimore and the greater Chesapeake region produced for the European market as did the tar kilns of the Carolinas, the rum distilleries of New England, the whiskey distilleries of Kentucky and Ohio, and the cotton gins of the South, but the smaller local operations produced most of the manufactured goods in the United States. Indeed, prior to the Civil War, flour milling, which relied heavily upon small mills, was the greatest manufacturing industry in the nation in terms of value of production.

American manufacturing, although improving, nevertheless lagged far behind the industrial leader, Great Britain. British inventions such as John Kay's flying shuttle (1733), Richard Arkwright's water frame (1769), James Hargreaves's spinning jenny (1770), and Samuel Crompton's "mule" (1779) helped in the development of water-powered and later steam-powered spinning and weaving machines that revolutionized the textile industry. The techniques developed for the textile industry spread throughout the British Isles and were adapted to other areas of manufacturing.

Although the British government attempted to prevent the diffusion of industrial technology beyond its borders by prohibiting the exportation of machines and the emigration of engineers and trained mechanics, still such knowledge spread. Some of the simpler devices such as Hargreaves's spinning jenny were easily copied, and American jennies were in use in Philadelphia as early as 1787. The transmission of the knowledge of more complex machines, however, required the skills of such individuals as Samuel Slater and Francis Cabot Lowell.

Samuel Slater, a young apprentice in a textile mill in Belper, England, memorized the equipment and layout of the English mill and carried his knowledge with him when he emigrated to New York in 1789 disguised as a farm boy. Early in 1790 Slater went to Providence, Rhode Island, where he formed an association with Moses

Brown. The Browns of Providence were wealthy merchants, and Moses was looking for new areas of investment after turning against the family's involvement in the African slave trade. Brown and Slater built a factory to produce machine-spun yarn.

As Slater had learned the business from his British employers, American workers at Slater's mill in turn were able to start their own operations. By 1810 there were ninety small cotton mills in operation throughout southern New England around Providence and Pawtucket, Rhode Island, and Fall River, Massachusetts. These early mills produced only cotton yarn; the cloth itself was still produced by weavers working in their own homes.

In 1814 Francis Cabot Lowell organized an operation at Waltham, Massachusetts, that combined the production of cotton cloth (spinning and weaving) within one factory. Lowell had gained the necessary technical knowledge by observing the English mills during a two-year visit to that country prior to 1812. Boston financiers provided the necessary $300,000 in capital. By 1816 the Waltham plan had proven itself, and the Boston group built a new factory town on the falls of the Merrimack River just over 20 miles from Boston. In 1826 this new town was named Lowell in honor of Francis Cabot Lowell. Between 1826 and 1840 the Boston financiers built other factory towns at water-power sites at Taunton, Massachusetts; Manchester and Somersworth, New Hampshire; Saco and Biddeford, Maine; and elsewhere. With the introduction of the power loom in the 1830s these mills mass-produced cotton cloth that not only won an increasingly larger share of the domestic market, but could meet the competition of the British giant in foreign trade as well.

The Lowell approach introduced innovation not only in the factory operation, but also in the labor force. In contrast to the Rhode Island mills, which hired local laborers from nearby communities, the Lowell system provided company dormitories to house the workers, who were primarily young New England farm women. This enabled the promoters to establish factories at water-power sites in rural areas where local labor might not be sufficient. Many of the women who took such employment did not intend to make it their permanent work, but rather viewed it as an occupation for a few years to supplement family income in declining agricultural New England and to save for a marriage dowry.

The "Lowell girls" found their lives in the dormitories highly regimented and, although provisions were made for attending church services and gaining some educational advancement, the women worked long hours for low pay. A twelve-hour-a-day, six-day week brought about $2.50 a week from which $1.25 was deducted to pay for room and board. Six to eight women shared a room in the dormitory and often had to sleep three to a bed. Protest was registered in an unsuccessful strike in Lowell in 1834, but on the whole little progress was made to improve working conditions.

PROFILE:

Alexis de Tocqueville's America

In 1831 and 1832 a young French aristocrat, Alexis de Tocqueville, visited the United States. The formal purpose of de Tocqueville's trip was to study American prison reforms, but his wider hope lay in gaining an understanding of the nation's democratic spirit. "I have long had the greatest desire to visit North America," he wrote in a letter prior to his departure. "I shall go see there what a great republic is like." De Tocqueville's observations, published between 1835 and 1850 as *Democracy in America*, offer a perceptive view of America's economic, political, and social institutions during the period of Jacksonian democracy.

One trait de Tocqueville saw as characteristically American was the drive for economic success. He noted that "the passions that agitate the Americans most deeply are not their political, but their commercial passions." De Tocqueville viewed the primary basis of distinction in America as monetary and believed that this induced a relentless quest for wealth. Some of this acquisitiveness, he thought, sprang from the social and political equality that tended to isolate men from each other and force their attentions inward. This self-concern produced a society in which individualism prevailed, and these self-made Americans sought wealth with a singleness of purpose.

In such a materialistic society it is not surprising that de Tocqueville found Americans to be serious, without humor, and insensitive to the arts. In one of the better known sections of his work, de Tocqueville described the rootless and mobile American who builds his house, plants an orchard, and then moves to another place before the trees are ready to bear fruit. He observed that Americans work so hard that they need yearly vacations. The vacations offer little relief, however, since during them Americans would travel hundreds of miles in a few days trying to satisfy their curiosity about distant places. This restless behavior he read as a rejection of permanence and a search for something newer and better. De Tocqueville saw an optimistic belief in the future as a preeminent quality of the American democrat.

The young Frenchman had an astute eye and captured the enthusiastic spirit of a growing nation. He marveled at the physical grandeur of America, calling it "the most magnificent dwelling place prepared by God for man's abode." De Tocqueville pointed to a darker side of the American system as well. Emphasis upon mass society could encourage quantity rather than quality. He warned of the "tyranny of the majority," although he looked upon education and a free press as protections against excesses in self-government. De Tocqueville returned from his nine-month trip across the United States deeply impressed by the vigor of American democracy despite its various blemishes. The dynamisn he observed in American society in the 1830s proved a prophetic assessment of the nation's economic future: "Of all the countries of the world, America is the one where the movement of thought and human industry is the most continuous and swift."

TARIFFS

This early promise of American manufacturing stimulated the movement for tariff protection. Alexander Hamilton had regarded tariffs as useful for protection of manufacturing as well as for revenue purposes. The Embargo of 1807, the Non-Intercourse Act of 1809, and the disruption of trade during the War of 1812 all curtailed imports and, in effect, protected American manufacturing. After the war, support for a formal policy resulted in the passage of the Tariff of 1816, which applied duties of 20 to 25 percent on manufactured goods and 15 to 20 percent on raw materials. The duty on cotton cloth effectively protected the American market from British production. The revenue generated from this tariff was to be used to retire the war debt.

There was some opposition to the Tariff of 1816, primarily in New England where merchant and shipowning interests, still stronger than the rising textile industrialists, found a spokesman in Daniel Webster of Massachusetts. New York, New Jersey, Pennsylvania, Ohio, and Kentucky, however, saw a need for an increased tariff. Iron was becoming increasingly important in New Jersey and Pennsylvania, while Ohio and Kentucky farmers sought protection for their wool, hemp, and flax. South Carolina and other southern areas showed promise of industrial development in 1816, and leaders such as John C. Calhoun applauded the bill.

The Tariff of 1824 increased rates on wool, cotton, iron products, and hemp, but did not go far enough for the woolen manufacturers. With textile manufacturing rising in importance, Daniel Webster shifted positions and now emerged as the champion of protection. South Carolina, meanwhile, had not developed along industrial lines, and John C. Calhoun changed to an anti-tariff position.

The Tariff of 1828, dubbed the "Tariff of Abominations," reflected more politics than economics. Andrew Jackson's supporters designed it to embarrass President John Quincy Adams by boosting tariff duties to unreasonably high levels on raw materials and ship supplies needed by New England manufacturers and merchants. The anticipation that Adams would veto the measure proved false. Daniel Webster summarized the bizarre legislative history of the tariff: "Its enemies spiced it with whatever they thought would render it distasteful; its friends took it, drugged as it was."

The reaction against the Tariff of 1828 came in the Tariff of 1832, which reduced duties to about the levels of 1824. Calhoun and other political spokesmen for planter interests were not appeased. They had moved to an increasingly intransigent position against protective tariffs, viewing them as undermining the southern economy. Economic historian Stuart Bruchey characterized the southern planters' attitude toward the tariff: "Already paying commissions, interest, and shipping charges to New York and other merchants engaged in marketing and financing the sales of their cotton, a tariff would squeeze them at the other end and push the real terms of trade—the amount of manufactured goods a given quantity of cotton would buy—further in their disfavor." Calhoun engendered a nullification crisis when South Carolina declared the Tariffs of 1828 and 1832 to be null and void within that state. This fundamental challenge to the authority of the federal government was ameliorated when Henry Clay of Kentucky sponsored the Compromise Tariff of 1833, which kept the duties of the act of 1832, but provided for a gradual reduction over the next years. The pro-tariff areas had their protection and the anti-tariff areas could look to gradual relief. The constitutional issue of state nullification of federal law had not been resolved, however, but simply deferred.

The Depression of 1837 stimulated a new wave of protectionism as American manufacturers blamed high unemployment on cheap imported goods. Substantially higher duties were incorporated into the Tariff of 1842, but the trend reversed in the Tariff of 1846, the "Walker Tariff," which significantly lowered duties, marking the closest the United States came to free trade in the period before the Civil War. In retrospect, it appears that American tariff policy before the Civil War had greater political than economic impact. It cannot be demonstrated that any major industries were either created or prevented by tariff legislation, and other factors, such as transportation and technology, proved more influential in shaping the nation's economic develpment during this period.

TRANSPORTATION

Transportation by the beginning of the nineteenth century had improved only slightly since colonial days. The eastern coastal regions were served by a network of rivers, but these rivers did not link region with region. Goods or passengers from Boston to New York, or New York to Philadelphia, moved largely by coastal sailing ships. In the interior, considerable commerce traveled down rivers such as the Ohio and the Mississippi, but only with the development of the steamboat could full economic advantage be taken of these waterways.

The application of steam power to riverboats represented the first technological breakthrough in transportation, one of particular importance for the economic growth of the Mississippi Valley. Some attempts had been made to apply steam power to river craft as early as the 1780s, but no successful commercial ventures followed. In 1804 John Stevens and his sons started construction of a 100-foot steamboat, the *Phoenix*, which used a high-pressure boiler and twin-screw propellers. In 1806 the *Phoenix* successfully traveled from New York to Philadelphia. The following year Robert Fulton's *Clermont* successfully steamed up the Hudson River from New York City to Albany.

Fulton had smuggled a Boulton and Watt engine out of England and had adapted it to operate the paddle-wheel drive of the *Clermont*.

Fulton and his business partner, Robert R. Livingston, one of the American negotiators for the Louisiana Purchase, obtained a franchise from New York State to hold exclusive control over steam navigation on New York waters for twenty years. It was not until 1824 that the Supreme Court (*Gibbons* v. *Ogden*), in ruling that only Congress could regulate interstate commerce, invalidated Fulton's monopoly.

Fulton, Livingston, and Nicholas Roosevelt became involved in river commerce in the Mississippi Valley in 1811 when their steamboat *New Orleans* made the trip from Pittsburgh down the Ohio and Mississippi rivers to New Orleans. In his work *The Transportation Revolution, 1815–1860*, George Rogers Taylor noted that from 1815 to the Civil War no section so completely depended upon steam for transportation as the great valley of the Mississippi. By 1820 sixty steamboats operated on western rivers, and by 1845 there were 557, carrying tonnage estimated to have been greater than the foreign trade of Great Britain. Louis Hunter, in his *Steamboats on the Western Rivers*, reminds us of the support structure that allowed for this achievement. "The history of the steamboat," he noted, "is also the history of foundry and machine-shop practice, of metalworking techniques and machine tools, and of the practical art of steam engineering."

Steamboats and other river craft made Pittsburgh, Cincinnati, Louisville, and St. Louis the great cities of the interior prior to the Civil War. New Orleans, which prospered from both river and ocean trade, became the third largest city in the United States after New York and Philadelphia.

Canals

A boom in canal construction hastened the economic development of other areas. Prior to 1825, there were only small canals such as the twenty-seven-mile Middlesex Canal connecting the Charles and Merrimack rivers in eastern Massachusetts. Canals allowed heavy, bulk commodities to be cheaply transported, but they were difficult to build over long distances and uneven terrain.

The most successful large canal, the Erie, was promoted by New

York Governor De Witt Clinton as a means of bringing the developing trade of the Great Lakes region to the port of New York. The projected 364-mile waterway would connect Buffalo with the Hudson River at Albany where river craft would then transport goods and passengers to New York City. Because much of the canal would be built through unsettled regions and because of the large expenses required for construction, private investors showed little interest in the scheme. The New York legislature agreed to fund the project, estimated to cost $5.7 million, and construction began on July 4, 1817. Since no American engineers had training in canal building, the men responsible for the construction of the Erie essentially had to learn on the job. James Geddes, Canvass White, and Benjamin Wright, local landowners with some surveying experience, developed construction techniques that earned the praise of European canal experts. The Erie Canal in turn became a training school for civil engineers who went on to build canals and railroads elsewhere.

Some 75 miles of the Erie Canal were completed during the first two years of construction, and as sections opened tolls quickly provided revenue to finance the venture. When the enormous project was concluded in 1825 at a total cost of $8.4 million, annual profits from tolls had already reached over half a million dollars. The Erie Canal afforded the areas south of the eastern Great Lakes—northern New York, Ohio, Indiana, and Illinois—a water connection to New York City and from there to the Atlantic coastal region. Along the canal Buffalo, Rochester, Syracuse, and Utica became important cities, and New York City emerged as the trade and financial center of the nation.

The success of the Erie Canal encouraged other states to sponsor projects. In 1826 Pennsylvania chartered the Main Line, a combination of canals and railroads, to run 400 miles from Philadelphia to Pittsburgh. To traverse the 2,000-foot elevation of the Allegheny Mountains, a rail system was developed, using stationary steam engines and cables to pull canalboats mounted on cars over tracks. The ambitious project took eight years to complete, and although it was a technical success, it never carried 10 percent of the volume of traffic of the Erie.

To the west, the state of Ohio built two canals linking Lake Erie with the Ohio River. The first, the Ohio and Erie Canal, completed in 1833, cost $8 million and connected Cleveland with Portsmouth,

Ohio. In 1815 the Miami and Erie, in the western part of the state, joined Cincinnati on the Ohio River to Toledo on Lake Erie. In Indiana, the Wabash and Erie, completed in 1843, tied in with the Miami and Erie at a point east of Fort Wayne and from there ran south to the Ohio River at Evansville. The Illinois and Michigan Canal, connecting Lake Michigan at Chicago with the Illinois River, was not completed by Illinois until 1848. Although quite costly to the state, it contributed to the growth of Chicago and continued in use long after the Ohio and Indiana canals fell into disuse. Although these midwestern canals helped develop their areas, they did not approach the volume of business on the Erie and proved more vulnerable to competition from the developing railroads.

Canals played an important role in linking the different areas of the nation economically. By 1840 some 4,000 miles of canal, which had cost $125 million to construct, were in operation. Canals had their disadvantages. Construction and maintenance proved costly, and use was limited during winters and periods of flood or drought. Still, only in the late 1850s did railroads outperform canals as freight haulers. In 1859 the ton-mileage on the canals totaled 1.6 billion, while the railroads surpassed 2 billion.

Turnpikes

Turnpikes played a lesser though still important role in the developing transportation structure in the period prior to 1840. The poor condition of public or common roads around 1800 encouraged private investments in toll roads. By 1830 some 11,000 miles of turnpikes were constructed in the northern states at a cost of $28 million. Turnpikes radiated out of cities and towns such as Boston, Concord, New Haven, New York, Philadelphia, and Baltimore. A few, such as the Philadelphia and Lancaster Road, connecting the rich agricultural region of the Pennsylvania Dutch with Philadelphia, proved profitable, but most did not. Many were eventually acquired by state and local governments and made into free roads.

The federal government's most ambitious undertaking in road construction was the National Pike. Begun at Cumberland, Maryland, in 1811, it had reached Wheeling, in what was then Virginia, by 1818. In 1833 it ran as far as Columbus, Ohio, and by the 1850s stretched to Vandalia, Illinois. The road was well constructed, with a thick base of crushed stone and a macadamized surface. It became a primary route for the Conestoga wagons carrying pioneers westward.

Railroads

As important as turnpike, river, and canal transportation was to the development of the interior regions of the United States, the coming of the railroad brought the transportation revolution to completion. Attempts had been made to apply steam power to rail transportation as early as 1802, but the principle did not achieve practical demonstration until George Stephenson's locomotive, the *Rocket*, successfully performed during the Rainhill Trials in England in 1829. In 1830 the *Rocket* was in operation providing rail service between Liverpool and Manchester.

At the time of Stephenson's achievement in England in 1829, the United States had no steam locomotives operating on rails, although the Baltimore and Ohio Railway had been chartered as the first railway company in 1827. By the end of 1830 the Charleston and Hamburg Railway of South Carolina was operating an American-built locomotive, the *Best Friend of Charleston*, over a six-mile section of track. When completed in 1833 the Charleston and Hamburg was the longest railway in the world, running over 136 miles of track. By 1835 the Baltimore and Ohio operated between Baltimore and Washington, D. C. In 1840 the railroad system of the United States was the most extensive in the world with over 3,000 miles of track, 45 percent of which lay in the mid-Atlantic states. This new mode of transportation had gotten off to an auspicious beginning in the 1830s, but in the succeeding two decades it would experience explosive growth, increasing tenfold by 1860.

Ocean Transportation

There was no application of steam power to ocean ships comparable to that which was transforming river transportation in this period. The American-built *Savannah* made the first transatlantic crossing by a steamship in 1819, but the ship's engine was used for only 80 hours out of the 29 days of voyage, with sail furnishing the power for the balance of the voyage. The United States lagged far behind Great Britain in the use of steam and iron for ocean ships, and the British were to use this new technology to overtake American merchant marine supremacy.

America's delay in developing steam-powered iron ships can be attributed partly to its mastery in the use of wood and sail. American clipper ships brought the age of sailing to its highest level in the period from 1830 to 1850. The clipper, distinguished by its low bow and raked masts, was designed for speed and distance. American clipper ships could travel as many as 400 nautical miles in a single day with cargoes in the range of 2,000 tons. Although the clipper ship brought the American merchant marine to a dominant position by the 1850s, it was becoming technologically obsolete in the face of British development. By the early 1860s, even though sailing ships still carried the bulk of world trade, it was apparent that the future lay with steam.

GOVERNMENT LAND POLICIES

The changes in transportation allowed accelerated settlement in the interior public-land regions of the United States. By 1815 much of the nation's basic land policy had already been established. The Land Ordinance of 1785 provided for a grid-work pattern of surveying with land measured in townships of 36 sections, each section consisting of one square mile, or 640 acres. Land was sold at public auction in minimum units of one section (640 acres) at a minimum price of $1 an acre. This system favored large purchasers and a partial remedy came with the Land Act of 1800, which reduced the minimum-sized tract to 320 acres, but kept the minimum price at the $2-an-acre figure that had been introduced in 1796. The Land Act of 1800 also had a credit provision designed to assist small purchasers, but in actuality it proved a boon to speculators. As little as 25 percent had to be paid at the time of purchase with up to three years allowed for payment of the balance. This enabled speculators to buy far larger quantities of land than their available funds allowed, and substantial profits could be made if the land increased in value and was sold before additional payments fell due.

The credit features of the Land Act of 1800 helped unleash rampant speculation in cotton lands after 1815 and contributed to the Panic of 1819. In the Alabama Territory in 1818 land auction prices shot up from around $8 an acre to as high as $70 an acre within a few months. Many speculators went into default during the Panic of 1819 when land prices dropped back toward the $2 minimum figure. Congress was called upon to provide relief for many of the distressed purchasers and abolished the credit provision in the Land Act of 1820. To assist small purchasers the Land Act of 1820 reduced the minimum price to $1.25 an acre and minimum purchases to 80 acres. In practice many settlers still did not have sufficient funds to pay cash at the time of purchase and were forced to obtain credit from the land companies and speculators.

The cry for additional land reform, and particularly for free land, continued not only from farmers, but from northeastern workingmen's associations. In New York City labor leader Thomas Skidmore condemned land monopoly, while George Henry Evans, editor of the *Workingman's Advocate* called for free homesteads for the surplus workers of the eastern cities.

Land reform sentiment in the West called attention to the squatters, those who had settled on federal lands before survey and often lost the lands they farmed when they were later auctioned. Squatters wanted special consideration to purchase the land they squatted on when it came up for sale. The Preemption Act of 1830 authorized settlers who had cultivated land on the public domain to purchase a maximum of 160 acres at the minimum price of $1.25 an acre.

The call for free land for homesteaders evoked controversy in the pre–Civil War years. Eastern manufacturers voiced opposition, fearful that homesteads would lure workers and create a labor shortage. Southerners were fearful that homesteads would develop the free areas of the West to the detriment of the slave states. Homestead legislation became caught up in the growing sectional disputes between the South and the rest of the nation during the 1840s and 1850s, with bills being passed in the House of Representatives in 1852 and 1854 only to suffer defeat in the Senate. In 1854 Congress passed the Graduation Act despite southern opposition. It provided that federal lands not sold after ten years should be offered for $1 an acre, and ranged down to land not sold for thirty years, which would sell for 12.5 cents an acre. Less than a year after the law went into effect, close to 40 million acres of public land had been sold.

Congress did not enact homestead legislation providing free land until after the outbreak of the Civil War. The Act of 1862 offered an adult citizen who was head of a family 160 acres of surveyed public domain for a small filing fee after five years of continuous residence. The Homestead Act met with approval from those who had long pressed the government for a free land policy. It did not, however, end speculation or curtail the acquisition of large tracts of the public domain by special-interest groups. Indeed, even though the act assisted many families in acquiring land for farming, it also was misused to extend the holdings of large landowners.

GOVERNMENT AND BANKING

The issue of the federal government's appropriate involvement in the economy arose in dramatic form during this period with President Andrew Jackson's attack upon the Second Bank of the United States. The Second Bank of the United States had been granted a twenty-year charter by Congress in 1816. The charter of its predecessor, the First Bank of the United States, had expired in 1811, and the Jeffersonians in power had hoped to do without the services of a central bank. By 1816, however, even the opponents of a federally chartered central bank had come to appreciate the value of such an operation. The Second Bank, like the First, was essentially a private bank operating under federal authority with specific functions. The bank was capitalized at $35 million, of which the federal government provided 20 percent. The President appointed five of the twenty-five directors. The bank served as a depository for government funds, but paid no interest for their use. The bank was required, however, to pay the government $1.5 million for the charter.

In many ways the Second Bank of the United States stabilized the nation's banking practices. It could restrict the ability of state and private commercial banks to issue paper currency by taking the notes it received to the bank of issuance for redemption in gold or silver. The bank had twenty-five branches in twenty states, which facilitated its policy of paper money redemption. The state and private commercial banks resented the Second Bank's ability to control their currency practices. The Second Bank also competed directly with them in lending funds and issuing paper money, prompting charges of monopoly and unfair competition. The state of Maryland moved against the Second Bank in 1818 by levying a tax on its Baltimore branch. The United States Supreme Court under Chief Justice John Marshall ruled unanimously against Maryland in *McCulloch* v. *Maryland* (1819), holding the bank to be constitutional and not subject to state taxation, since "the power to tax involves the power to destroy."

The bank faced a more implacable foe a decade later when Andrew Jackson began his presidential term (1829–1837). While it had prospered under the management of Nicholas Biddle (1823–1836), it had also acquired a variety of enemies. The currency-starved sections of the developing South and West opposed the bank's curtailment of paper money issuance by state and private commercial banks. Martin Van Buren and his New York supporters viewed an attack upon the Philadelphia-based bank as a means of promoting the interests of Wall Street. State bank supporters envied the Second Bank's role as a depository for federal funds. States' rights advocates in the South regarded the bank as unconstitutional.

Jackson, who displayed an agrarian distrust of all banks, opened the assault upon the Second Bank in his first annual message in 1829. He challenged the bank's constitutionality, and charged that it had failed to establish a sound and uniform currency. Jackson took the position that the bank was monopolistic and the protector of the special interests of the wealthy. As the champion of the common man, Jackson called for the bank's destruction.

Since it was apparent that Jackson did not plan direct action against the bank until after the presidential election of 1832, Nicholas Biddle, at the urging of presidential contender Henry Clay, decided to force Jackson's hand by applying for a renewal of the bank charter prior to the election. The recharter bill passed Congress, but was vetoed by Jackson in July, 1832. In his veto message, Jackson attacked the "exclusive privilege" the bank had been accorded. When such benefits "make the rich richer and the potent more powerful," Jackson argued, "the humble members of society—the farmers, mechanics, and laborers—who have neither the time nor the means of securing like favors to themselves, have a right to complain of the injustice of their Government."

Jackson made opposition to the bank the central issue of his campaign. Easily reelected, he began early in his second term to move against the bank. Jackson selected as the agent of destruction Roger Taney, a foe of the bank who, as attorney general, had drafted Jackson's veto message in 1832. As secretary of the treasury in 1833 Taney announced that after September 26 federal funds would no longer be deposited in the Second Bank. The measure was instrumental in precipitating the bank's demise, but it was a boon to the twenty-three state "pet banks" selected as new depositories. The destruction of the Second Bank, which had acted as a restraint upon the lax paper money issues of state banks, gave a free hand to various paper money schemes, which fueled the inflation preceding the Panic of 1837.

Much of the rhetoric employed by the Jacksonians against the Second Bank was couched in terms such as "aristocracy," "monied power," and "monopoly" and reflected the Jeffersonian heritage of the Democratic party along with Jackson's "common man" perspective. As Bray Hammond noted, however, the cause of the Jacksonians was far more complex than simply a Jeffersonian-rural attack upon privilege. Hammond saw the struggle as a rising capitalistic group moving against an established capitalistic group. The rising entrepreneurs wished greater freedom of action to further their interests and opposed the restraints imposed by the dominant group. Hammond offered a caustic assessment of the Jacksonians' goals in attacking the bank: "They did not seek reform or correction. They sought to end the bank's life, impelled by the entrepreneur's desire for abundant credit, the sectional politician's jealousy of federal powers, the self-made man's envy of those whom he had not yet supplanted, and New York's impatience with Philadelphia's remnant of financial primacy."

LABOR

The American labor force by 1840 consisted of 5.7 million workers— 4.2 million free laborers and 1.5 million slaves. Agriculture continued as the dominant occupation, employing approximately seven out of every ten workers.

Trade unions grew slowly during the early decades of the nineteenth century, in part because of their doubtful legal status. A Philadelphia shoemakers' union that struck in 1806 was prosecuted as a conspiracy in restraint of trade and found guilty. Similar prosecutions took place in Pittsburgh and New York City. Organized labor eventually won a landmark victory in 1842 when the supreme court of Massachusetts, in the case of *Commonwealth v. Hunt*, ruled that trade unions were legal and that a strike to achieve a closed shop was permissible.

By the mid-1830s bakers and printers, masons and sailmakers, and skilled and semi-skilled workers in dozens of other occupations had organized trade unions. They pressed for higher wages and shorter working hours, but also advocated broader social programs such as free public education and the ending of imprisonment for debtors. These concerns took on political expression with the founding of workingmen's parties in various parts of the country, which were encouraged by the removal of property qualifications for voting.

In 1834 central labor councils from seven cities met in New York to form the National Trades' Union. This initial attempt to establish a national labor federation proved short-lived. The NTU and many of the individual unions failed to survive the financial Panic of 1837 and the ensuing economic downturn that lasted until the mid-1840s.

PANIC OF 1837

Business activity had quickened in 1834, spurred by railroad and canal construction and land speculation. Foreign investment, particularly British, fueled the upswing along with increasing federal deposits in state banks. The national debt was retired in 1834, and over the next two years the federal government raised its bank deposits fivefold. Land sales furnished much of this revenue, jumping from $2.6 million in 1832 to $24.9 million in 1836. President Jackson, anxious about this rapid expansion, ordered Treasury Secretary Levi Woodbury to issue a specie circular in July, 1836, providing that, with few exceptions, only gold and silver would be accepted in payment for federal lands after August 15. Land sales declined quickly in the West, with gold and silver in short supply throughout the country. The Bank of England's decision in late 1836 to curtail the flow of British capital to the United States exacerbated the situation.

The financial crisis began in May, 1837, with most banks suspending specie payments. After a brief respite, the nation plunged into the worst depression it had experienced. Prices fell 40 percent between 1838 and 1843, railroad construction declined by almost 70 percent, and canal building by 90 percent. Large-scale unemployment developed, and serious food riots broke out in New York City. An upswing did not develop until 1844 when the economy entered what Walt Rostow has characterized as its "take-off" phase into sustained industrial development.

FIVE

AN ACCELERATING ECONOMY:
1840–1865

The American economy experienced a vigorous revival as it emerged from the depression induced by the Panic of 1837. Recovery proved steady from 1844 to 1848, with a boom developing in 1849, stimulated in part by the discovery of gold in California. The economy was shaken by a sharp but short-lived financial panic in 1857, but prosperity resumed in 1859, lasting until the outbreak of the Civil War in 1861. Business faltered at the start of the war, but heavy government spending and an inflationary price increase unleashed a boom in the northern states. The boom lasted for the duration of the war. The South's defeat produced a collapse of its currency and retarded its economic development.

The most significant advances in economic growth during this period came in manufacturing, mining, railroad expansion, and agriculture. The magnitude of these changes and the speed with which they transpired suggests that an examination of Walt Rostow's "take-off" analysis might offer some useful insights.

THE TAKE-OFF STAGE IN ECONOMIC GROWTH

Rostow describes five stages of economic development that a country passes through before becoming a fully mature industrial nation: (1) traditional society, (2) preconditions for take-off, (3) take-off, (4) drive to maturity, and (5) age of high mass consumption. The take-off stage marks that phase when the country is clearly developing into an industrialized nation. Rostow located the take-off point for the American economy in the years 1843 to 1860. He viewed it as the culmination of two separate periods of expansion. The first period, during the 1840s, was characterized by railway and manufacturing development, primarily in the East, along with a high level of national savings. At the same time, the West and the South were consolidating the extensive agricultural expansion that had occurred during the 1830s. The second expansionary period in the take-off phase came with the great railway penetration into the Midwest during the 1850s, marked by a heavy inflow of foreign capital. By the opening of the Civil War the American economy in the North and the West, in Rostow's estimation, had achieved the take-off stage of development.

Rostow regarded the railways as a catalyst, inducing growth in the iron, coal, and steel industries. In turn the expansion of these industries stimulated other areas of the economy. Rostow's thesis has not gone unchallenged, however. Paul A. David and others have rejected the take-off analysis, arguing that the growth of the American economy during the 1840s and 1850s did not mark a substantial shift from the growth rates of previous decades. Even if a take-off did not occur in the nation's economic development, the economic activity underway during the two decades before the Civil War represented a distinct focus. The United States was moving in the direction of industrial development, and the railway, coal, iron, and steel industries played critical roles in these changes. Even in agriculture, still the mainstay of the economy, a new level had been gained with the appearance of horse-powered harvesting machines and steel plows. The movement into a more commercialized agriculture signaled, as well, this new direction.

AGRICULTURAL TECHNOLOGY

By the 1840s horse-powered machines could be seen on many American farms. Harvesting, the most labor-intensive agricultural activity, proved a prime target for mechanization. Cyrus McCormick and Obed Hussey, two American inventors, independently developed effective reapers. McCormick's reaper went into production in 1840. The invention of a horse-drawn hay rake in 1856 substantially lessened the labor requirements of this major cash crop.

Plowing underwent important technological change as well. In 1837 John Deere introduced a steel plow. The advantages of steel were that it held a sharp edge and sticky soils would not cling to the moldboard. The steel plow had major impact in the midwestern states where the tough prairie sod had presented problems to farmers equipped with cast-iron or wooden plows. Moreover, Deere's plow was assembled from interchangeable parts, simplifying manufacture and repair. By 1858 Deere's Moline, Illinois, factory had a yearly output of 13,000 plows.

Significant changes took place on the farmlands as well. Pipe tiles, introduced from Scotland in 1840, drained vast, swampy regions of Ohio, Indiana, and Illinois. Commercial fertilizer first appeared in the United States in 1830 with the importation of a boatload of Chilean nitrate. During this period, Peruvian guano (bird dung) and fish guano served as the two primary commercial fertilizers. In 1832 Edmund Ruffin of Virginia published *An Essay on Calcareous Manures,* calling attention to soil acidity as a factor in fertility. His recommendation that lime be added to the soil to neutralize the "vegetable acid" of previous crops greatly increased yields throughout the acid-soil regions of the eastern United States by 1850. In a related area, in 1860 E. W. Hilgard, a pioneer in soil science in America and at that time state geologist for Mississippi, issued a report critical of the exploitative practices of American farmers who would farm an area until the soil was depleted and then move on. His report anticipated the later consciousness about the need to maintain a sound ecology for future generations. Hilgard insisted that it was the right of Americans "to use, but not to abuse, the inheritance which is ours, and to hand it down to our children as a blessing, not as a barren, inert incubus, wherewith to drudge through life as a penalty for their fathers' wastefulness."

The Northeast

The regional agricultural specialization noted in the earlier period continued into the decades before the Civil War. More and more northeastern farmers geared their production to the needs of urban populations, with beef, vegetables, and dairy products becoming increasingly important. Dairying now existed as an industry in its own right and not just as a sideline for farmers. The first large shipment of fresh milk from the country arrived in New York City in 1842. From this point on, the urban centers of the Northeast received supplies of milk, butter, and cheese from New England dairy farmers. The first ice cream plant opened in Baltimore in 1851, and by 1860 American cheddar cheese had become an export item.

PROFILE:
Cyrus Hall McCormick

Cyrus Hall McCormick (1809–1884) played a pivotal role in the revolution underway in American agriculture, a transformation resulting from mechanization and the opening of the vast regions of the interior to agricultural production. Although McCormick had no formal engineering training, he developed his mechanical abilities on the family farm in Virginia, which housed a sawmill, a gristmill, and a smelting furnace. McCormick's father, Robert, had worked unsuccessfully for two decades to build a mechanical reaper. Cyrus, at age twenty-three, achieving what had eluded his father, demonstrated his invention in 1832.

Cyrus McCormick's horse-drawn reaper contained a basic cutting bar consisting of short, triangular, reciprocating knives with cutting edges serrated like sharks' teeth, a design still used in modern grain-cutting machinery. During the 1830s McCormick continued to improve his reaper and began commercial manufacturing on the family farm in 1840. By 1844 fifty reapers had been sold, and these new labor-saving machines began attracting attention both in the United States and abroad. The productivity gains afforded by McCormick's invention were indeed startling. Leo Rogin has estimated that a man with a sickle could cut one-half to three-quarters of an acre of wheat a day; with a reaper, he could cut ten to twelve acres a day.

Demand for McCormick's reaper soon outstripped the productive capacity of his facility on the Virginia farm. In 1847 McCormick started a factory in Chicago and by 1851 was turning out 1,000 reapers a year. McCormick demonstrated his mechanical reaper at the London

Great Exhibition of 1851 and at fairs in Paris, Hamburg, and Vienna, adding European markets to the growing domestic one. By 1860 McCormick had sold close to 80,000 reapers.

The mechanical reaper was not the "pure" invention of Cyrus McCormick. Its essential elements had already appeared in English patents by 1825. McCormick possessed, however, what Sigfried Giedion, the historian of mechanization, has described as "the American secret of making things work and at the same time exploiting them." McCormick's success lay as much in his business abilities as his inventiveness. He employed labor-saving, mass-production machines in his factory and used field trials, deferred payments, and advertising to market his wares. McCormick combined the qualities of the inventor, manufacturer, financier, salesman, and public relations man.

McCormick's reaper dramatically altered the economics of American agriculture. Wheat production shot up 75 percent in the 1850s, and it became a primary northern export during the Civil War years. The productivity increases generated by the reaper reduced demand for farm labor and encouraged the eventual shift of large numbers of workers from agriculture to industry. The census of 1860, surveying the state of the American economy, noted McCormick's contribution when pointing to "the evidences of improvement in some of the most important agricultural operations, proving that our farmers are fully in sympathy with the progressive spirit of the age, and not behind their fellow-citizens engaged in other industrial occupations."

The West

Considerable expansion of agriculture took place in the prairie regions of the Central West during this period, hastened by improved rail access and the significant gains in agricultural technology. Pork, wheat, corn, oats, and hay constituted the important cash crops of this region, with much corn still converted into whiskey. Beef cattle were also important, but the urban growth of the area could not yet support a dairy industry comparable to that of the Northeast. Fruits, hemp, flax, and tobacco played a lesser role in the area's agriculture.

Much additional farmland in the West became available during these years. The Kansas and Nebraska territories, containing close to 160,000 square miles, opened to settlement in 1854. In the Far West the agricultural potential of the Pacific Coast and Great Basin regions (646,000 square miles) was added to the United States after the resolution of the Oregon boundary dispute with Great Britain in 1846 and the war with Mexico in 1848. Irrigation, an agricultural practice so closely identified with the Far West in the twentieth century, dates from 1847 when the Mormon settlers in Utah first employed it near Salt Lake City.

The South

The South also experienced territorial expansion in this period with the annexation of Texas in 1845. Although cotton could be cultivated only in the eastern sections of Texas using the farming practices of that time, the central and western sections of the state offered good grazing areas, and the range cattle industry developed there. Cotton, tobacco, sugarcane, and rice still served as the South's major cash crops, with considerable corn grown for farm consumption.

SLAVERY

The institution of slavery provided a massive work force for southern agriculture. The number of slaves stood at approximately 700,000 in 1790, but by 1830 that figure had virtually tripled to two million. By the eve of the Civil War, it had jumped to close to four million. Virginia, North Carolina, South Carolina, Georgia, Tennessee, Alabama, Mississippi, and Louisiana all held more than a quarter of a million slaves in 1860. One out of four southern families in 1860 owned slaves, with 88 percent possessing fewer than twenty.

Economic historians have long debated the profitability of slavery and its role in the economic development of the South. In his major work, *American Negro Slavery* (1918), historian Ulrich B. Phillips analyzed the question and concluded that slavery had become unprofitable by the early part of the nineteenth century and had retarded southern economic growth. Phillips noted that the price of slaves, after the legal termination of the slave trade in 1808, had increased far more rapidly than cotton prices. In addition, the high prices of slaves absorbed much of the South's capital and diverted it from more productive areas. Phillips also saw the South's heavy concentration on slave-based agriculture as placing the region in a position of dependence upon the manufacturers and middlemen of the North. In Phillips's opinion, slavery by the mid-nineteenth century could not be defended in economic terms, but only as an institution for maintaining white control.

More recent historians have come to assess slavery as economically profitable. One of the most elaborate statements of that position is *Time on the Cross: The Economics of American Negro Slavery* by Robert W. Fogel and Stanley L. Engerman. The work employs the techniques of quantitative history, relying heavily upon computer analysis of a large volume of data.

In *Time on the Cross* Fogel and Engerman offer the following "corrections" of the traditional characterization of the slave economy:

1. Slavery proved profitable to the slave owners, with its profitability increasing just prior to the Civil War.
2. Slave agriculture was not inefficient compared with free agriculture. Because of economies of scale and good management, southern slave agriculture operated 35 percent more efficiently than the northern system of family farming.
3. The typical slave was not lazy, inept, and unproductive. Slave owners developed incentive systems, and the average slave was harder working than his white counterpart.
4. Slaves employed in industrial jobs in cities compared favorably with white workers, and the demand was increasing for slaves in urban areas.
5. The family remained the basic unit of social organization under slavery. It was economically advantageous for slave owners to encourage the stability of slave families and most of them did so.
6. The material (not psychological) conditions of slave life compared favorably with those of free industrial workers.
7. The per capita income of the South increased more rapidly than that of the rest of the nation in the period from 1849 to 1860.

A number of economic historians have subjected certain of Fogel and Engerman's data, techniques, and conclusions to a powerful barrage of criticism. Other historians have been disturbed that Fogel and Engerman's economic accounting of slavery as a successful institution can tend to blur its moral bankruptcy. Martin Duberman criticized this effect of *Time on the Cross*, pointing out that "in focusing on the *material* conditions of slavery, in totaling up 'positive' findings about diet, housing, et al., and wholly omitting the 'negative' psychological costs, the net result *is* to present slavery in a favorable light. This result may be unintentional and undesired, but it is the result."

The controversy that enveloped *Time on the Cross* immediately upon its publication has had some positive effects. There has been a revitalization in the historiography of slavery, and more scholarly attention is being paid to the "peculiar institution" and its relation to the larger southern economy.

INDUSTRIAL GROWTH

Although industry had developed in all parts of the country by 1860, the Northeast provided 70 percent of the nation's manufacturing. Industrialists and finance capitalists gained increasing economic power. By 1850 New York, Philadelphia, and Boston could each boast of some twenty millionaires, whereas in 1800 a sum of $50,000 was considered a sizable fortune.

In 1860 New York, Pennsylvania, Massachusetts, and Ohio were the leading industrial states. New York had become a center for flour, men's clothing, refined sugar, and leather. Pennsylvania profited from its iron and coal deposits. Massachusetts and the rest of New England led in the production of cotton and woolen goods. Manufacturing in Ohio centered around agricultural implements, machinery, and pork packing.

Internal Transportation

The Northeast had a decided edge in developing manufacturing because of the linkage of its transportation system. By 1840 there were 3,326 miles of canals in the United States, mainly in the Northeast, furnishing inexpensive water transportation. The canal boom, however, had peaked, and no major new canals were built after that date. By 1850 railroads had cut into revenues for many canals, but profitable ones, such as the Erie, were enlarged and continued to be important freight carriers. The extension of the Erie Canal in 1853 and 1854 cost $44.5 million, more than five times the initial outlay. As late as 1860 the total volume of freight hauled by canal came close to the amount transported by rail. Railroads, however, offered much broader possibilities than canals as a means of transportation. The drive to tie the various parts of the nation together by rail during this period proved a major stimulant to the American economy.

Railroads

The expansion of America's railway system during the years from 1840 to 1860 had enormous implications for the entire economy. Agriculture reaped immediate benefits, because the coming of the railroad meant increased farmland prices and more efficient and inexpensive access to markets. Industry grew as rail lines knit together wider regional markets. The large sums of capital required for railroad development spurred the growth of the nation's investment banking. The railroads became, according to Alfred D. Chandler, Jr., America's "first modern business enterprises." They employed great numbers of salaried managers, he pointed out, and offered the first model of "a large internal organizational structure with carefully defined lines of responsibility." They served, as well, as a training ground for scores of young businessmen who would move into leadership in a variety of industries in the post–Civil War years.

Railroad expansion stimulated the iron, coal, and steel industries, as well as creating new industries producing locomotives and rolling stock. When Matthias Baldwin died in 1866, his Philadelphia factory had produced 1,500 locomotives. Although American railroads purchased most of their rails from England until the mid-1850s, the Salvage Iron Works in Maryland began manufacturing iron rails in 1844, and by 1850 fifteen American firms were in the business.

American rail trackage rose from 3,328 miles in 1840 to 8,879 by 1850 and then jumped to 30,600 by 1860. Boston became the first city to develop a railway network, connecting it with Albany in 1841, and by 1850 having rail links with New York, Portland, Maine, and Montreal as well. During the 1850s the New York Central offered service to Buffalo, the Pennsylvania connected Philadelphia with Pittsburgh, the Baltimore and Ohio reached Wheeling, and the Illinois Central connected Chicago with Cairo, Illinois. By 1860 St. Louis, Memphis, New Orleans, Milwaukee, and Chicago all had rail service, and westward construction had reached the Missouri River at St. Joseph, Missouri.

On the eve of the Civil War railroads had become the second leading sector of the economy, surpassed only by agriculture. According to the 1860 census, the total construction cost of this railroad network had slightly exceeded $1 billion. Because of these large capital requirements, most railroads were organized as corporations in order to provide a broad base for financing. The New York Central had some 2,500 stockholders, some of them relatively small investors. In addition states, counties, and cities provided funds for railroads through bond subscriptions and stock purchases. In the South, for example, the cost of the 9,211-mile system in operation by 1860 was listed by the census of 1860 at $242 million. Slightly more than half of this amount had come from government. Public funding for railroad development ran higher in the South than in other sections of the country. It has been estimated that 25 percent of the cost of railroad development by 1860 came from public funds, a much lower proportion than the 75 percent invested in canal construction.

Coal

The growth of railroads triggered the expansion of the coal industry. As early as 1840, anxiety about forest depletion in some sections of the Northeast focused attention on coal as the primary resource to meet the nation's future energy needs.

America possessed large supplies of anthracite and bituminous coal. Anthracite deposits lay in Rhode Island and Massachusetts, near Worcester, and in northeastern Pennsylvania. Anthracite was burned as a fuel in Philadelphia as early as 1820, and by 1840 yearly production reached 845,000 tons. Twenty years later, it had risen to 9.6 million tons. Anthracite, or "hard coal," was almost pure carbon, usually dark gray in color. It served as an excellent fuel for steam boilers, iron making, and heating buildings.

By 1840 only a start had been made in bituminous coal mining, although mines in Virginia had provided some bituminous coal to New York and Philadelphia as early as 1815. By 1850 studies indicated that many areas in the eastern half of the United States had abundant bituminous coal deposits, and within ten years production reached six million tons annually.

Western Pennsylvania, where coal, limestone, fireclay, and iron alternated in layers, seemed destined to become a major iron center of the nation. The great Allegheny coal basin extended some 600 miles from Meadville, Pennsylvania, southwest to Huntsville, Alabama. The coal-bearing beds in the Wheeling area measured 2,000 to 3,000 feet thick. Contemporary observers noted that this area alone was larger than all of England and Scotland, yet the United States had more. The lower Ohio River coal basin covered an area some 300 miles long, running northwest to southeast across Illinois, southwestern Indiana, and into Kentucky. Although smaller in size than the Allegheny coal basin, this area, too, had deposits greater than those of the industrial leader, Great Britain. Beyond the Mississippi River coal was found from Iowa to Arkansas, but in 1860 little was known of its quality and potential.

When compared with anthracite or charcoal, bituminous coal presented certain difficulties. When burned in its raw state, it was sooty, left hard residues called "clinkers," which were difficult to remove from grates, burned out fire grates quickly, and contained impurities that lessened its suitability for iron making. Although techniques to burn it in its raw state were developed during the 1850s, the greatest advance for iron and steel making came through converting the bituminous coal into coke. Coke was produced by heating the coal in closed retorts and driving off the bituminous substances. The remaining material, coke, was light in weight, clean-burning, and cheaper than anthracite. It proved invaluable for America's developing steel industry.

Bessemer Steel

Steel was expensive and available only in relatively small quantities until the middle of the nineteenth century. It was used primarily for tools, cutlery, springs, and weapons. Henry Bessemer, an English inventor, conducted a series of experiments, starting in 1854, in hope of producing steel in quantities sufficient to cast into cannon. Bessemer found that sizable quantities of steel could be produced by blasting compressed air through a mass of molten iron. In 1856 Bessemer demonstrated his process and started selling licenses for the manufacture of steel in this fashion.

Earlier, in 1847, a Kentucky iron maker named William Kelly had produced small quantities of steel using a similar process. Neither inventor knew of the other's work until, in 1857, Kelly heard of Bessemer's demonstration in England. He quickly applied for an American patent, and his claim was accepted. In 1866 an agreement was reached between Kelly and Bessemer. The Bessemer process required iron ore low in phosphorus and sulfur, but many of the American ores, particularly those from the great Mesabi Range of Minnesota, proved suitable. Beginning in the 1860s sizable quantities of Bessemer steel were made, with almost all of the early production going into the manufacture of rails for the nation's expanding transcontinental railroads.

TRANSCONTINENTAL RAILROADS

The settlement of the Oregon boundary dispute with Great Britain in 1846 and the victory over Mexico in 1848 created a nation that stretched from the Atlantic to the Pacific oceans. The development of this vast expanse generated interest in a transcontinental railroad. This issue had first been raised in 1845 when Asa Whitney, a New York businessman and Far East trader, proposed that Congress grant a 60-mile-wide belt of land from Lake Superior to Puget Sound to any company willing to build a railroad connecting these two regions. Although Congress did not respond to Whitney's proposal at the time, by the early 1850s the need for a transcontinental railroad was widely acknowledged, along with the assumption that governmental assistance would be required to undertake such an extensive project.

A first step came in 1853 when Congress authorized the army to survey potential routes. Proponents of a southern route had a decided advantage, since all of the territory the line would cross had already been politically organized. In 1854 Senator Stephen A. Douglas of Illinois, a promoter of Chicago as the eastern terminus, sought to enhance chances for a northern route by securing passage of the Kansas-Nebraska Act, organizing these previously unorganized territories.

The sectional controversies of the 1850s, however, negated any serious possibility of congressional action on the transcontinental railroad. The South looked upon territories in the West as not suitable for a slave economy and as a threat to the slave system of the South. The new Republican party gained considerable support in the West by advocating federal assistance for a Pacific railroad, and Lincoln's election in 1860 gave promise of action. The opportunity came after the southern secession. Four California railroad promoters—Leland Stanford, Collis P. Huntington, Mark Hopkins, and Charles Crocker—sought federal support in building a railroad eastward out of San Francisco. On July 1, 1862, Congress passed the Pacific Railway Act authorizing the Central Pacific to build east from San Francisco, while the Union Pacific would build west from the 100th meridian, cross the Rocky Mountains at South Pass, and connect with the Central Pacific in the Great Basin. The federal government provided grants of five square miles in alternating sections as well as loans of up to $48,000 for each mile of track laid. During the period from 1850 to 1871, federal land grants to all railroads came to a quarter of a million square miles.

CENTRAL PACIFIC RAILROAD AND UNION PACIFIC RAILROAD JOIN LINES AT PROMONTORY POINT, UTAH, MAY 10, 1869.
Library of Congress

The construction of the transcontinental railroad became one of the most colorful episodes in America's past. The Central Pacific started first, but encountered difficulties crossing the Sierra Nevada. With labor scarce in the frontier regions, the company imported gangs of pigtailed Chinese coolies, and the crest of the Sierras had been reached by the summer of 1867. The Union Pacific moved quickly across the relatively easy terrain of Nebraska and Wyoming before confronting the more formidable mountain conditions in Utah. The meeting of the two lines came in May, 1869, at Promontory Point, Utah, near Great Salt Lake.

LABOR

The Chinese coolies building the Central Pacific and Irish construction workers on the Union Pacific serve as a small but dramatic illustration of the changes linking immigration and labor during this period. The years 1843 to 1857 witnessed a great wave of immigration, a development that affected all of American society but had particular consequences for the labor movement.

Trade unionism gained ground in the 1850s as business conditions improved after the depression of the early 1840s. Organized labor's growth during these years followed the business cycle very closely, and the downswing in 1857 crushed many unions. Locomotive engineers, stonecutters, typographers, hat finishers, molders, and machinists formed national unions in the 1850s. These organizations, generally avoiding the wider social reforms sought during the Jacksonian period, pursued straight business considerations of higher pay and better working conditions. Some success came in the area of reducing work hours. In 1840 President Martin Van Buren, by executive order, had established a ten-hour day for all laborers and mechanics employed on federal public works. By 1850 most skilled workers in the large cities had also attained the ten-hour day. Attempts to reduce work hours in the textile mills met with less success. The average working day for all nonagricultural employees stood at eleven hours in 1860.

During the decade of the 1850s the cost of living increased 12 percent, while wages rose only 4 percent. Much of the deterioration in the wage structure came as the result of the influx of immigrants willing to work for lower wages. These immigrants came to constitute America's first permanent industrial labor force, as Irish workers replaced the farm girls in the textile mills of New England.

IMMIGRATION

The first federal census conducted in 1790 revealed that slightly more than 60 percent of the white American population were of English stock. From 1790 until 1820 the disruptions of war limited the flow of European immigrants to the United States to less than a quarter of a million. During the years 1820 to 1860, however, economic and political upheavals in Europe and the promise of America attracted close to 5.5 million immigrants.

TABLE 5:1
Immigration to the United States: 1820–1859

Years	Numbers of Immigrants
1820–1824	38,689
1825–1829	89,813
1830–1834	280,442
1835–1839	307,939
1840–1844	400,031
1845–1849	1,127,306
1850–1854	1,917,527
1855–1859	896,027

Source: U.S. Department of Commerce, *Historical Statistics of the United States, Colonial Times to 1970.*

The Irish and Germans constituted the principal non-English groups accounting for this flood of immigration. Ireland provided 44 percent of America's immigrants in the 1830s, and 49 percent in the 1840s. The potato famine of 1845 to 1847 triggered a greater outpouring, with more than 100,000 Irish immigrants arriving during each year from 1847 to 1854. The 1850 census reported an Irish population of one million in America, with 40 percent of them residing in large cities.

Germans made up 30 percent of the immigration of the 1830s, but their number swelled over the next two decades. Poor farming conditions and the Revolution of 1848 caused a surge of German immigration, with a peak arrival of 215,000 in 1854. By 1860 more than half of the residents of Chicago, Milwaukee, and St. Louis were foreign born.

America benefited enormously from this pre–Civil War wave of immigration. John Smith's assertion back in the early seventeenth century that this country was long on land and short on men still largely held true more than two centuries later. These millions of immigrants provided needed labor for all segments of the American economy, but particularly for its rapidly expanding industrial sector. Many had been involved in the trade union movement in Europe, and their experience influenced the growth of organized labor in America. Overall, they added a cultural diversity that, despite nativist resistance, enriched American life.

MECHANIZATION

The increased availability of labor resulting from the influx of immigrants in the 1840s and 1850s did not lessen demand for mechanization as might have been expected. The relatively high wages of the pre-1837 period have been explained in part by the labor shortage caused by the abundance of cheap land. Entrepreneurs thus turned to labor-saving devices, interchangeable parts, and other features associated with American technological development. The expansion of the labor force caused by immigration with the resultant drop in real wages, however, did not significantly dampen demand for labor-saving technology. Anticipation of eventual rising labor costs as well as a persistent American fascination with the machine ensured continuing technological innovation.

At the great Crystal Palace Exhibition in London in 1851, the American exhibits attracted little initial interest. Indeed, for a time it appeared as though there would be no American exhibits, because Congress had authorized funds to ship the products to England, but not sufficient money to unload them at the dock. Finally, George Peabody, an American banker living in London, advanced the money, and the displays were sent on to the Crystal Palace exhibition hall.

The field trials of agricultural machinery clearly established the superiority of the McCormick reaper. Top awards and medals went to Charles Goodyear for his India rubber products and to Gail Borden for a special meat biscuit. (Borden, reflecting the American cult of efficiency, wrote, "Time was when people would... spend hours at a meal. Napoleon never took over twenty minutes.... I am through in fifteen.") Samuel Colt's revolver and Robbins's and Lawrence's rifles epitomized for Europeans the success of the "American system" of manufacturing with interchangeable parts. The results of the Crystal Palace Exhibition proved gratifying. The United States, still in the early phases of industrialization, had given notice that it could successfully compete with the most technologically advanced nations in the world.

THE CIVIL WAR

The Civil War, that centerpiece of American history, holds a particular interest for economic historians. Along with analyzing the economic aspects of that conflict, they have attempted to assess its long-term effect on American economic development. The prevailing view had long been to view it as a pivotal moment that accelerated the industrialization of America. That interpretation has come under challenge, and it would be valuable to examine that debate as well as look at the more immediate economic dimensions of the war.

Economic Comparison of the Union and the Confederacy

The Union entered the war with an overwhelming economic advantage. It held 70 percent (21.3 million) of the nation's population, and 75 percent of its wealth. It also controlled 85 percent of the nation's manufacturing, 72 percent of the railroad mileage, and 64 percent of all improved farmland. In contrast, the Confederacy had a population of 9.1 million, of whom about 3.5 million were slaves. Although it possessed close to 9,000 miles of railway, many of these railroads were in poor repair. Southern railroads had been built mainly to haul cotton from the interior to the port cities and offered no railway network to permit the easy transit of men and materials throughout the different sections of the Confederacy. The southern economy relied heavily on exports of cotton and imports of manufactured goods, and this dependence on foreign trade made it vulnerable to a northern blockade.

King Cotton

Southern leaders, recognizing that a prolonged war would bring the superior potential of the Union into play, hoped that a series of early military victories would achieve the desired independence for the Confederacy. Should that fail, they believed the force of cotton in world trade would prove decisive. Senator James Hammond of South Carolina had warned, "You dare not make war upon our cotton. No power on earth dares make war upon it. Cotton is King."

Great Britain, the world's industrial leader, imported 80 percent of the cotton for its textile industry from the American South. Confederate leaders believed that the necessity of obtaining cotton to keep their textile factories operating would inexorably force the British to offer recognition and protect that trade. The sale of cotton, in turn, would provide the capital for purchasing needed war supplies. Great Britain, with the greatest navy in the world, became the Confederacy's trump card.

As it turned out, southern cotton never provided sufficient leverage to achieve Confederate aims. Bumper crops in 1859 and 1860 filled British warehouses so that there was no initial economic pressure. In addition, the British textile mills, still recovering from the depression of 1857, were operating at reduced levels. As the war progressed, cotton was shipped to England by Union forces as they penetrated the Confederacy. Finally, Great Britain developed alternative sources for cotton in Egypt and India, thus further reducing the impact of the loss of southern imports. The lack of access to southern cotton, while eventually somewhat disruptive to the British textile industry, thus never attained the coercive power that had been expected.

Some northern leaders correctly anticipated that England's need for Union wheat would exert greater economic leverage than its demand for southern cotton. England had become a food importing country as early as 1815, and wheat from the United States became an important part of its food requirements by the 1860s. Poor harvests in 1861 and 1862 increased English imports of American wheat from 17 million bushels in 1860 to 62 million bushels in 1862. Wheat had proved more of a king than cotton.

Other factors as well helped ensure British neutrality. The Lincoln administration, aware of the enormous problems English intervention would pose, worked effectively at maintaining good diplomatic relations. Although some sympathy for the Confederacy existed among the English aristocracy, strong anti-slavery sentiment on the part of industrial workers reduced the possibilities of British recognition. Whatever lingering chance of English intervention remained ended with Lincoln's issuance of the Emancipation Proclamation in September, 1862. That statement, for all its limitations (freeing only those slaves in areas in active rebellion on January 1, 1863), defined the war in terms that made British involvement impossible. The Civil War, in John Hope Franklin's words, had been "transformed from a struggle to preserve the Union into one in which the crusade for human freedom became an equally important goal." The Confederacy, having lost its final hope of outside intervention, was doomed to carry on the struggle with its own limited resources.

The Wartime Economy

Economic uncertainties accompanied the outbreak of the war. Many southern banks suspended specie payment before hostilities commenced. More northern banks failed during the early months of the war than had collapsed during the Panic of 1857. Not until late 1862 did the northern economy experience a wartime boom. By that time the flood of war orders had stimulated an economic upswing, and northern manufacturing flourished.

The demand for iron for war materials boosted iron manufacturing. Shipments of iron ore from the Lake Superior region doubled during the war period. Pittsburgh's mills expanded production, while Cleveland became established as a new iron processing center. The Morrill Tariff of 1861 and its subsequent revisions effectively eliminated any threat of foreign competition. The heavy demand for uniforms for the Union army, 1.5 million a year, stimulated the woolen textile industry of the Northeast. By war's end, domestic consumption of woolen textiles had tripled from the prewar figure. The cotton textile industry, on the other hand, suffered from the curtailment of southern cotton. On the whole northern manufacturers, by expanding facilities and, in many cases, increasing mechanization, largely satisfied military and civilian needs. War profits produced a new class of millionaires, and the foundation for many of the great postwar fortunes (Carnegie, Rockefeller, Armour) was laid during these years.

While northern industry met its needs and expanded during the war, southern industry faltered despite herculean efforts. The South organized its limited resources well. The Tredegar Iron Works at Richmond cast cannon, armor plate, and other articles of war. Gunpowder plants were established at Richmond, Selma, Raleigh, and Augusta. Such efforts, however, proved insufficient, and shortages of food and equipment plagued the Confederacy throughout much of the war. In addition, the effectiveness of the Union naval blockade precluded any sigificant supply of materials from abroad. By the end of 1864 the South had lost the war on both the military and the economic fronts.

Northern agriculture matched the strong performance of manufacturing. Even though thousands of northern farm youths served in the Union army, corn, wheat, pork, and wool production all substantially increased during the war period. Farmers offset labor shortages by increased mechanization, with the number of reapers on wheat farms rising from 125,000 in 1859 to 375,000 in 1865. A ready domestic cash market for farm products plus increased European demand drove farm prices to their highest level in the nineteenth century. Southern agriculture, on the other hand, found the markets for its staples, cotton, and tobacco, largely cut off and had to turn to beef, corn, and other food crops to support the war effort. Even this effort, however, was often frustrated by the inability of the southern railway system to deliver the foods where they were most needed.

Financing the War

The war disrupted the finances of both the Union and the Confederacy. This period, however, also witnessed a long-range financial accomplishment, the establishment of the National Banking System, the first national-level banking structure since the destruction of the Second Bank of the United States in 1836.

The Confederacy faced serious financial problems throughout the war. It proved unable to borrow substantial sums from foreign bankers, and the predominantly agricultural base of its economy made it difficult to raise taxes. The Confederacy issued more than $1.5 of unbacked paper currency during the war. This paper money deteriorated rapidly in value. The level of the resultant inflation can be measured by the price of salt, which sold for eighty cents a bushel in 1861 and had jumped to thirty dollars a bushel by 1863. At the war's end, flour was selling for $1,200 (Confederate currency) a barrel. By 1865 Confederate money, valued at 1.6 cents on the dollar, was barely worth the paper it was printed on.

The North proved to be more successful in financing the war than the South was. The Union also experienced wartime inflation, but nothing matching the fire storm that ravaged the South. Consumer prices in the Union rose 75 percent between 1861 and 1865. The Morrill Tariff of 1861 (amended in 1862 and 1864) reached a duty level of 47 percent by war's end, producing substantial revenues. Government borrowing, both domestically and abroad, raised $2.6 billion, approximately three-quarters of the war's cost. Congress, in February, 1862, authorized treasury notes dubbed "greenbacks" because of the green ink used for printing. Almost $450 million in greenbacks, backed not by gold but by the general credit of the government, were issued during the war. The value of these notes fell as low as 39 cents on the dollar during the summer of 1864 before beginning a rise toward the end of the war. The redemption of greenbacks in gold at face value became a major political issue in the post–Civil War era.

Congress enacted the first income tax in American history in August, 1861. The initial rate of 3 percent on incomes in excess of $800 increased in succeeding years, but the income tax raised only $55 million in the course of the war. By 1866 the national debt stood at $2.8 billion, a level that would not be reached again until World War I.

The National Banking System

To strengthen the Union's finances and to provide a uniform currency, Secretary of the Treasury Salmon P. Chase recommended to Congress in 1861 that a national banking system be established. Congress responded in February, 1863, passing the National Banking Act and amending it in June, 1864. This law established a system of national banks that were required to have one-third of their capital invested in U.S. securities, which were deposited in the treasury. They could then issue paper currency up to 90 percent of their U.S. bond holdings. The imposition of a 10 percent tax on state bank notes in 1865 drove the 7,000 different types of these notes out of circulation. The deflationary effects of this curtailment of state bank currency was more than offset by the inflationary impact of the new national bank notes. Indeed, these new national notes might have stimulated serious inflation except for the growth and expansion of business and industry during this period. By the end of 1865 more than 1,500 banks had joined the national banking system.

Costs of the War

The most devastating cost of the Civil War lay in its enormous toll in human lives. The Union dead totaled 360,000, while Confederate losses amounted to 258,000. Overall costs of the war, including pension benefits, have been estimated to have run as high as $20 billion. The abolition of slavery represented a capital loss of $2.7 billion. The South's rail system, agriculture, and cities suffered major damage. By 1870 the production of cotton, corn, rice, sugar, and tobacco still remained below prewar levels. The North, in contrast, appeared at the war's end to be vibrant, ready to devote its full energies to economic progress. The Republican party had successfully promoted a wartime package of long-range economic legislation such as the Homestead Act, the Pacific Railway Act, the National Banking Act, and the Morrill Tariff. A new surge of industrial development seemed in the offing.

Until relatively recent times historians have assumed that the Civil War marked a major watershed in American economic history, accelerating the process of industrialization in the North. In *Triumph of American Capitalism,* Louis M. Hacker asserted the accepted view that extensive expansion in the iron, machinery, farm implements, shoe, clothing, and food industries moved the nation onto a higher level of industrial development. In 1961 this view was challenged by Thomas C. Cochran in an article provocatively titled, "Did the Civil

War Retard Industrialization?" Cochran concluded that the Civil War did retard industrialization and that its primary positive role lay in freeing the slaves. He attempted to show that important areas of the economy such as railroad construction, copper and iron production, cotton consumption, and immigration showed only modest growth or no growth during the war period.

Although some scholars have criticized Cochran, maintaining that he looked only at short-term results, whereas the Civil War served as a long-term stimulant, others have lent support to his argument. Albert W. Niemi's study of "Structural and Labor Productivity Patterns in United States Manufacturing, 1849–1899" concluded that the Civil War had little or no influence on the basic structure of American manufacturing. A trend toward increased concentration in the metals and machine industries existed prior to the war, and it simply continued during the war and afterward. Niemi's conclusions essentially agree with Rostow's position that the United States was a rapidly developing industrial state by the eve of the Civil War. The last three decades of the nineteenth century witnessed the fruition of that development as the United States emerged as the world's leading industrial nation.

SIX

AMERICA'S RISE TO INDUSTRIAL POWER:
1865–1900

Much of the history of the pre–Civil War decades can be explained in terms of the tension between nationalism and sectionalism. The motto *"E pluribus unum"* (one from many) had increasingly lost its validity as sectional antagonisms became paramount. The Civil War's resolution, in David Potter's phrase, "gave *unum* the upper hand." The preservation of the union by force of arms ensured that America would remain a single strong nation growing immensely more powerful in the decades ahead. The war left a host of problems in its wake—the political and economic reconstruction of the South, the transition of close to four million blacks from a condition of servitude to the status of freedmen—but it did clearly resolve one persistent question. America would enter the last third of the nineteenth century as a unified nation, embarking upon a period of unprecedented economic growth.

The generation from 1865 to 1900 witnessed change so extensive and intensive that it fundamentally altered American society. A new America, shaped by pressures of industrialization, immigration, and

---

urbanization, was emerging during this period. Most Americans responded to these rapid changes with ambivalence, marveling at the technological advances and enormous leaps in productivity while simultaneously feeling a nostalgic sense of loss for an older America and some anxiety about the political and economic implications of these new relationships.

By 1894 the United States had become the leading manufacturing nation in the world, while continuing its dominant role in agriculture. During this time the relative position of agriculture in the American economy declined. In 1870 slightly more than one-half (6.9 million) of the total labor force of 13 million engaged in agriculture, whereas manufacturing employed 2.1 million. By 1900 the proportion of agricultural workers had fallen to approximately one-third (10.9 million) of the labor force of 29 million, and 6 million now worked in manufacturing.

This shift toward a more diversified economy made many uneasy. Farmers felt their status threatened and looked upon the general decline of agricultural prices during this period as proof that the new industrialized America was detrimental to their interests. Workers in the expanding manufacturing sector often believed that they were not adequately benefiting from this new economic order, which seemed characterized by millionaires, booms, and depressions. In 1873 and again in 1893 the economy suffered serious disruptions marked by runs on banks, collapses of the stock market, dramatic business failures, high unemployment, and prolonged moods of public pessimism.

This period, which afforded large-scale material progress, also saw develop a concern whether such abundance could last. In 1893 historian Frederick Jackson Turner delivered an address entitled "The Significance of the Frontier in American History." Turner's thesis held that American democracy and development had been shaped by the abundance of free land and an expanding frontier. Turner, drawing upon data from the census of 1890, concluded that the frontier had come to an end and that considerable adjustments lay in store for American agriculture, labor, and democracy.

A neo-Malthusian fear troubled many Americans. Would there be sufficient coal or forests for future generations? Arthur Abbott, in *A Treatise on Fuel* published in 1891, posed a troubling question: "The coal mines are finite; at the present rate of consumption but a few centuries will elapse ere they will become exhausted. From whence, then, shall man draw those enormous supplies of energy which to him are now even more than the bread of life?" That same year, Congress passed the Forest Reserve Act, and before the decade ended Presidents Harrison, Cleveland, and McKinley had all set aside forest reserves. This conservation movement would grow in the early twentieth century under the enthusiastic support of President Theodore Roosevelt.

This fear of scarcity also found expression in the campaigns to prohibit alien ownership of land and to restrict immigration. Some states enacted laws against alien land ownership, and Congress in 1882 restricted the immigration of specific groups, primarily Chinese laborers.

AGRICULTURE

The decline of agriculture relative to manufacturing and farmers' complaints about the new industrialized society tend to obscure the great strides agriculture made during this period. More land came under cultivation between 1860 and 1890 than during all of the nation's previous history. The value of farmland and farm buildings more than doubled between 1870 and 1900, and the value of implements and machinery almost tripled. The most notable change for the individual farmer was the shift from a self-sufficient, slightly commercial operation to one primarily commercial. The American farmer increasingly produced for a market beyond his locality and relied upon a price structure often set by world markets. The Jeffersonian vision of the self-subsistent yeoman was being replaced by the reality of the agricultural businessman, challenged by economic factors beyond his control.

TECHNOLOGY AND AGRICULTURE

Many of the changes affecting agriculture came about because of technological development both on the farm and beyond, particularly in the areas of transportation and marketing. The application of steam power to shipping had revolutionized river transportation, and steam locomotives on rails had opened up the interior regions of the United

States to general development. Ocean transportation became the next area to be affected by the technology of steam power. With the development of the compound marine steam engines of the 1870s and 1880s, steam-powered ocean vessels became dependable and efficient. Earlier, steamers required about 80 percent of their hull capacity for coal, allowing only 20 percent for cargo. By the 1880s, that ratio was reversed. Refrigeration now allowed perishable products such as meat, as well as grain and cotton, to be shipped to European markets. The first shipment of refrigerated beef in a steam freighter arrived in Liverpool from New York in 1875.

Closely paralleling the technological advances in steam engines came the telegraph and ocean cable. The telegraph allowed rapid communication within the nation and the ocean cable, first laid across the Atlantic in 1866, facilitated international communication. These changes in transportation and communications extended world commodity markets. Liverpool became the center of trade for cotton and wheat. By the mid 1880s an American wheat farmer found that the price of the wheat he sold was set in Liverpool, not at his local mill. His price became the Liverpool price minus transportation charges. He took his wheat to the nearest railroad freight station where it was graded and stored in bulk in grain elevators. From there it went to Kansas City, Minneapolis, or other milling centers, or on to a seaport for shipment to overseas markets. Agricultural exports rose from slightly less than $300 million in 1870 to more than $840 million in 1900.

Increased farm output in the post–Civil War era can be attributed in large part to expanded usage of farm machinery—the "horsepower revolution" in agriculture. Total value of farm implements and machinery rose from $271 million in 1870 to $750 million in 1900. By the early 1880s horsepowered machines such as spring-toothed harrows (1877), chilled iron plows (1870), gang plows (1880), twine binders (1878), and automatic binders added to the productivity of the American farmer.

REGIONAL SPECIALIZATION

The changes in transportation and marketing resulted in considerably greater regional specialization than had been practiced before 1865. Northeastern farmers found themselves unable to compete in corn, wheat, and beef production with areas to the west. The Northeast encompassed most of the urban centers, however, and farmers more and more turned to providing dairy products, poultry, fruits, and vegetables for these markets.

The development of the canning industry allowed a wider distribution of fruits and vegetables. Prior to the Civil War few canneries existed, and most canned goods were packed in Baltimore, New York City, Boston, and Portland, Maine. They consisted primarily of oysters, lobsters, fish, peaches, and corn. These were expensive items, consumed only by the wealthy as luxury foods, or by travelers and seamen. After the war the industry expanded into agricultural areas away from the cities. By 1880 there were over four hundred fruit and vegetable canneries in the United States, compared to less than one hundred in 1870. By 1900 Maryland, New York, Pennsylvania, New Jersey, Ohio, Indiana, Illinois, and Wisconsin had all become important canning states, and to the west California was becoming the leader. By the turn of the century over $60 million had been invested in the food industry. Production had risen (over 6 million cases of canned corn, over 9 million cases of tomatoes), and prices had dropped sufficiently that canned foods were no longer a luxury item but a regular part of the diet of urban Americans.

Regional specialization resulted: the central states from the Dakotas to Oklahoma became dominant in wheat, while Ohio, Indiana, Illinois, Iowa, and Missouri became the corn belt. Particular adjustments often proved necessary. In Kansas the first attempts to grow wheat met with little success. Farmers planted the varieties they were familiar with from areas farther east, but insect and weather problems negated their efforts. Some of the new immigrants arriving in Kansas in the 1870s and 1880s were German-Russian Mennonites attracted to the lands being sold by the Kansas Pacific and other land-grant railroads. These immigrants brought with them winter wheat from regions of Russia north of the Black Sea. These new hard varieties of winter wheat thrived in the soil of Kansas, but they presented special problems to American millers used to softer types of the grain. During the 1870s and 1880s steel rollers and other technological refinements were developed to handle the new hard varieties of winter and spring wheat, and by 1900 such wheat came to be highly regarded in the American market and abroad.

Specialization characterized livestock production as well. Since most of the nation's corn went for animal feed, animal production, especially pork, proved economically important for the corn belt. In the Northeast, the emphasis lay with dairy animals for the urban centers. To the west the range-cattle industry became dominant. During the Civil War large herds of beef cattle, estimated at more than four million, had built up in Texas. After the war hundreds of thousands of these animals were driven north to Abilene and Dodge City, Kansas, and other railheads for shipment to the markets of the East. Some of them were used to stock the northern plains, and by the early 1880s the range-cattle industry stretched from Texas to the Canadian border.

The semi-wild Texas longhorns survived well on the Great Plains, but their tough and stringy meat did not earn good market acceptance. On the other hand, many of the eastern meat breeds such as the Angus and shorthorn were not suitable for the range environment of the Great Plains. The Hereford proved ideal. This Scottish breed could handle western Texas summers and North Dakota winters. It thrived on the grasses of the plains and with a final fattening of corn produced a high quality of beef that won good market acceptance.

These cattle operations soon became big business, and cattlemen were among the largest landowners in the country. The XIT ranch in Texas, organized by Chicago entrepreneurs in 1879, held some three million acres of land. In addition cattlemen regularly grazed their herds on federal lands. By the mid 1880s many of the grasslands of the Great Plains suffered from overgrazing. The industry experienced a severe setback during the blizzard of 1886–1887 when many cattle perished. The cattlemen recovered but were forced to modify their operations. Farmers moving into the region had restricted the amount of land available for grazing. Cattlemen now had to fence in their herds and raise hay crops for feeding purposes. J. F. Glidden had developed barbed wire in the early 1870s and, within a decade, his company produced 600 miles of fencing a day.

The marketing of beef grew more sophisticated. Range-grown Herefords, first taken for final fattening to the corn areas of Iowa, went from there to the slaughterhouses of Omaha, Kansas City, or Chicago. The new refrigerated railroad car allowed the dressed animals then to be carried to the markets of the Northeast. George Henry Hammond, Gustavus F. Swift, and Philip D. Armour pioneered this development. Swift achieved domination when he captured the New York market in 1882. He shipped dressed beef in refrigerator cars—insulated cars cooled by blocks of ice—to a refrigerated warehouse in New York where it was distributed to butcher shops. The savings in freight charges proved considerable as a 1,000-pound steer dressed out to only 550 pounds. Refrigerated beef encountered some initial public opposition as consumers were hesitant to eat meat a week or more after slaughter, yet its price sufficiently undersold locally slaughtered beef that such prejudices diminished. *Harper's Weekly* soon proclaimed, "This era of cheap beef."

The cash crops in the South continued to be cotton, tobacco, rice, and sugar, but southern agriculture had suffered severe disruption from the Civil War. By 1870 cotton production stood at only 60 percent of its prewar level, while rice had fallen to 40 percent and sugar to 45 percent. Buildings were rebuilt and lands recultivated, but serious problems continued in the area of farm labor.

Although some of the newly freed slaves went to southern cities such as Jacksonville and Memphis, and a few traveled to the North, most stayed with the occupation they were most familiar with, agriculture. Some blacks obtained farms through the Homestead Act in states such as Florida where public lands could be found, but most sought employment as agricultural laborers. Some planters initially tried to hire the freedmen as laborers, but a shortage of currency rendered this difficult. Instead sharecropping and tenancy became the rule throughout the South.

Various individual arrangements could be made for sharecropping and tenancy. A common form involved a division of the harvested crop into thirds. If the landowner supplied the seed, fertilizer, and mules as well as the land, he would receive two-thirds. If the landowner supplied only the land, his portion was one-third. Sharecroppers worked the land according to the wishes of the landowner and had little freedom of operation from an economic standpoint. Some land was rented on a cash basis in which case the technical arrangement was tenancy rather than sharecropping. A tenant presumably had more freedom of action than a sharecropper, but this was not always true in practice.

All too often tenants and small landowners had to obtain credit from the local country store for the seed, fertilizer, clothes, food, and other items necessary for the maintenance of the family and the farming operations. Customarily, the credit would be granted with the future crop pledged as security (crop lien). The store owner (who was frequently also the landowner) could dictate to the tenant or small landowner the conditions of operation, crops to be planted, and so on; in practice tenants and small landowners rarely got out of debt.

From the economic standpoint the sharecrop-tenancy-crop lien structure of southern agriculture proved inadequate. The planters themselves did not profit well from its operations. Soil depletion and low prices prevailed in the cotton and tobacco areas. Its most destructive aspect, however, lay in its role in race and class suppression. Southern poor white and black farmers were locked into a structure that restricted their opportunities and kept them in a subservient position. Poverty, malnutrition, and low educational levels plagued the sharecropping and tenancy areas of the South.

Although there was nothing intrinsically evil about such devices as tenancy and sharecropping, and lending arrangements such as mortgages and crop liens, the way they were utilized in the South caused them to be viewed as vicious devices. In other parts of the United States both crop and land mortgages and sharecropping worked reasonably well, but there they were employed as business devices and not for class and racial suppression. In such areas they essentially reflected the growing commercialization of agriculture, with farmers increasingly unable to own the land and provide the capital and labor needed to operate it. As industry developed from the individual craftsman to the corporation, a separation of ownership, management, and labor had taken place. American agriculture did not fully follow this pattern in the nineteenth century, but mortgages and tenancy devices paralleled the corporation functions of accumulating capital and limiting risk. The farmer might own the land but would mortgage it to another to obtain operating capital. The banker or merchant advancing the money might require certain farming practices (crop selection or tillage techniques, for example) to be followed, and thus the farmer yielded his management prerogative. This arrangement, however, often proved quite profitable to both farmer and lender.

RURAL UNREST

Difficulties in adjusting to the new commercialized agriculture lay at the root of many of the problems farmers faced in the period from

1865 to 1900. Many farmers, however, viewed these difficulties as the product of conspiracies organized by monopolistic middlemen and bankers. Economic historian Douglass C. North classified such farmers' complaints into three basic categories. First, agricultural prices declined at a rate greater than prices of other goods because of monopolistic elements in the economy. Second, monopolistic middlemen such as railroad owners and grain elevator operators were able to absorb the profits from agriculture, ensuring that farmers did not benefit from improvements in transportation. Third, the usurious interest rates of moneylenders, in effect, robbed the farmer.

North finds that an analysis of these issues as they affected farmers in the Midwest, one of the major areas of unrest, fails to support the farmers' contentions. He concludes that farm prices actually fell less than overall prices during the period from 1867 to 1900. He also notes that declining railroad rates paralleled the decline in farm prices. North acknowledges that interest rates were higher in midwestern agricultural regions, but does not find the differences sufficient to explain the hardships that farmers complained about. Moreover, these sections with higher interest rates were developing areas where shortages of capital and greater risks would normally result in raised interest rates.

Even though the charges of a great conspiracy of the money interests against the farmer do not stand up, the agricultural sector, nonetheless, suffered from many problems. New England witnessed a decline in rural population. Between 1880 and 1900 farm acreage declined between one-third and one-half in Maine, New Hampshire, and Vermont. New England farmers who could not survive were forced to try their hand in newer agricultural regions or to become factory workers. In the South cotton production expanded beyond the needs of the market and, by the 1890s, could not be raised profitably on many of the sharecropping and tenant operations. Overexpansion in the West resulted in a price collapse aggravated by drought and other natural disasters so that many Kansas, Nebraska, and other midwestern farmers reversed the westward movement and went back to older regions farther east. It is estimated that some 180,000 people left Kansas between 1887 and 1891. "In God we trusted, in Kansas we busted" became a familiar refrain.

This disruption of life in the agricultural regions had a deleterious effect upon rural populations. The Jeffersonian vision of the farm as the foundation of American society seemed under assault. In its place, rising cities, teeming with foreign immigrants and luring youth away from the land, looked to farmers like a poor alternative. They found no consolation in the realization that these growing urban centers provided markets for the increased farm production. Instead they saw themselves becoming a minority in an America where they had once been dominant. The demoralization of the rural communities and the small towns that served them proved one of the most destructive aspects of the general adjustments being made to the new commercialized agriculture. Successful farmers tended to be the larger, more efficient operators, while the great number of small farmers found it increasingly difficult to turn a profit.

Farmers' Political Movements

Disgruntled farmers looked to the political process for redress of their grievances. The Grange, founded in 1867 as a social and cultural organization to improve the quality of farm life, branched out into politics in the 1870s, advocating antimonopoly and programs of reform. Grangers gained considerable strength in state government during this decade, particularly in Illinois, Wisconsin, Iowa, and Minnesota, but Grange influence could be felt from Pennsylvania and Georgia in the East to Kansas and Texas in the West. The Grange boasted a membership of 800,000 in 1874, but by 1880 it had fallen to 150,000. Its main area of legislative success came in obtaining state regulation of railroad freight rates and grain elevator and warehouse fees. In 1877 the United States Supreme Court ruled in *Munn v. Illinois*, a case involving state-imposed rate limitations on Chicago grain warehouses, that the state had a right to regulate businesses involved with "a public interest." However, the effectiveness of this decision was lost in 1886 when the Supreme Court, in the Wabash case, ruled that such state measures infringed upon Congress's exclusive control over interstate commerce.

Greenbackers

Farmers also looked to currency schemes to help resolve their difficulties. Farmers in debt readily understood how declining prices deepened their indebtedness. Simply put, if the prices of corn, tobacco, wheat, cotton, meat, and other farm products dropped, increasingly greater production would be required to remove the debt. This increased production further glutted the market and prices fell even lower. Many farmers looked upon the deflationary policies of the federal government as greatly contributing to their problem and argued that an increase of paper money would raise prices and relieve their burdens. The Civil War greenbacks were viewed as the best strategy to accomplish this.

After the war there had been considerable debate over whether to resume specie payments for the close to $500 million greenbacks in circulation. A political movement, the Greenbackers, urged an increase in the number of greenbacks in circulation. Calling a national convention in Indianapolis in May, 1876, they sought repeal of the Specie Resumption Act of 1875, which was to reduce greenbacks in circulation to $300 million and require redemption in gold by 1879. In the November, 1876, election Greenback presidential candidate Peter Cooper of New York received only 81,000 votes. In the congressional races two years later, the Greenback Labor party attracted over one million votes nationally, electing fourteen congressmen, but enthusiasm for the "greenback solution" eroded after this date.

Farmers' Alliance

Greenbackism and the Grange declined during the late 1870s when a temporary rise in farm prices lessened the farmers' woes. Agrarian activism next appeared in the various farmers' alliances. Around 1875 a group of farmers in Lampasas County, Texas, formed an organization, an alliance, for catching horse thieves and recovering stray cattle. They also opposed the large land and cattle companies, which they regarded as monopolistic. Other local clubs began and by 1885 the Grand State Alliance in Texas had 50,000 members. From Texas the movement spread throughout the South. Merger with the Louisiana Farmers' Union in 1887 and with the Agricultural Wheel of Arkansas in 1888 resulted in the formation of the Farmers' and Laborers' Union of America. The North Carolina Farmers' Association had 42,000 members by 1888. Black farmers in the South joined the Colored Farmers' National Alliance.

The National Farmers' Alliance, commonly called the North-western Alliance, had its strength in the wheat states. By 1890 Kansas had 130,000 alliance members, with Nebraska, the Dakotas, and Minnesota close behind. The alliance groups favored the abolition of national banks, a graduated income tax, nationalization of the railroads, the prohibition of alien land ownership, and the free and unlimited coinage of silver. The southern alliance also favored a subtreasury plan whereby the federal government would build and maintain warehouses for basic agricultural commodities (cotton, corn, wheat, tobacco, sugar, rice, wool, oats, and rye). Farmers could store their products and receive receipts that could be used as currency for up to 80 percent of the value of their commodities. The farmer would thus have the use of 80 percent of the cash value of his crop while still being in a position to withhold sale until the market turned favorable.

Populism

The most significant transition from farm protest groups to direct political action at the national level came in June, 1890, with the formation of the Peoples' Party, better known as the Populist Party. A national convention was held in Omaha in July, 1891, attended by alliance groups, the Knights of Labor, and various reform groups. That political action offered the key to solving economic problems was underscored by Populist leader Mary Ellen "Yelling" Lease of Kansas, who delighted the faithful by telling them they should "raise less corn and more hell." At Omaha the Populists nominated James B. Weaver of Iowa for President and put forward an economic platform calling for the free and unlimited coinage of silver, a graduated income tax, postal savings banks, government ownership of railroads and of telegraph and telephone operations, prohibition of alien land ownership, immigration restriction, and an eight-hour work day.

Free Silver

The Depression of 1893 intensified the farm protest movement. As the election of 1896 neared, inflationists singled out the issue of free and unlimited coinage of silver as the key to prosperity. Silver had been used for currency along with gold since the colonial period. Alexander Hamilton had argued for the use of both precious metals, and other supporters of hard currency such as Andrew Jackson accepted silver along with gold. In the 1830s the federal government set the value of silver coined into money at the ratio of 16 to 1 (16 ounces of silver equaled 1 ounce of gold). On the London market, however, silver brought a higher price, and little silver ended up in coins. In 1873 such a small amount of silver was being presented for coinage that Congress discontinued the practice. Congress's elimination of silver came at the very time that major discoveries in the Far West lowered the world price of silver, which would have made it attractive for mine owners to coin their silver if the old ratio had still been in effect. Advocates of silver coinage looked upon the Act of 1873 as a "crime" promoted by a conspiracy of international bankers and Wall Street.

In 1878 silver proponents led by Missouri Representative Richard "Silver Dick" Bland pressured Congress into passing the Bland-Allison Act, which provided for the monthly coinage of two to four million dollars of silver at the ratio of 16 to 1. Farmers and other debtors favoring an increase of money in circulation gained little from this act as pro-gold administrations never purchased more than the two-million-dollar minimum, and most of that stayed in government vaults. In 1890 silverites bolstered with alliance support prompted the passage of the Sherman Silver Purchase Act, which required the treasury to purchase 4.5 million ounces of silver each month using legal tender treasury notes as payment. The act had the effect of increasing paper money in circulation and weakening the federal gold reserve. It was repealed during the Panic of 1893 as President Cleveland sought to lessen the drain on the gold reserve. Cleveland's action did little to stem the panic but much to antagonize the silverites in his party.

The free silver promoters gained control of the Democratic party in the election of 1896 and nominated William Jennings Bryan of Nebraska. The Populists also endorsed Bryan, and both groups pushed for the free and unlimited coinage of silver to inflate currency, raise prices, and end the depression. Republicans argued that surplus production, not monetary policies, caused the low prices, and so the Republicans nominated the goldbug conservative William McKinley of Ohio. McKinley won, and the Currency Act of 1900 (Gold Standard Act) declared the gold dollar as the standard unit of value. The Democratic party ran Bryan and free silver for a second time in the election of 1900, but the return of prosperity sounded the death knell for the silver issue.

THE COMING OF BIG BUSINESS

The post–Civil War decades witnessed striking economic growth. The American population climbed from 40 million in 1870 to 76 million by 1900. The labor force experienced an even larger rate of increase, rising from 13 million to 29 million over these three decades. During these years, as well, industry passed agriculture in economic importance. In 1870 agriculture provided 57 percent of value added and industry 43 percent. By the turn of the century those positions had reversed, with industry responsible for 65 precent of value added, and agriculture down to 35 percent.

Industry's surge to the dominant position in the American economy came about because of the emergence of big business. Industry produced more than it had in the pre–Civil War years, but its ability to achieve such an expansion of production can be traced to the new structure of business organization. According to Alfred Chandler, "The major innovation in the American economy between the 1880s and the turn of the century was the creation of the great corporations in American industry."

Although the terms *industrialization* and *big business* are sometimes used interchangeably, they represent different stages of American economic development. The industrialization process had gotten well under way in America by the second decade of the nineteenth century, with the coming of the textile mills to New England. However, with the exception of the railroads, big business did not evolve until the post–Civil War era. Until that time, as Glenn Porter explains, business "continued to be done in single-plant operations, ownership of individual units was still concentrated among small numbers of people, ownership and management still usually went hand in hand, manufacturers specialized in a single product or a single line of goods, and industry had not yet become the province of complex, bureaucratically administered managerial networks."

The rise of big business fundamentally altered these earlier relationships. The scale of business operations changed dramatically. The largest pre–Civil War businesses, again with the exception of the railroads, had less than $1 million in capitalization. By the end of the nineteenth century, many businesses had tens of millions of dollars in capitalization, and some hundreds of millions. United States Steel, organized in 1901, for example, consisted of 156 factory units and was capitalized at $1.4 billion.

The extended scope of business in the postwar era created large capital demands. The corporation, with its access to larger pools of capital and its protection of limited liability, replaced partnerships and proprietorships as the significant form of business organization. With ownership resting with the shareholders, and policy emanating from the board of directors, a new managerial class developed to oversee the daily operations of these large enterprises. This new corporate structure, maximizing production for the national and international markets, proved the vehicle for America's rise to global industrial leadership by the end of the nineteenth century.

THE INDUSTRIAL PROCESS

The American industrial strategy can most readily be seen in those consumer-goods industries that utilized mass-production methods, particularly meat packing, clothing, footwear, watches, and bicycles. By the late 1890s the larger meat-packing houses had been highly mechanized. As the animals moved along a power-driven disassembly line, individual workers performed the chores of killing, skinning, and making the carcasses ready for refrigerated shipment to the consuming public.

Not until the introduction of the sewing machine in 1846 did the manufacture of clothing cease to be a hand operation. By 1860 over 100,000 sewing machines had been sold in the United States. During the Civil War the demand for uniforms was met with factory-made clothes, and after the war such operations provided ready-to-wear clothing for civilians. Because of greater variations in style, factory-made women's clothing appeared later, but by 1900 American men could cheaply purchase good quality factory-made suits.

The shoe industry evolved in a similar way. Although still requiring a large number of hand operations, factory production of boots and shoes developed during the Civil War. The application of mass-production techniques produced large quantities of low-cost, good-quality footwear. The McKay sole-sewing machine of 1864 cut the cost of attaching soles to uppers from the hand-sewing cost of 75 cents a pair to 3 cents. By 1895 some 25 million pairs of factory-made shoes were produced annually, and in 1900 the U.S. Bureau of the Census judged the boot and shoe industry as "a perfect system of continuous manufacturing."

Watch and bicycle manufacturing best demonstrated the American system of assembly-line manufacturing using interchangeable parts. The use of interchangeable parts allowed the American worker to average 150 watches a year compared to his Swiss counterpart who averaged 50 with his hand-fitted parts. Bicycle manufacturing in the United States achieved a high degree of standardization. By 1900, less than two decades after they first appeared in England, bicycles equipped with pneumatic tires and coaster brakes were being ridden by some four million Americans. Bicycle riders promoted better roads, and much of the mobility we associate with the automobile was actually under way during the age of the bicycle.

DISTRIBUTION AND MARKETING

The establishment of department stores in the larger urban centers and the appearance of mail-order houses to serve the rural areas facilitated the distribution and sale of the growing volume of American products. Department stores offered a wide variety of merchandise at relatively low prices, along with such services as free delivery and charge accounts. Chain store organizations offering specialized lines of merchandise such as groceries, hardware, and drugs became popular in the medium- and smaller-sized cities. In the rural areas Americans had access to a wide variety of goods through mail-order houses such as Sears Roebuck and Montgomery Ward. These mail-order houses, chain stores, and department stores purchased in large quantities directly from the manufacturer and offered substantial savings over the existing manufacturer-to-wholesaler-to-retailer pattern. R. H. Macy's slogan in 1887 promised, "Goods suitable for the millionaire at prices in reach of the millions." By 1900 the linking of mass production and nationwide distribution had established the groundwork for a consumer society.

Prototypes of Big Business: Steel and Oil

The steel industry offers a prime example of the surge of big business in the late nineteenth century. Although steel had been in limited use since antiquity, not until the development of the Bessemer process of the 1850s could it be produced in sufficient quantity for uses other than instruments, tools, cutlery, and small objects. The Bessemer process required low-phosphorus iron ore and presented problems of quality control, but by the 1880s refinements in the process plus the introduction of open-hearth furnaces had resolved most of the technological difficulties. The new process created a large enough volume of steel for bridge building and other structural applications, as well as for replacing iron railroad tracks. The strength of steel rails allowed much heavier loads to be hauled, and they offered five times the durability of iron rails.

Large-scale production enhanced steel-making cost efficiency. Carnegie sold steel rails for over $100 a ton in 1873. By 1875 his price had dropped to $50, a decade later to $20, and toward the end of the 1890s, it had fallen to $12. The industry operated behind a wall of tariff protection that enabled entrepreneurs like Andrew Carnegie, even with lowering prices, to earn large profits. By the late 1880s demand for steel rails had decreased, and Carnegie moved into structural steel to meet the needs of the developing cities. Carnegie Steel absorbed less efficient competitors and by 1892 had become the largest steel operation in the United States.

PROFILE:

Andrew Carnegie and John D. Rockefeller— Robber Barons or Industrial Statesmen?

America's new industrial leaders have not been universally regarded as men of virtue who secured their fortunes through honesty and hard work. Indeed the years of their dominance have been described as the "age of the robber barons" or, in Mark Twain's phrase, the "Gilded Age," conveying his sense that the era was overlaid with an ornate veneer, but lacking in underlying substance. The robber baron analogy likens the leaders of big business to the medieval robber barons who lived by plunder and force. The term "robber baron," although used as early as the 1880s to attack certain business practices, came into wider prominence with the publication of Matthew Josephson's book with that title in 1934. Josephson's *The Robber Barons: The Great American Capitalists, 1861–1901* offered a portrait of the "small class of men who arose at the time of our Civil War and suddenly swept into power." Josephson acknowledged the gains in productivity and efficiency introduced into the economy by many of these entrepreneurs, but indicted their rapacity: "To organize and exploit the resources of a nation upon a gigantic scale, to regiment its farmers and workers into harmonious corps of producers, and to do this only in the name of an uncontrolled appetite for private profit—here surely is the great inherent contradiction whence so much disaster, outrage and misery have flowed." Let us briefly examine the careers of the two preeminent industrialists of that age, John D. Rockefeller and Andrew Carnegie, and see how valid this indictment is in their cases.

John D. Rockefeller, son of a patent medicine salesman, was born in Richford, New York, in 1839. By the age of nineteen he had his own produce commission business in Cleveland and soon earned substantial profits selling salt and pork to the Union army. Scouting about for investment opportunities, Rockefeller settled on the emerging oil industry. The first oil well had been sunk in 1859 in Titusville, Pennsylvania, and this new product offered substantial possibilities as an industrial lubricant and a source of kerosene for illumination. Rockefeller decided to enter the refining sector of the business, determined to impose order and efficiency on a chaotic enterprise. He had a talent for persuading older, more experienced businessmen such as Samuel Andrews and Henry Flagler to join him in his venture. This partnership, formed in 1867, became incorporated as Standard Oil of Ohio in 1870, with Rockefeller owning two-thirds of the shares. The new corporation held less than 10 percent of the nation's oil refining capacity at this time, but Rockefeller had immediate plans to move into a more dominant position in the industry.

Rockefeller's goal was to systematically eliminate competition and move toward a monopolistic position in the oil refining business. His first avenue of attack lay in developing an advantageous relationship with the lifelines of the industry, the railroads that hauled the crude from the oil fields to the refineries and from there to the marketplaces. Early on, Rockefeller's volume of traffic enabled him to negotiate a discount (rebate) on the business he supplied the railroads. As his volume increased, Rockefeller insisted upon and won "drawbacks," rebates on all of the oil being carried on these rail lines. Rockefeller had placed himself in the extraordinary position of being subsidized by his competitors. An attempt to counter Rockefeller's advantageous relationship with the railroads by building a pipeline evoked a no-holds-barred economic assault by Standard Oil. Throughout the 1870s Rockefeller's competitors yielded to the awesome pressure he brought to bear against them, and by the end of the decade he controlled 90 percent of the nation's oil refining capacity.

Rockefeller now moved to consolidate his position by creating the nation's first trust in 1882. The Standard Oil Trust consisted of forty companies whose shares were transferred to a board of trustees in return for trust certificates. The obvious economic power built into such an arrangement quickly attracted imitators in other industries. It provoked, as well, an outraged public reaction and a number of lawsuits. The supreme court of Ohio dissolved the Standard Oil Trust in 1892, but it reorganized as a holding company. New Jersey had revised its incorporation laws in 1888 to allow corporations to purchase and "hold" shares in other corporations. This became the new strategy of imposing control in an industry. The U.S. Supreme Court in 1911 dissolved Standard Oil into thirty-three constituent companies, and Standard of New Jersey, now Exxon, has risen to be the world's largest corporation.

At the time of the Supreme Court's action, John D. Rockefeller had reduced his active role in the management of Standard Oil. He had amassed a fortune of close to a billion dollars, and he dispersed part of it to philanthropies such as the University of Chicago, the Rockefeller Institute of Medical Research, the General Education Board, and the Rockefeller Foundation. His defenders, such as historian Allan Nevins, emphasize his philanthropic contributions, his innovations in American business, and portray him as a "captain of industry" who brought stability and efficiency to the chaotic oil industry of late-nineteenth-century America. His critics, such as Henry Demarest Lloyd and Ida Tarbell, see him instead as a ruthless competitor, driven to use any means to dominate the market.

Rockefeller clearly does not merit being bracketed with men like Daniel Drew and Jim Fisk, the spoilsmen of the railroads, in the category of robber barons. Drew and Fisk, and others like them in that era, functioned as parasites, draining all the economic substance from an enterprise and leaving a hulk in their wake. Rockefeller built, at times in unscrupulous and unsavory ways, an economic empire. His genius lay, as one commentator has noted, not in the technology of oil, but in the technology of control. His skills might have been applied in any of a number of ventures, but the newly emerging oil industry offered the widest range for his talents. He was, in his own words, "all business," and his driving ambition for mastery led him to shape the rules and break the rules in the tumultuous business environment at the end of the nineteenth century.

Andrew Carnegie followed a pathway different from Rockefeller's in shaping an extraordinarily successful career. Born in Scotland in 1835 Carnegie came to the United States in 1848 with his poverty-stricken parents and started work at the age of thirteen as a bobbin boy in a cotton mill, earning $1.20 a week. A year later he became a messenger boy in the Pittsburgh telegraph office, and by 1853 served as personal telegrapher to Thomas Scott, general superintendent of the Pennsylvania Railroad. In 1860, at the age of twenty-five, Carnegie was appointed superintendent of the Pittsburgh division of that railroad.

Had he stayed with the railroad Carnegie would undoubtedly have become a wealthy man, but after the Civil War he resigned his position to pursue wider possibilities in iron and oil. Beginning in 1873 he devoted himself exclusively to steel, insisting that his avenue to success lay in "putting all my eggs in one basket and then watching the basket." Carnegie paid close attention to his basket, since it expanded very quickly. During the Depression of 1873–1878, he bought out four of his competitors. Upon the advice of Henry Clay Frick and other of his managers, Carnegie integrated his operations vertically and acquired sources of coking coal and iron ore. By 1900 Carnegie Steel dominated American production and turned out more steel than all of Great Britain's mills combined. After selling his company to Morgan and the interests who formed the U.S. Steel Corporation, Carnegie retired from the steel business and devoted himself to disbursing his $250 million in accordance with his "Gospel of Wealth" philosophy.

Carnegie believed that a rich man before he died had an obligation to dispose of the bulk of his fortune on projects that would benefit mankind. Carnegie was a firm adherent of Social Darwinism, which held that a process of natural selection operated in the human as well as the animal world and that the fittest survived. Accordingly, business leaders who had demonstrated their fitness by accumulating vast fortunes should view themselves as trustees of this wealth and use it during their lifetimes to support institutions that uplifted the community.

Carnegie assessed the worthiness of projects for his philanthropy in the following order: (1) universities (2) free libraries (3) hospitals (4) parks (5) concert and meeting halls (6) swimming baths (7) churches. The relegation of churches to the last category rankled religious leaders and prompted theologian William Jewett Tucker to challenge Carnegie's "Gospel of Wealth" on the grounds that it was simply charity and did not deal with fundamental issues of economic justice and the distribution of wealth in society.

Before his death in 1919, Carnegie had given away more than $350 million, including $60 million for close to 3,000 free public libraries. Carnegie had discovered that his fortune grew more rapidly than his ability to properly disperse it so, in 1911, he established the Carnegie Corporation with an endowment of $125 million plus the undistributed portion of his estate. Carnegie, in the last decade of his life, had thus created another behemoth. Joseph Wall, Carnegie's biographer, noted, "As United States Steel had been the supercorporation in industry, so the Carnegie Corporation of New York became the first supertrust in philanthropy."

IMMIGRATION AND URBANIZATION

Just as Andrew Carnegie and his parents had left Scotland in the 1840s in search of a better life in America, millions of other Europeans followed that same path across the Atlantic in the years after the Civil War. These "new" immigrants were predominantly southern and eastern Europeans: Italians, Greeks, Poles, Russians, and Slavs. They arrived in America in breathtaking numbers, over 26 million in all between the end of the Civil War and the beginning of World War I.

These immigrants settled in large numbers in America's cities and, joined by the stream of those leaving the nation's farms, tripled the urban population between 1870 and 1900. By 1880, some 87 percent of Chicago's residents were foreign-born or the children of immigrants, and the percentages for other urban areas were almost as high: Milwaukee, 84 percent; Detroit, 84 percent; New York, 80 percent; Cleveland, 80 percent; San Francisco, 78 percent.

These new Americans, eager to work and make their way, filled a rapidly industrializing society's voracious demands for labor. The vast majority of these immigrants, Carl Degler has noted, came "in the prime of life—in the working years between fourteen and forty-five." In 1900, for example, 80 percent of those arriving in America fell into that age range. Economist John R. Commons acknowledged, in 1906, the bonus afforded the host country in such a migration: "Thus, immigration brings to us a population of working ages unhampered by unproductive mouths to feed. Their home countries have borne the expense of rearing them up to the industrial period of their lives, and then America, without that heavy expense, reaps whatever profits there are on the investment."

TABLE 6:1
Immigration to the United States: 1865–1914

Years	Numbers of Immigrants
1865–1869	1,374,018
1870–1874	1,886,501
1875–1879	885,636
1880–1884	3,037,594
1885–1889	2,210,974
1890–1894	2,320,645
1895–1899	1,373,649
1900–1904	2,855,149
1905–1909	4,947,239
1910–1914	5,174,701

Source: U.S. Department of Commerce, *Historical Statistics of the United States, Colonial Times to 1970.*

This tidal wave of immigration undoubtedly proved a bonanza for employers seeking an ample and inexpensive work force. American workers, however, viewed the surge of immigrants with ambivalence or, at times, antagonism, fearful of their own ability to improve their bargaining position in the midst of a constantly swelling labor force.

LABOR

The period from the end of the Civil War to the turn of the century proved contentious for America's workers. The rise of larger, more impersonal business units placed unorganized laborers in an increasingly disadvantageous position. The flood of immigrants undercut their bargaining power, particularly that of unskilled workers. Attempts to organize labor met with fluctuating success, ebbing and flowing in response to the overall health of the economy. A number of strikes, often called not to press for improved conditions but to protest wage cuts, frequently flared into violence. Industrialists used private police forces, as well as calling for state and federal troops, to curb protests by discontented workers.

Trade unions showed strong development following the Civil War, reaching a total membership of 300,000 by 1872. An attempt to unite labor unions and reform associations came in 1866 with the formation of the National Labor Union. The original objective of the movement was an eight-hour workday. During the presidencies of William Sylvis (1868) and Richard F. Trevellick (1869), however, the union turned increasingly to politics but collapsed with the failure of the National Labor Reform Party in 1872.

The Depression of 1873–1878 had a shattering effect on labor unions, plunging their membership to around 50,000. Labor disputes erupted into violence, most notably in the anthracite region of eastern Pennsylvania with the Molly Maguire incident, and during the general strike of 1877. The Molly Maguires were a secret group of Irish coal miners who employed violence against the coal companies and railroads. Based upon evidence provided by an infiltrator into the group, twenty Molly Maguires were convicted in 1876 and hanged for murder.

The following year, 1877, witnessed the most extensive industrial violence of the nineteenth century. An announcement by the Baltimore and Ohio Railroad of its third wage cut since 1873 triggered a walkout that quickly spread, shutting down two-thirds of the rail lines across the country. Striking workers battled state militia in Buffalo, St. Louis, Chicago, San Francisco, and Pittsburgh, where the Pennsylvania Railroad yards were set ablaze and more than twenty-five persons lost their lives. President Hayes dispatched federal troops to quell the rioting. The scope of this industrial warfare stunned many Americans. Historian James Ford Rhodes observed, "We had hugged the delusion that such social uprisings belonged to Europe and had no reason of being in a free republic where there was plenty of room and an equal chance for all."

Later large-scale strikes repeated the harsh lessons of 1877. The 1892 strike in Homestead, Pennsylvania, against Carnegie Steel brought state militia intervention and left the once-powerful Amalgamated Association of Iron and Steel Workers shattered. Two years later, a strike by the American Railway Union, led by Eugene Debs, against the Pullman company was broken by federal troops, and Debs ended up in prison on contempt charges. Labor clearly lacked the economic and political strength to successfully challenge powerful corporations. Its hope of gaining that ability lay in developing an effective national organization.

The Knights of Labor had seemed for a time to be moving in that direction. Organized in 1869, it had gained over 700,000 members by the middle of the 1880s. This organization differed markedly from the trade unions in that the Knights formally renounced strikes. Going beyond the usual wage and hours considerations, it sought instead to establish worker-run producers' cooperatives. Terence V. Powderley, head of the Knights, proclaimed, "There is no good reason why labor cannot, through cooperation, own and operate mines, factories, and railroads." The Knights' membership peaked in 1886 and then declined precipitously. The Haymarket Affair in May, 1886, helped hasten the Knights' demise. A labor protest rally in Haymarket Square, Chicago, ended tragically when a bomb was tossed as police were breaking up the meeting. An often indiscriminate outrage at labor agitation provoked by this event unfairly tarnished the Knights' reputation. An even more fundamental problem dividing the Knights of Labor lay in the uneasiness many workers felt with the utopian goals being pursued. The creation of a new national organization, the American Federation of Labor, committed to traditional "bread and butter" unionism sealed the fate of the Knights.

The American Federation of Labor was a federation of independent craft unions composed of skilled workers. When organized in Columbus, Ohio, in 1886 it consisted of some twenty-five labor groups representing about 150,000 members under its first president, Samuel Gompers. The AFL limited its objectives to the pragmatic goals of higher wages and better working conditions. It made major gains after the Depression of 1893–1896, despite a massive anti-union campaign by the newly organized National Association of Manufacturers. As of 1900, however, little had been accomplished in organizing the millions of unskilled and semi-skilled industrial workers in the great manufacturing concerns. Concentration on skilled tradesmen gave the AFL a short-term strength, but postponed the basic problem of organizing most of the key industries until well into the twentieth century.

GOVERNMENT AND THE ECONOMY

The relationship between government and the economy somewhat shifted during this period, as witnessed by the railroad regulation and antitrust movements. Public resentment of high rates, corruption, and other abuses in railway transportation resulted in a variety of bills being considered by Congress. In 1874 a special committee headed by Senator William Windom of Minnesota recommended competitive routes and raised the possibility of a government-owned railroad to serve as a regulatory guide. This and similar bills failed, leaving railroad regulation to the states during the 1870s. The issue took on a national focus again in 1886 when the Supreme Court in the Wabash case stripped the states of their regulatory powers over interstate carriers. The following year Congress passed the Interstate Commerce Act, which prohibited discriminatory rate structures by interstate carriers, but did not specifically authorize rate-setting. The commission created by the act (Interstate Commerce Commission) was denied the power to fix rates in a series of Supreme Court decisions in 1896 and 1897. These decisions determined that Congress had not given the commission the power to set rates of any kind. By 1900 the ICC could do little more than prepare reports and make recommendations. Of far greater significance in rate reduction were the technological developments of steel rails, air brakes, couplers, and other devices that allowed larger trains to haul products more efficiently. Improved signal equipment also reduced accident rates and lowered costs. During the early twentieth century Congress would again consider railroad regulation, encouraged in part by the railroads themselves seeking more order and stability for their industry.

SHERMAN ANTI-TRUST ACT

The anti-trust movement followed the pattern of railroad regulation by moving from the state to the national level. Much of the opposition to those big businesses commonly labeled "trusts" came from small farmers and businessmen who were at a severe disadvantage in coping with the tactics of the large corporations. By 1890, twenty states had some type of prohibition against monopoly or restraint of trade. But, as in the case of railroad regulation, states had little power over interstate corporations, and the demand intensified for federal action. The Sherman Anti-Trust Act (1890) was put forward by Senator John Sherman of Ohio, although he was assisted in its preparation by Senators George F. Hoar of Massachusetts and George F. Edmunds of Vermont. The act authorized the federal government to dissolve trusts that engaged in illegal restraints of interstate trade and commerce, but the terms proved too vague to allow effective policing. Prior to 1901, the act served more as a weapon against labor unions than against big business. The Pullman strike of 1894 resulted in the issuance of injunctions under the Sherman Act against Eugene Debs and other labor leaders. The Supreme Court upheld Debs's conviction for contempt in violating the injunction, and the use of injunctions emerged as a powerful restraint on labor unions.

AMERICA AT THE END OF THE NINETEENTH CENTURY

As the nineteenth century closed, the nation had embarked on a new wave of prosperity. The dynamism of American life mirrored the enormous physical energy that had been harnessed over the previous century. Energy released from coal and transferred through steam had added a new dimension to the quest for power beyond that provided by muscle or by wind, water, or horse. There had seemed virtually no limit to the multiplication and application of this power, and in the last decades of the century new energy sources of petroleum and of electricity from coal and water had expanded future potentialities. This massive increase in energy was matched by a wide range of new processes and materials. The developing technology of industrial chemistry promised a cornucopia of products from coal, petroleum, and other organic materials.

This glorification of material well-being was not without its critics. Historian Henry Adams expressed doubt that technological advancement reflected true progress. Some scientists had doubts as well, not about the value of the gains, but about whether the nation's natural resources could sustain such growth far into the future. The misery experienced by many workers during the Depression of 1893–1897 and the cramped, squalid tenements of the nation's cities served as painful reminders of underlying problems in the economy. But despite these concerns, the majority of Americans welcomed the new century in a mood of profound optimism. The American feast was just beginning.

SEVEN

AN EXPANDING INDUSTRIAL POWER: 1900–1913

Richard Hofstadter summarized much of America's economic, social, and political history when he noted that the United States had been born in the country and moved to the city. That shift from a rural to an urban society took place, in large part, in the generation following the Civil War. During those years, the interconnected pressures of urbanization, industrialization, and immigration reshaped America. By 1900 a "new" nation had emerged.

AMERICA IN 1900

In 1900 there were 76 million Americans, 40 percent of whom lived in urban areas. The nation's population had virtually doubled since 1870, and that increase was most visible in the cities. In 1870 no American city had a million residents, and only two had more than half a million. By 1900 New York, Chicago, and Philadelphia had passed the million mark while Baltimore, Boston, and St. Louis counted more than a half-million residents.

This surge of urban population had been fed by streams of immigrants—millions of Germans, Irish, English, and, more recently, Russians, Italians, and Slavs. More than three-quarters of New York City's population in 1900 consisted of immigrants and their children. They had fled Europe, lured by the promise and opportunity of America. By the turn of the century, however, many Americans had begun to feel doubt and uncertainty about the changes that had transformed the nation since the Civil War. America had become a "new" nation so suddenly that there had been little time to reflect on the implications of the emerging economic and social order. The populists in the 1890s had raised their voices in protest against the diminished status of the farmer. Now, in the first years of the twentieth century, a new movement—progressivism—sought to redress the grievances that plagued the American economic and political systems.

THE PROGRESSIVE MOVEMENT

The perception of American life that generated progressivism was, according to Richard Hofstadter, the sense that while the nation had experienced an extraordinary release of productive energy in the last decades of the nineteenth century, its "moral energies had lain relatively dormant." The Progressives sought "to develop the moral will, the intellectual insight, and the political and administrative agencies to remedy the accumulated evils and negligences of a period of industrial growth." The problems of overcrowded tenements, exploited workers, and industrial concentration would not, the Progressives believed, resolve themselves. The solutions lay with an effective reform movement and an enlightened and outraged public.

Investigative journalism proved to be one of the most potent forces in shaping public attitudes on the problems of industrial America. President Theodore Roosevelt, fearful of the revolutionary potential of these analyses, characterized some of the writers as muckrakers. Despite Roosevelt's attack, these explorations of the darker side of American life attracted a large audience. Readers discovered the harsh realities of child labor in John Spargo's *The Bitter Cry of the Children*. Upton Sinclair's *The Jungle* graphically documented the primitive

BREAKER BOYS AT A MINE IN PENNSYLVANIA, 1911.
National Archives

health standards and the abysmal working conditions in Chicago's meat-packing plants. *McClure's*, a popular magazine, became a major contributor to this growing body of criticism. In a series of articles in *McClure's* on municipal corruption, eventually collected and published as *The Shame of the Cities*, Lincoln Steffens depicted the collaboration between the business community and the urban political machines. The most detailed and devastating indictment of that period, however, was provided by Ida M. Tarbell in her *History of the Standard Oil Company*, which ran for eighteen monthly installments in *McClure's*.

Tarbell wished to expose the evolution and inner workings of a trust and chose Standard Oil as her case study. Two criteria determined her selection. First, Standard Oil was the prototype of the trust, "The one whose story is best fitted to illuminate the subject of combinations of capital." Second, extensive documentation on the operation of Standard Oil was available because the trust had been under investigation by Congress and the state legislatures of Pennsylvania, New York, and Ohio almost continuously since its creation.

Ida Tarbell, who grew up in the oil region of Titusville, Pennsylvania, set out to analyze the role of John D. Rockefeller in attaining domination of the oil industry. She examined his collusion with the railroads, his effectiveness in driving out competition, and his ability, once the trust was in place, to exercise "power over prices with almost preternatural skill." Tarbell's study, published in book form in 1904, contained over 500 pages of text and a 200-page appendix filled with tables, contracts, and testimony before legislative bodies. Historian Allan Nevins, a later, more sympathetic biographer of Rockefeller, acknowledged the Tarbell work as "the most spectacular success of the muckraking school of journalism, and its most enduring achievement."

Tarbell's indictment of Standard Oil served to focus Progressive anxieties about the dangers of business combinations. From 1898 to 1903 there had been a wave of business mergers that far surpassed the trust movement ten years earlier. The first surge of consolidations primarily involved industries producing consumer goods; the later one was concerned with producers' goods. They differed as well in the financial leadership of the movements. The first wave of combination had been primarily funded by the industrialists themselves. The later merger movement was largely orchestrated by the investment banking houses. J. P. Morgan provided the most dramatic example of the new trend, organizing the largest industrial unit in the world, United States Steel, capitalized at more than one billion dollars.

This merger wave at the turn of the century, according to Robert Heilbroner, fundamentally altered the structure of American industry. At the end of the Civil War no single company dominated any industry. By 1904, "one or two giant firms—usually put together by merger—controlled at least half the output in 78 industries."

John Moody, in an attempt to dispute the "agitators" who were attacking big business, published The Truth about the Trusts in 1904. Moody catalogued 318 industrial combinations as of 1903, representing 40 percent of the manufacturing capital in the nation. Exactly 184 of these consolidations had been developed since 1898. Overarching these combinations Moody found "two mammoth groups," the Rockefeller and Morgan, which constituted "the heart of the business and commercial life of the nation." This interlocking network of big business, which Moody viewed as "industrial progress," appeared to most Progressives as the strangulation of economic opportunity. They pressed for the breaking up of these "trusts," often using the term loosely to include any business organization designed to restrict competition. Their hope for restoring a competitive framework for the economy lay with the federal government.

President Theodore Roosevelt's assessment of trusts proved less condemning than many Progressives would have preferred. Roosevelt saw such combinations as "an inevitable development of modern industrialism." Trusts were not intrinsically evil, and he believed the government should move against them only when the public interest demanded it.

Early in his administration, Roosevelt challenged a "bad" trust. The Northern Securities Company, a consolidation of the James J. Hill–J. P. Morgan and the E. H. Harriman railway empires, controlled the northern rail routes from Chicago to the west coast. In 1902 Roosevelt instructed Attorney General Philander Knox to bring suit against the company as being in violation of the Sherman Anti-Trust Act. The Supreme Court in 1904, by a 5–4 vote, dissolved the Northern Securities Company, thwarting plans to create a national railroad monopoly.

Two years later, in 1906, the Roosevelt administration took on the preeminent trust, Standard Oil. The case was not decided by the Supreme Court until 1911, after Roosevelt had left office, but it represented a double-edged victory for T. R. Not only did the court determine that Standard Oil had to be broken up into its constituent parts, but it also accepted Roosevelt's distinction between "good" and "bad" trusts. The majority opinion, written by Chief Justice White, enunciated the "rule of reason," that the Sherman Anti-Trust Act outlawed only "undue" or "unreasonable" restraints of trade. Justice John Marshall Harlan, dissenting, attacked the "rule of reason" as "judicial legislation" and a "perversion of the plain words of an act in order to defeat the will of Congress."

Roosevelt's attacks against some industrial combinations earned him the reputation of "trust buster," but except in the case of the railroads, the attacks did little to resolve the problem of concentration. Economic historian Thomas Cochran, describing the operations of the individual Standard Oil companies after the court-ordered dissolution, characterized them as functioning "with such synchronization that they might almost have remained one company." Roosevelt himself, in a speech given at the 1912 Progressive party national convention, acknowledged the limited effectiveness of anti-trust litigations. The Sherman Act had provided "no real check on the great trusts." The solution lay in government as regulator, not dismantler. Roosevelt, in his summation, insisted that the new economic order required acceptance of a more assertive government role. Once, he said, individual liberty was equatable with limited government. Now, however, the limitation of governmental action "means the enslavement of the people by the great corporations who can only be held in check through the extension of governmental power."

Federal regulatory power was extended in several sectors of the economy during Roosevelt's presidency. The Interstate Commerce Commission was strengthened by the Elkins Act (1903) banning railroad rebates, and the Hepburn Act (1906) granting it greater authority to regulate rates. Congress, prodded by public outrage evoked by Sinclair's *The Jungle*, passed a pure food and drug bill and a meat inspection bill in 1906. Roosevelt, an ardent proponent of conservation, pressed for a larger governmental responsibility in protecting the environment. The Newlands Act (1902) committed federal funds to reclamation projects and dam construction. In addition, President Roosevelt issued an executive order in 1907 creating 17 million acres of forest preserves. The following year, he convened a National Conservation Congress at the White House to attempt to develop systematic programs to safeguard natural resources.

The legislative successes of the Progressives in the first decade of the twentieth century, both on the state and federal levels, in mitigating the worst effects of industrialization were limited. Indeed, New Left historian Gabriel Kolko argued that they were not even "progressive" but represented a "triumph of conservatism." What Kolko found striking about this period was "the large area of consensus and unity among key business leaders and most political factions on the role of the federal government in the economy." Kolko's assertion that the Progressive economic reforms did not move much beyond a conservative consensus is largely accurate. However, that consensus itself had shifted considerably over the previous generation in its willingness to accept governmental economic intervention.

For William Allen White, the essence of progressivism was its insistence on using the government "as an agency of human welfare." That principle would be evoked again in the 1930s to justify far more substantial governmental reform and regulation of the American economy.

Scientific Management

Progressivism laid great stress on planning and effective organization, what Samuel Hays has called "the gospel of efficiency." The most widely acclaimed preacher of this gospel in the business community was an engineer named Frederick Taylor.

Taylor had been preparing for a career in law when he suffered a breakdown because of nervous exhaustion. His physician recommended that he take up manual work for therapeutic reasons, so Taylor took a job in a machine shop. He went on from there to become a foreman in a steel mill and obtained a degree in mechanical engineering by attending night classes.

Taylor's emotional difficulties had reflected a compulsive need for order, and his life, even after the nervous disabilities had been cured, reflected that persistence. His interest in efficient production resulted in a range of inventions, the most important being a steam hammer and a new process of tempering steel to be used in high-speed metal-cutting machinery. His fame, however, ultimately rested on his experiments in the human side of the productive process, what he called scientific management.

What Taylor set out to establish was a scientific standard for industrial labor output. Taylor claimed that each specific job could be broken down into its smallest components; each of those steps could be analyzed to determine the optimum mode of performance; and thus the "one best way" of performing that job could be scientifically ascertained. "Taylorism" unleashed an array of "efficiency engineers," stopwatches and clipboards in hand, committed to increasing labor productivity. Taylor himself insisted in testimony before a congressional committee that scientific management was not simply a scheme to squeeze more work out of the labor force. His program required a "complete mental revolution" on the part of management and workers. Rather than battling over the division of surplus, both sides should use these techniques to increase the surplus until it is so large "that it is unnecessary to quarrel over how it shall be divided." Taylor shared with the congressmen his visionary sense of the possibilities of scientific management. It offered hope for "the substitution of hearty brotherly cooperation for contention and strife; of both pulling hard in the same direction instead of pulling apart; of replacing suspicious watchfulness with mutual confidence; of becoming friends instead of enemies...."

Labor

American workers proved less enamored with Taylor's theories than the business community was. Despite Taylor's selling of scientific management as a blessing for all, labor perceived it as a more sophisticated version of the hated speed-up.

The civilian work force during the Progressive era reflected the shift away from an agrarian-based economy. In 1900 there were 11 million persons involved in farm labor and 16 million in nonagricultural employment. By 1913, although the agricultural labor force still stood at 11 million, nonfarm employment had risen to slightly more than 26 million.

The mature industrial economy that had emerged by the beginning of the twentieth century placed labor at an increasing disadvantage. Powerful corporate enterprises such as U.S. Steel, which had 20,000 employees, possessed extraordinary leverage in determining working conditions. Labor sought to resolve this imbalance by developing comparable organization. The American Federation of Labor led the way in this struggle, guided by the values and aspirations of its founder, Samuel Gompers.

PROFILE:
Samuel Gompers

Samuel Gompers, born in a London slum in 1850, began working as a cigarmaker's apprentice at the age of ten. Three years later the Gompers family migrated to America, arriving in New York City in the midst of the Civil War draft riot. Gompers took up his craft in his new country, immediately joining the cigarmakers' union. Work in the cigar factory provided Gompers with a livelihood and an opportunity for further education. Since a skilled roller could shape perfect cigars almost mechanically, the workers in the factory took turns reading to their colleagues from a wide assortment of books and journals. Gompers, in his memoirs, fondly recalled "the educational value of the little forum existing in each shop."

At the age of twenty-five, Gompers, married and with a family, working a ten-hour day, took on the additional responsibility of serving without pay as president of the New York local of the cigarmakers' union. Over the next decade he became increasingly involved in union organizing. His dedication to the trade union movement was rewarded when, in 1886, the newly founded American Federation of Labor selected the thirty-six-year-old Gompers as president with an annual salary of $1,000. He would continue as president of the federation, except for a one-year break, until his death in 1924.

The AFL institutionalized Gompers's sense of what realistic opportunities lay open for labor. He had broken with his socialist past and insisted that labor must persuade business that, rather than wanting to undermine the capitalist system, workers were simply seeking a more equitable share of its rewards. Gompers wished to end the stereotyping of labor organizers as radicals and anarchists. His goal was the acceptance of labor unions as an integral part of the economic system.

SAMUEL GOMPERS, 1904.
Library of Congress

By 1900 the federation had eighty-two affiliated unions with an enrollment of 548,000. The ranks rose slowly until World War I, when a surge brought membership up to four million by 1920. The end of Gompers's tenure as president marked the beginning of the lean years for organized labor, with membership declining by over one million during the 1920s.

Gompers's dominant role in the labor movement evoked controversy in his own lifetime and has continued to do so among historians ever since. Gompers stressed "bread and butter" unionism, the improvement of the economic lot of organized workers. He generally avoided political activism and larger social concerns. The membership gains made by the AFL during the Gompers years consisted mainly of skilled workers in craft unions. They could be more readily organized because employers could not easily dismiss them and find adequate replacements. With the exception of the coal miners, industry-wide organizing of all categories of workers did not succeed until the 1930s.

Critics then and since have charged Gompers with trying to isolate and immobilize elements of the labor movement who pressed a more radical position than he could accept. They attacked his involvement in the National Civic Federation, meeting with industrialists and financiers, as evidence that he was a disguised capitalist. Finally they argued that, based on the ultimate criterion of success—the ability to organize the unorganized—the AFL under Gompers's leadership fell short.

Much of the criticism leveled at Gompers has substance, but it needs to be balanced by a realistic assessment of the economic and political context in which he operated. At the time of the founding of the AFL and for years afterward, the labor movement faced entrenched opposition. Strikes, often called not to press for pay increases but to protest pay cuts, were usually broken, often by federal or state troops, and strike leaders found themselves unemployable. The courts followed a conservative path, and anti-trust litigation and injunctions were used against unions. The New York Times in a 1903 editorial claimed the need "to call the public attention to the dangerous and criminal character of so many of the labor organizations, and to the dangerous and criminal spirit which, we are sorry to have to say, is coming to characterize labor organizations." The labor force, swollen by millions of immigrants, had its own racial and ethnic divisions.

Gompers may have placed too great a value on winning legitimacy for labor unions, but many subsequent gains emerged from organized labor's increased acceptance. At the time of Gompers's death the labor movement was experiencing a new wave of attacks. The institution Gompers had helped mold, the American Federation of Labor, was by then strong enough to ride out that crisis and stand ready to expand in the more favorable political environment of the New Deal.

THE PERFORMANCE OF THE AMERICAN ECONOMY: 1900-1913

By 1900 the United States had developed the leading industrial economy in the world. In that year America produced over 11 million tons of steel, more than the combined output of Germany and France. By 1913 the nation's factories and mills were responsible for one-third of the world's industrial production.

This remarkable expansion can be attributed to several factors: on the supply side, increased capital investment, technological innovation, and productivity growth; on the demand side, domestic market development, particularly in the urban areas, and increased exports.

Alfred Chandler has traced the shifts in the dynamic sectors of the post–Civil War American economy. Until the end of the 1870s the laying and developing of a railroad network absorbed capital and provided impetus for the economy. From 1880 until just after the turn of the century, the growth of a national market (created in large measure by the railroads) and urban markets served to accelerate economic expansion. From the early 1900s until 1920 the integration of electricity and the automobile into American life spurred the economy.

The growth of the American economy in the nineteenth century can be traced in the movement from local to regional markets and then on to a national market. By 1900 this market was held together by a grid of railroad lines, totaling more than a quarter of a million miles of track.

Within this national market, the highest demand sectors were the rapidly expanding cities. Not only did the growing population require a large volume of consumer goods, but the physical development of the cities—housing, bridges, water and sewage systems—demanded enormous investment.

American manufacturing production doubled between 1900 and

1913, and a rising portion of this output flowed into foreign markets. The composition of the nation's international trade reflected the changes that had taken place in the structure of the American economy. As of 1900 agricultural products still constituted the largest category of exports, but by 1912, they were surpassed by industrial exports.

TABLE 7:1
Value of Exports: 1900–1913
(In millions of dollars)

Year	Agricultural Products	Industrial Products
1900	788	487
1912	985	1,020
1913	1,050	1,185

Source: U.S. Department of Commerce, *Historical Statistics of the United States, Colonial Times to 1970.*

The United States enjoyed a favorable balance of trade during each year of the period from 1900 to 1913, with total exports approximately $26 billion and total imports approximately $19 billion. Despite America's creditor status in international trade, the amount of foreign capital investment in this country continued to keep the nation in a debtor category until World War I.

TECHNOLOGY

The opening years of the twentieth century witnessed innovations in the technology of energy that transformed the character of American life. Thomas Alva Edison had developed the electric light bulb and opened a power generating station in New York City by 1882. Within a few years, George Westinghouse had organized a competing system of electricity transmission utilizing alternating current that could be sent far greater distances. By 1895 a giant hydroelectric unit was operating at Niagara Falls.

TABLE 7:2
Growth of the Automotive Industry: 1900–1913

| | Motor Vehicle Factory Sales | | | | |
| | Passenger Cars | | Trucks and Buses | | |
Year	Number in Thousands	Wholesale Value in $ Millions	Number in Thousands	Wholesale Value in $ Millions	Motor Vehicle Registrations in Thousands
1900	4.1	4	—	—	8
1908	63.5	135	1.5	2	198.4
1913	461.5	399	23.5	44	1,258

Source: U.S. Department of Commerce, *Historical Statistics of the United States, Colonial Times to 1970.*

The effect of this readily available electrical power was immediately apparent, particularly in the cities. Electricity drove trolleys and subways and illuminated homes and factories. Equally important, it provided abundant power for the nation's growing production needs. Henry Ford noted that it was "the fashion to call this the age of industry. Rather, we should call it the age of Edison. For he is the founder of modern industry in this country." Edison's claim to that title would not rest with any of his particular inventions, but rather with his strategy of invention. Norbert Wiener saw in Edison's laboratory at Menlo Park, New Jersey, the prototype for the industrial research laboratory that would be established by General Electric in 1900 and Du Pont in 1902. "Invention," said Wiener, "came to mean, not the gadget-insight of a shop-worker, but the result of a careful, comprehensive search by a team of competent scientists."

In 1896 Edison met a young engineer, Henry Ford, at the annual meeting of the Association of Edison Illuminating Companies. Ford described in some detail his plans to produce a gasoline-powered automobile. Edison responded enthusiastically, "Young man, that's the thing! You have it—the self-contained unit carrying its own fuel with it! Keep at it!"

Ford kept at it, but so did a host of competitors in this new industry. By 1903 he had organized the Ford Motor Company, capitalized at $28,000. Ford's long-term strategy lay not in immediately producing the least expensive car, but in developing a durable, well-designed automobile. Once that had been achieved, cost could be reduced through efficiencies of high-volume production. In 1908 Ford introduced his "car for the great multitude," the Model T. That first year he sold fewer than 6,000 cars at $850 each, but by 1913 he had increased sales to 183,000, and the price of a Model T had dropped to $550. The age of the automobile was under way, with motor vehicle registrations passing the one million mark for the first time in 1913.

In 1913, there were approximately seventy American firms producing automobiles, but the Ford Motor Company was moving toward a dominating position. Using a stationary assembly line, the company had increased output until it captured more than a third of the market. However, looking toward larger and more efficient production, Ford began experimenting in May, 1913, with a moving assembly line. By the following year, the system was fully operative. America's productive potential was about to take a quantum leap.

EIGHT

Reform and War:
1913–1920

OVERVIEW

Woodrow Wilson, campaigning on the Democratic ticket in 1912 against Progressive Theodore Roosevelt and Republican William Howard Taft, warned his audiences that the electoral decision they were about to make would determine "the future economic development of the United States of America." The choices Wilson posed for the voter were either expanding consolidation and control—monopoly—or his New Freedom offering—the restoration of competition and the reopening of the avenues of economic opportunity.

Wilson entered the White House in 1913, and his years as President did, in fact, greatly affect the nation's future economic development, but not precisely in the ways he had anticipated. In his first two years in office, new tariff and anti-trust laws were enacted, and the Federal Reserve System and Federal Trade Commission were created. The passage of this legislation, however, did not signal the beginning of a frontal assault on business concentration. The federal government continued in the economic role of regulator, not dismantler. America's entry into World War I initiated an unprecedented level of governmental economic planning. More than 5,000 agencies directed industrial and agricultural mobilization.

The war marked the emergence of the United States as the world's leading economy. America moved from debtor to major creditor in the international economic order; New York replaced London as the financial capital. The war years proved a boon for organized labor as well. Its ranks doubled between 1913 and 1920. Labor's war-induced success, however, would erode almost as quickly as it had been gained. Postwar attempts to organize key industries, particularly steel, were crushed. An anti-union movement emerged and would draw strength in the 1920s from a political environment sympathetic to business interests.

WILSON'S NEW FREEDOM AND TARIFF REFORM

Wilson, in his inaugural address on March 4, 1913, enumerated the economic problems calling for immediate legislative attention. At the top of his list he placed the tariff, "which cuts us off from our proper part in the commerce of the world, violates the just principles of taxation, and makes the government a facile instrument in the hands of private interests." The President, on his first day in office, called a special session of Congress to take up tariff reform.

For over half a century the nation had maintained the high-tariff policy initiated by the Morrill Tariff of 1861. In challenging this pattern, Wilson broke with an even older tradition. No President had spoken before Congress since John Adams, but Wilson emphasized his commitment to tariff revision by addressing a joint session on April 8, 1913. Wilson noted that during a period in which the American economic system had undergone a "radical alteration," tariff policy had stood immune from basic change. For too long, Wilson charged, tariff schedules had been established "to give each group of manufacturers or producers what they themselves thought that they needed in order to maintain a practically exclusive market as against the rest of the world." The new goal of tariff policy, Wilson insisted, must be the assurance of "effective competition, the whetting of American wits by contest with the wits of the rest of the world."

While Congress deliberated on the Underwood-Simmons tariff

bill, Wilson kept up the pressure. On May 26, he issued a statement to the press attacking those interest groups seeking to influence the legislation. "Washington," he protested, "has seldom seen so numerous, so industrious or so insidious a lobby." Wilson's efforts were rewarded when on October 3, 1913, he signed the Underwood bill into law, lowering tariff rates to pre–Civil War levels. The average duty now stood at about 25 percent, and wool, sugar, iron, and steel were added to the free list.

Because the federal government derived its financial support from customs duties and excise taxes, some provision had to be made for the anticipated loss of revenues under the new tariff schedule. The Sixteenth Amendment, ratified in February, 1913, had authorized a federal income tax. The Underwood Act provided for a 1 percent tax on personal and corporate incomes over $4,000. Incomes in excess of $20,000 would be taxed on a graduated basis, with the maximum rate set at 7 percent.

BANKING REFORM

The 1913 special session of Congress dealing with tariff revision had another far-reaching economic proposal on its legislative agenda: banking reform. Persistent criticisms of the nation's monetary and banking system had come to a head after the Panic of 1907. A National Monetary Commission, appointed by Congress in 1908, did a comprehensive study of American banking. Its report, presented in 1912, catalogued a long series of inadequacies in the nation's banking structure. Representative Arsene Pujo (D., La.), chairman of the House Banking and Currency Committee, served on the monetary commission and took issue with its conservative orientation. Pujo chaired a House subcommittee that conducted its own investigation of investment banking and the "money trust," calling J. P. Morgan, among others, to testify. The report of the Pujo subcommittee in February, 1913, described the heavy concentration of financial power in a few investment banking houses. The Pujo findings received wider public attention when they served as the basis of articles by Louis Brandeis entitled "Breaking the Money Trust," published in *Harper's Weekly* in August, 1913. Brandeis's articles later appeared in book form, entitled *Other People's Money and How the Bankers Use It*.

While Congress discussed banking reform during the summer of

1913, a number of alternative approaches drew support. Senator Nelson Aldrich (R., R.I.), chairman of the National Monetary Commission, advocated a privately controlled central bank. Progressives insisted that a decentralized, government-operated system of reserve banks be created. The Wilson administration supported a compromise proposal sponsored by Representative Carter Glass (D., Va.) that became, on December 23, 1913, the Federal Reserve Act.

The Federal Reserve System created by the act marked the first fundamental restructuring of the nation's banking organization since the Civil War. The system consisted of twelve regional Federal Reserve banks (bankers' banks) whose stock was owned by member banks. Each regional Federal Reserve bank had a board of nine directors, six of whom were elected by the member banks. The remaining three were appointed by the Federal Reserve Board, a seven-member panel appointed by the President to oversee the system.

The regional Federal Reserve banks provided a variety of services for the member banks of the system. They were depositories for a specified portion of their member banks' reserves. They could make loans to these banks, with commercial paper as security, a transaction known as rediscounting. By raising or lowering the rediscount rate—the interest rate paid by member banks on these loans—the Federal Reserve banks could encourage or discourage borrowing. Payment to member banks could be made in a new currency, Federal Reserve notes, which was backed by a 40 percent gold reserve. Finally, the Federal Reserve banks could further influence the availability of credit by engaging in open market operations, that is, the buying and selling of government securities. Buying government securities would expand the money supply, whereas selling them would make money "tighter."

This new national banking system left some dissatisfied. Senator Aldrich's call for a central bank had been answered instead by the creation of a dozen central banks. Progressives, such as Senator Robert La Follette, were critical of the degree of private control in the system. The new structure, however, clearly had strengths. It provided a more flexible currency and a better regional distribution of credit resources. The Federal Reserve System would eventually require substantial modification to more effectively perform its banking and monetary responsibilities. However, even in its original arrangement, it marked a distinct improvement over the outmoded national banking system developed a half-century earlier.

ANTI-TRUST

Having achieved tariff and banking reform legislation during his first year in office, President Wilson turned directly to the issue of the trusts. Wilson addressed Congress on January 20, 1914, assuring his audience that "the best informed men of the business world condemn the methods and processes and consequences of monopoly as we condemn them." However, because of the confusion created by the Supreme Court's "rule of reason" opinion in the 1911 Standard Oil case, Wilson claimed the business community was now unsure of the permissible limits of concentration. His solution was legislation that would list unfair business practices "explicitly... in such terms as will practically eliminate uncertainty."

The Clayton anti-trust bill, introduced in April, 1914, attempted to provide the specificity that Wilson desired. It soon became apparent, however, that framing a statute which catalogued every improper business practice was an impossibility because, in historian Otis Graham's words, "No law could keep abreast of entrepreneurial inventiveness." Wilson, therefore, moved away from reliance on the Clayton approach toward acceptance of a permanent regulatory agency. In so doing, Wilson had basically adopted the Roosevelt position which he had previously attacked.

The Federal Trade Commission Act of September 26, 1914, created a five-member body to investigate unfair methods of competition in all areas of business except banking and common carriers. The commission would investigate alleged unfair trade practices and, on the determination that such practices had been followed, would issue a cease and desist order. Failure to obey such an order would result in prosecution.

The Clayton anti-trust bill, now reduced in significance because of Wilson's acceptance of a regulatory commission strategy, became law on October 15, 1914. It defined illegal practices in the areas of price discrimination and interlocking corporate directorates. In addition, it declared that unions were not illegal combinations in restraint of trade, and prohibited the use of injunctions in labor disputes "unless necessary to prevent irreparable injury to property."

By the end of 1914 Wilson felt satisfied that the new legislation in the areas of the tariff, money and banking, and trusts had accomplished the economic reforms pledged in his 1912 campaign. He defended these accomplishments, claiming that new "American business and life and industry have been set free to move as they never moved before."

Others offered a less glowing assessment of these achievements. Many saw the Wilsonian program as imposing more order and efficiency on the economy, without resolving deeper problems. They were additionally disappointed at Wilson's conservative appointments to the regulatory commissions and the restrained policies consequently adopted. Organized labor, which initially viewed the Clayton Act as its "Magna Carta," grew disenchanted when the courts interpreted it differently.

Wilson, however, insisted that the economic reforms of 1913–1914 would introduce a period of "cooperation, of new understanding, of common purpose." His focus now increasingly turned from domestic politics to a world plunged into war.

WORLD WAR I AND THE AMERICAN ECONOMY

When war began in Europe in August, 1914, President Wilson enunciated America's response in absolute terms: "We must be impartial in thought as well as in action, must put a curb upon our sentiments as well as upon every transaction that might be construed as a preference of one party to the struggle before another." That same month Secretary of State William Jennings Bryan asserted that "loans by American bankers to any foreign nation which is at war are inconsistent with the true spirit of neutrality."

Those sentiments, however, proved inadequate in the face of strong pro-Allied sympathy and the economic advantages of expanded wartime trade. The first breach in the wall of neutrality came in November, 1914, when the State Department allowed the National City Bank to extend $10 million in short-term credits to France. That initial commitment quickly developed into full-scale backing of the Allies so that by 1916, as Arthur Link described it, "The United States became virtually an Allied warehouse, from which munitions, food, and other vital raw materials flowed in an increasing stream."

The statistics of America's international trade during this period confirm the erosion of neutrality. American commerce with the Allies increased almost 400 percent from 1914 to 1916, rising from $825 million to $3.2 billion. Trade with the Central Powers virtually disappeared, declining from $169 million in 1914 to $1 million in 1916. This shifting commercial pattern reflected not only American partisanship for the Allied cause, but the effectiveness of the British blockade. Even if the United States had been desirous of pursuing a more even-handed trading policy, the British navy stood between American producers and German ports.

The funding for Allied purchases came principally from two sources: the sale of their holdings in American securities and the extension of loans. The liquidation of British and French investments in the United States could not, of itself, provide sufficient funds to ensure the flow of war materials. The additional financial support came from loans raised by American banking houses. By the time the United States entered the war, the Allies had been lent over $2.3 billion. Loans extended to the Central Powers during that period came to only $27 million.

By early 1917 American sympathies and greatly expanded trade had forged close economic ties with the Allied cause. The final step into full-scale partnership in the war effort came with Germany's announcement of unrestricted submarine warfare. On April 2, 1917, President Wilson, who had been reelected five months previously on the slogan "He kept us out of war," called upon Congress to recognize that the German attack on neutral rights required a declaration of war. Within four days both the Senate and the House had committed the nation to entering the first world war.

America's entry into the war placed an enormous strain on the economy. Not only would the supplying of the Allies have to continue, but an American Expeditionary Force had to be raised and equipped. These enormous demands led to an unprecedented level of government economic planning and direction.

Congress had taken the first step in this direction when it created a Council of National Defense in August, 1916. The council, made up of cabinet members, had an advisory body consisting of representatives from business, industry, transportation, and labor. The task of organizing a wartime economy, however, required more than a single administrative structure, no matter how powerful.

Modern warfare demanded economic as well as military mobilization. Production priorities had to be established; the flow of scarce resources channeled in the most efficient manner. A host of boards and agencies, eventually running into the thousands, was assigned this responsibility. The War Industries Board, eventually chaired by Bernard Baruch, had the broadest authority, making resource allocations, pricing decisions, and production determinations. A Food Administration, headed by Herbert Hoover, pressed the slogan "Food will win the war." Programs were developed to increase agricultural productivity, reduce domestic consumption of items in short supply, and increase food exports to the Allies. A snarled transportation system came under federal control with the creation of the United States Railroad Administration, directed by William Gibbs McAdoo, former treasury secretary. These and the many other agencies brought increasing order and efficiency to a burgeoning wartime economy. They represented as well, according to William Leuchtenburg, a "bold new departure" from the accepted relationship of the government to the economy. The wartime emergency had "raised the federal government to director, even dictator, of the economy." Washington stepped back from this role after the war ended, but when a new crisis emerged in the 1930s, a model existed for strong presidential action and new executive agencies in the economic sphere. Economic planning during World War I proved, according to Leuchtenburg, a significant moment in the "genealogy of the New Deal."

The costs of the war proved staggering, both in human and economic terms. Although United States participation lasted little more than a year and a half, 116,000 Americans lost their lives (more than half from disease) and more than 200,000 others suffered wounds. The federal government, whose annual expenditures had never reached $1 billion before 1917, spent approximately $35 billion on war-related expenses between 1917 and 1920, slightly less than $10 billion of which went for government loans to the Allies.

President Wilson, in his call for a declaration of war, had expressed the hope that the cost could be "sustained by the present generation" through a program of "well conceived taxation." New

TABLE 8:1
Federal Government Finances: 1916–1919
Fiscal Years Ending June 30
(in millions of dollars)

Year	Receipts	Expenditures	Surplus or Deficit (−)	Total Public Debt
1916	761	713	48	1,225
1917	1,101	1,954	−853	2,976
1918	3,645	12,677	−9,032	12,455
1919	5,130	18,493	−13,363	25,485
1920	6,649	6,358	291	24,300

Source: U.S. Department of Commerce, *Historical Statistics of the United States, Colonial Times to 1970.*

TABLE 8:2
Economic Performance: 1913–1920

Year	Gross National Product Current Prices Total $ Billion	Per Capita (Dollars)	Constant (1958) Prices Total $ Billion	Per Capita (Dollars)	Unemployment Number Unemployed (Millions)	Percent of Civilian Labor Force
1913	39.6	407	131.4	1,351	1.67	4.3
1914	38.6	389	125.6	1,267	3.12	7.9
1915	40.0	398	124.5	1,238	3.38	8.5
1916	48.3	473	134.3	1,317	2.04	5.1
1917	60.4	585	135.2	1,310	1.84	4.6
1918	76.4	740	151.8	1,471	.54	1.4
1919	84.0	804	146.4	1,401	.55	1.4
1920	91.5	860	140.0	1,315	2.13	5.2

Source: U.S. Department of Commerce, *Historical Statistics of the United States, Colonial Times to 1970.*

revenue acts were passed in 1917 and 1918; these acts increased individual and corporate taxes by broadening the range of taxable income and increasing the rates on a progressive basis. Fewer than 500,000 individual tax returns had been filed in 1916. The following year that figure rose to 3.5 million, and by 1919 it reached 5.3 million. Additional excise, estate, and excess profits taxes were included, but the entire wartime tax program fell short of Wilson's desire for a "pay-as-you-go" war. Approximately one-third of the war's cost was paid out of tax revenues, the remainder by government borrowing.

War-related spending in the period from 1916 to 1918 brought a surge to an economy that had been lagging from 1913 to 1915. Real economic growth, which had declined at an annual rate of 2.6 percent from 1913 to 1915, rose at an annual rate of 6.8 percent from 1916 to 1918. The postwar period witnessed a business boom with heavy inflation preceding a slide into a depression in the early 1920s.

Unemployment, which stood at 8.5 percent in 1915, diminished under the twin pressures of expanding defense production and conscripting an army. By 1918 it had fallen to less than 1.5 percent.

The nation's basic industries grew enormously during the war years, winning production contracts in the tens of millions of dollars. The American chemical industry benefited particularly, since the government seized all German-owned patents and made them available on a licensing basis. It was during this period as well that, in Walt Rostow's words, "The automobile revolution took hold as a mass phenomenon." The automobile moved into the forefront of the American economy and the guiding figure behind this "revolution," Henry Ford, achieved a global reputation.

PROFILE:
Henry Ford

In the early weeks of 1914 the Ford Motor Company made two innovations that would profoundly affect the direction of American industrialization. The first, the moving assembly line, represented the refinement of production experiments begun in the previous summer. Horace Arnold, an industrial engineer, enthusiastically chronicled the increasing success of the new technique. In August, 1913, stationary assembly of a chassis took 12 hours, 28 minutes of labor time. On October 7, 435 chassis units were produced on a 150-foot moving line, with an average assembly time of 2 hours, 57 minutes. On April 30, 1914, with three longer lines operative, chassis units were assembled in 1 hour, 33 minutes. After less than a year's experimentation, this new technique had increased production more than eight times.

The second innovation, announced on January 5, 1914, affected the human side of production. Ford instituted a reduced workday, from nine hours to eight, and doubled the basic daily wage to five dollars. Ford justified his plan, which was essentially a profit-sharing arrangement, saying, "We want to make men in this factory as well as automobiles." Whatever altruistic motives he had in significantly raising industrial wages, there were clear practical advantages as well. The company had been plagued by labor turnover. Over 50,000 men had to be hired in a single year to maintain a constant work force of 14,000. The improved wage situation largely resolved that problem. Another benefit accruing from the wage hike reflected Ford's vision of the auto industry. The logic of mass production required mass consumption. Ford's goal of selling millions of cars annually required a market that included working-class Americans. His wage increase, with the pressure it placed on other industrial employers, was a large step toward creating that market.

Ford now stood poised to perform what John D. Rockefeller called "the industrial miracle of the age." Model T sales leaped from 261,000 in 1914 to 355,000 in 1915, and then 577,000 in 1916, and 803,000 in 1918. By the early 1920s the Ford Motor Company was producing 60 percent of the cars in America and half the world's output. Ford's reputation as the genius of industrialization stood unchallenged.

Within a few years, however, Ford's supremacy would be tested and overturned by General Motors, led by Alfred Sloan. Ford's commitment to the Model T as a durable, efficient vehicle failed to take into account the changing tastes of the American public. Ironically enough, as David Riesman pointed out, Ford, with his moving assembly line and $5 a day wage, was "instrumental in creating an economy far too bounteous to be satisfied with the Model T." By the time the last of the more than 15 million Model T's rolled off the assembly line in May, 1927, Ford had dropped to second place among automobile manufacturers. The company would, with a few brief exceptions, continue there for the next half-century.

Why the abrupt turnaround for Ford? His competitor, Alfred Sloan, wrote that "the old master had failed to master change." That is a fair enough description of what happened, but does not explain why it happened. Ford saw the essential strength of his productive technique as developing a good automobile and then, through economies of scale, selling it at a constantly lower price. The changes he failed to master, such as styling and new models, were ones he dismissed as irrelevant and price inflationary. Ford judged the shifts in automobile purchasers' tastes as a pursuit of false values, and he resisted aiding their quest.

Ford eludes simple categorization. He was hailed as a revolutionary who had harnessed productive potential in a way that would transform industrial America. Yet he was a man whose values reflected a preindustrial society, and he sought to preserve part of that life-style by recreating a nineteenth century American village in Dearborn, Michigan. He published an anti-Semitic newspaper but escaped other prejudices common to his time. He hired ex-convicts, individuals with a variety of physical handicaps, and Ford employed more blacks than any other company. He was applauded for his wage breakthrough in 1914 but spent the latter part of his career imposing rigid controls on his workers and battling any attempts to organize at the Ford plants. He was, in short, an extraordinarily complex figure. If we focus, however, on the production strategy he implemented in the first two decades of this century, we can see the merit of Allan Nevins's simple assessment that Ford's was "the most spectacular career in American industrial history."

THE ECONOMIC AFTERMATH OF WORLD WAR I

The armistice in November, 1918, set in motion not only the demobilization of the armed forces but also the phasing out of the government's wartime structure for administering the economy. President Wilson, in an address to Congress in December before leaving for Versailles, described the government's role in focusing economic energy to maximize wartime production. That intervention, he assured the congressmen, had largely ended; the "harness" was now off.

Wartime inflation carried over into the postwar period. The Consumer Price Index (1967 = 100) had risen very slowly in the two decades prior to 1915. It was 25 in 1895, increased to 27 in 1905, and stood at 30.4 in 1915 when the economic impact of the war began to be felt. By 1917 it had climbed to 38.4, and the following year jumped to 45.1. It continued to surge right after the war, moving to 51.8 in 1919 and reaching 60 in 1920, the high-water mark. That level would not be regained until the post–World War II period. This rampant inflation helped trigger widespread labor unrest and strikes.

Labor

The World War I years proved a boon for segments of the labor force. The American Federation of Labor grew from less than two million in 1915 to over four million in 1920. The war strengthened labor's position in a number of ways. Labor's long-time insistence that the flood of immigration be closed off was finally met, not through legislation, but by the travel limitations imposed by war. The reduced flow of immigrants, the drafting of an army, and increased production requirements created a labor demand that enhanced bargaining.

Samuel Gompers, who had constantly pressed for the acceptance of the trade union movement's legitimacy, found a responsive political environment. President Wilson appointed Gompers to the advisory committee of the Council of National Defense, and union officials served on many of the government committees overseeing the wartime economy. The need for full-scale, uninterrupted production led Wilson, according to Melvyn Dubofsky, "to admit 'loyal' labor leaders to the inner ranks of the national political establishment."

Other labor leaders, who opposed the war and challenged the economic system, were harassed and imprisoned. Socialist Eugene Debs, leader of the Pullman strike in 1894, received a ten-year sentence for giving a speech against the war. The Industrial Workers of the World, known as the "Wobblies," were fervent opponents of the capitalist system and were committed to "one big union" of all workers. Their attempts to organize copper and iron miners and lumbermen were met with governmental harassment and vigilante justice.

Gompers repudiated these more radical labor spokesmen and pledged the full commitment of America's work force to winning the war. Many workers, however, squeezed by inflation and aware of their stronger bargaining position, still chose to go on strike. There were close to 3,800 work stoppages in 1916, more than double the previous year's total, and that figure rose to 4,450 in 1917. Hoping to limit labor unrest and ensure continued production, President Wilson created the National War Labor Board in April, 1918. The board, jointly chaired by former President William Howard Taft and labor lawyer Frank Murphy, operated under the following guidelines: no strikes or lockouts during the war, workers had the right to organize in trade unions and bargain collectively, equal pay for equal work for women, and "minimum rates of pay shall be established which will ensure the subsistence of the worker and his family in health and reasonable comfort." The board served as final arbiter in 1,251 labor disputes before it was dissolved in August, 1919.

Production workers in manufacturing made sizable wage gains in their race to offset inflation. Average hourly earnings of 22 cents in 1914 had increased to 47 cents in 1919. Average hours worked per week had dropped slightly, from 49.4 to 46.3. However, many other workers lost ground in their battle to keep pace with the rising cost of living.

No sooner had the armistice been signed than a movement emerged to roll back labor's wartime gains. William H. Barr, president of the National Founders' Association, declared in a speech on November 13, 1918, that "there is no one who will seriously contend that with the return of peace we can continue to operate our mines and factories and compete in the world of trade if we are to operate on a national eight-hour day and pay the wages which have been imposed during the stress of political opportunity."

Samuel Gompers responded to this challenge, asserting that "notice is given here and now that the American working people will not be forced back by either Barr, his association, or all the Bourbons in the United States." He added, "The time has come in the world when the working people are coming into their own. . . . They have made the sacrifices, and they are going to enjoy the better times for which the whole world has been in a convulsion."

Postwar America, at least for the next two years, proved to be a far from peaceful environment. Fear of social upheaval, triggered by the Bolshevik revolution and the founding of the American Communist Party in 1919, unleashed a "red scare." Aliens and dissenters were rounded up and many deported, with wholesale violations of civil liberties. Hundreds of thousands of southern blacks had moved into northern industrial areas during the war, and they suffered racial attacks and lynchings during this period.

Four million workers went out on strike in 1919, fueling the imaginations of those who saw a radical conspiracy abroad in the land. A general strike took place in Seattle, textile workers struck in Massachusetts, and Boston's police force walked out demanding unionization. The largest of this wave of strikes occurred in September, 1919, when a quarter of a million steelworkers left their jobs.

The steel strike proved the pivotal confrontation of the postwar period. The war had provided a bonanza for the steel industry. Otis Graham described the substantial gains: "The profits of U.S. Steel went from a prewar average of $76 million to $478 million in 1917. In 1918 the profits of the ten largest steel mills ranged from 30 percent to 319 percent of invested capital, and a grateful management of Bethlehem Steel voted its top four officers a shared bonus of $2.1 million."

Steelworkers felt that they were entitled to enjoy some of these benefits. Their wages had improved during the war, and their demands dealt primarily with hours of work and union recognition. A church study indicated that the average work week at United States Steel was 68.7 hours, with approximately half the work force on twelve-hour shifts.

The strike, begun with great enthusiasm, soon faltered under widespread accusations of radicalism. Judge Elbert Gary, chairman of the board of United States Steel, stood adamant in his opposition to collective bargaining. While testifying before a Senate investigating committee during the strike, Gary was asked, "You recognize the right of the men to form unions?" Gary acknowledged he did. Senator Walsh continued, "But you refuse to confer with the representatives of the unions?" Gary: "Yes."

The strike continued for four months. Even before its conclusion many of the men, sensing the hopelessness of the situation, drifted back to work. On January 5, 1920, the strike ended; the steel companies had won an unconditional victory.

The defeat of the steelworkers marked the first of a series of setbacks for labor in the 1920s. The "New Era" of business ascendancy would force labor into a defensive posture for the next decade.

NINE

Prosperity and Collapse:
1920–1932

The decade of the 1920s has captivated the nation's historical imagination. Mention of the "roaring twenties" evokes a flood of vivid images: flappers and bathtub gin, newspapers headlining the exploits of a Babe Ruth, a Red Grange, or a Jack Dempsey, photographs of a grim-faced Al Capone or of a smiling Charles Lindbergh stepping out of his plane at Le Bourget airport. Commentators spoke during those years of America's having gained "a permanent plateau of prosperity."

Reality proved much harsher. The twenties began with a short-run depression that had bottomed out by July, 1921. The economy, with the significant exception of agriculture, then entered a long expansionary cycle that was fed by an emerging consumer culture. However, the structure of this prosperity was riddled with numerous flaws that toppled it by the end of the decade. The stock market crash in October, 1929, and the waves of bank failures marked the descent into the nation's worst economic trauma in the 1930s. The anticipations of material success widely shared in the 1920s gave way to more modest ambitions during the years of the Great Depression.

MCCORMICK REAPER STILL IN USE IN 1916.
National Archives

THE AMERICAN ECONOMY IN 1920

The most striking development since the Civil War had been the shift from a rural, agrarian economy to an urban, industrialized one. The year 1920 marked a significant moment in that process. The census of that year indicated that, for the first time, the majority of Americans now lived in urban areas. Agricultural workers made up one-quarter of the labor force in 1920, and farm production constituted only one-sixth of the gross domestic product. Farm prices fell precipitously after the wartime boom, and the 1920s proved a bleak decade for the nation's farmers.

AGRICULTURE IN THE 1920s

America's farmers had prospered during World War I. Expanded domestic demand plus the war-induced growth of the export market drove up farm income. Net income of farm operators more than doubled between 1915 and 1919, rising from $4.3 billion to $9.1 billion. Farmers reinvested much of this income in mechanized equipment to allow greater productivity. The number of tractors rose tenfold between 1915 and 1920, jumping from 25,000 to 246,000. Other farm vehicles increased at a less dramatic rate, trucks going from 25,000 to 139,000 and automobiles from 472,000 to 2.1 million.

The war's end and the termination of the European loans that had propped up the agricultural export market had a devastating impact on the American farmer. Net farm income slipped from $9.1 billion in 1919 to $7.8 the following year. And then 1921 proved a crushing year for the farmer, with income falling to $3.4 billion.

A listing of individual crop prices between 1919 and 1921 reads like a catalogue of disaster for the farmer. Corn fell from $1.50 a bushel to 52 cents, wheat from $2.19 to $1.03, barley from $1.31 to 48 cents, cotton from 35 cents a pound to 17. Farm prices began a slow upswing in 1922, but farm income would not regain its 1920 level until World War II.

The farmers' dilemma lay in the fact that the more successful (i.e., productive) they became at their occupation, the less profitable it proved. Increasing production of a crop that had relatively inelastic demand served to drive prices down. American agriculture in the

1920s, according to Donald McCoy, "basically continued to be un-coordinated economically either from within or from without its ranks. Therefore, it was subject to the caprices of markets with which individual farmers could not effectively cope."

The acute distress of the nation's farmers led to the creation of a congressional farm bloc in 1921. Agricultural organizations had acted politically in the past seeking to curb the powers of railroads and banks and pressing for monetary reform. They now mounted a new political campaign to improve the farmers' position in the economy. Their goal lay in winning governmental approval of the concept of parity (the restoration of the farmers' purchasing power as of 1909–1914) through a price support system.

The basic strategy of the farm bloc in pursuing parity was to seek adoption of the McNary-Haugen bill. This proposed legislation, in-troduced in January, 1924, provided for purchase by the government at prewar average prices of certain surplus farm commodities for sale abroad. The difference between the price paid by the government and the world price would be made up by the producers through an equal-ization fee. The measure failed to win congressional passage in 1924 and 1926, but gained the necessary votes in 1927 and 1928, only to be vetoed by the President. The bill, which evoked opposition from other sectors of the economy, was dismissed by President Coolidge in his 1928 veto message as a "preposterous economic and commercial fallacy."

With the demise of the McNary-Haugen approach, Congress, with President Hoover's encouragement, adopted a farm bill that gave the government a less direct role in improving agricultural prices. The Agricultural Marketing Act, passed in June, 1929, sought to encourage farmers to exercise their own initiative in raising prices by forming marketing cooperatives in the basic commodities. The Federal Farm Board, created by the act, could lend up to $500 million to these cooperatives to assist them in limiting production and marketing their commodities advantageously. The act also created government-fi-nanced stabilization corporations to maintain price levels by pur-chasing commodities that had developed excessive surpluses. Hoover hoped that agricultural marketing cooperatives, like the trade asso-ciation he recommended in business, would enable the farmer to voluntarily control his production and improve his economic posi-tion, to "attain his independence and maintain his individuality."

Unfortunately, shortly after the act went into effect, the stock market crashed, and farm prices dropped rapidly. The cooperatives proved ineffective in limiting production and defaulted on government loans. The Federal Farm Board had lost $345 million by 1931.

Agriculture throughout the 1920s failed to keep abreast of the rest of the economy. Legislation enacted in the early 1920s providing farm loans, greater competition in the stockyards, and representation for agriculture on the Federal Reserve Board, although helpful, did not resolve the central difficulty. Agricultural production consistently exceeded demand, and until these could be brought into balance, the farmer would continue to be in a precarious position.

GOVERNMENT AND BUSINESS

Warren Harding, in his inaugural address on March 4, 1921, stressed the new administration's desire for a closer working relationship with the business community. The war, he noted, had launched a "delirium of expenditure," and the time had now come to put "our public household in order." That would be achieved by ending "government's experiment in business" and allowing "for more efficient business in government administration." A first step in that direction, Harding insisted, lay in "lightened tax burdens," and the new secretary of the treasury, Andrew Mellon, became the architect of that tax-reduction program.

PROFILE:
Andrew Mellon

When sixty-six-year-old Andrew Mellon joined President Harding's cabinet in 1921, his personal fortune stood as one of the two or three largest in the nation. Mellon's economic empire radiated out from Pittsburgh, Pennsylvania, encompassing vast aluminum, steel, oil, and banking holdings. His acceptance of the position of secretary of the treasury necessitated his stepping down from the more than fifty directorships he held.

Mellon placed federal tax reduction at the top of his agenda. He argued that continuation of wartime rates of taxation would "tend to destroy individual initiative and enterprise, and seriously impede the development of productive business." Mellon's comprehensive tax program faced resistance by Democrats and Progressives when proposed in 1921 and again in 1923 and secured only partial adoption. The third attempt in 1926, aided by additional Democratic support, earned what the New Republic labeled "the victory of Mellonism." The tax rate in the highest bracket, 73 percent when Mellon entered office in 1921, dropped to 56 percent in 1922, fell further to 46 percent in 1924, and stood at 24 percent in 1929.

Mellon won further admiration from the business community for his success in reducing federal expenditures and retiring the public debt. Government spending dropped from $5 billion in 1921 to $3.1 billion in 1929. Over that same period, the public debt fell from $24 billion to $17 billion.

Mellon's reputation grew enormously during these years. The claim that government was simply a business that needed the best businessmen to direct it drew heavily on Mellon's success. Mellon was increasingly described as "the greatest secretary of the treasury since Alexander Hamilton," and Senator Reed Smoot expressed doubt that even Hamilton belonged in the same class. The mystique of Mellon's financial wizardy found its fullest expression in the only slightly tongue-in-cheek claim that "three Presidents served under him."

Herbert Hoover was less enamored with Mellon's abilities than his two predecessors in the Oval Office had been. Hoover, according to his biographer, David Burner, saw Mellon as a "hopeless reactionary," but hesitated to replace him because Mellon "was so venerated in the business world that his departure would have raised problems."

In September, 1929, Andrew Mellon assured the American people that the "high tide of prosperity will continue." The stock market crash the following month did little to dampen his public expressions of confidence. In January, 1930, Mellon stated that he saw "nothing in the present situation that is either menacing or warrants pessimism."

President Hoover, in his memoirs, recounted the secretary of the treasury's private assessment of how the economic crisis should be dealt with. "Mr. Mellon," Hoover recollected, "had only one formula: 'Liquidate labor, liquidate stocks, liquidate the farmers, liquidate real estate.'" Mellon insisted that the purging of the American economic system had to be allowed to run its course. Only then will people "work harder, live a more moral life. Values will be adjusted, and enterprising people will pick up the wrecks from less competent people."

In February, 1932, as the economy slid toward the trough of the depression, Mellon resigned as secretary of the treasury. His eleven-year tenure in that position had been exceeded only by that of Albert Gallatin. Mellon, now seventy-six years old, was named United States ambassador to Great Britain and served the remaining year of the Hoover administration in that position.

Whatever dreams Mellon had of peaceful retirement were shattered when, in March, 1934, the government charged him with having filed fraudulent tax returns. The grand jury failed to indict him, and Mellon, seizing the offensive, claimed that he had overpaid his taxes and sued for a refund.

The prolonged litigation proved a double setback for Mellon. The government, in making its case, furnished evidence that while secretary of the treasury he had sought and received from Internal Revenue "a memorandum setting forth the various ways by which an individual may legally avoid tax." In December, 1937, the United States Board of Tax Appeals, after examining a court record that ran more than 10,000 pages, ruled that Mellon was not entitled to a refund but rather owed the government $668,000 in taxes and interest. This liability, however, lay with the estate of Andrew Mellon, who, at the age of eighty-two, had died the previous August.

ORGANIZED LABOR IN THE 1920s

Organized labor found itself on the defensive throughout the 1920s, struggling with limited success to prevent the erosion of the gains made during the war years. The principal threats to labor came from the business community's anti-unionism campaign and a series of judicial rulings that thwarted labor's goals in key areas.

Organizations such as the National Association of Manufacturers and the United States Chamber of Commerce led the assault on unionism in the 1920s. They pressed the case for the open, or nonunion, shop, labeling it the "American" way of employment. The "American Plan," announced at a national convention in Chicago in January, 1921, stressed its concern with preserving individualism. Its title clearly sought to draw strength from the postwar patriotic mood and the anti-radical fervor of the period.

The attack on unions went beyond rhetoric. A number of techniques were employed that sapped the strength of the labor movement. Company unions were established, "yellow dog" contracts (signed pledges before being hired that the employee would not join or help to organize a union) were widely utilized, and infiltrators were employed in many cases to keep management informed about pro-union sentiment. This campaign took its toll on labor organization. By 1930, despite a growing labor force, there were 28 percent fewer union workers than there had been in 1920.

The reverses labor experienced in organizing were matched by defeats in the courts. The Supreme Court, with William Howard Taft as Chief Justice, handed down a number of decisions during the 1920s that severely damaged the labor movement. The Clayton Act of 1914, which Gompers had hailed as labor's "Magna Carta," suffered a continuous paring down of its protective provisions by the judiciary. The Supreme Court in the 1920s struck down laws on child labor and minimum wages for women, and it restricted peaceful picketing. A study by Edwin Witte of the issuance of labor injunctions by federal and state courts in the period from 1880 to 1930 revealed that one-half of all the injunctions during this fifty-year period came during the decade from 1920 to 1930.

Organized labor made no vigorous counterattack to the challenges it faced in the 1920s. In the early 1920s an elderly Samuel Gompers presided over an American Federation of Labor that consisted largely of conservative craft unions. Gompers's last years in office, marked by a precipitous decline in union rolls, had only one redeeming feature. Immigration restriction, which he and the labor movement had long championed, was accomplished with enactments in 1921 and 1924. Gompers died on December 13, 1924, having led the AFL for close to forty years.

William Green, from the United Mine Workers, succeeded Gompers as president of the AFL. Green, accepting the pro-business mood of the era, stressed labor's willingness to work in concert with management. "More and more," he stressed in 1925, "organized labor is coming to believe that its best interests are promoted through concord rather than by conflict." Green's conservative, unimaginative leadership in the face of a concerted drive against unions and restrictive judicial rulings accentuated what historian Irving Bernstein has described as "the paralysis of the labor movement" in the 1920s.

THE PERFORMANCE OF THE ECONOMY IN THE 1920s

The beginning of the 1920s found the American economy in a vulnerable position. The erosion of European markets for agricultural products triggered a rapid drop in farm income. Government spending in the postwar period dropped precipitously, falling from $18.5 billion in fiscal year 1919 to $6.4 billion in fiscal year 1920. The rate of unemployment shot up, moving from 1.4 percent in 1919 to 5.2 percent in 1920, then more than doubling to 11.7 percent in 1921. The nonfarm unemployment figure for 1921 was an even more drastic 19.5 percent.

By midsummer, 1921, the low point of the short-run depression had been reached. Economic recovery began, and between 1921 and 1929 the average annual growth rate of the GNP was a booming 6 percent. This surging prosperity, however, masked certain underlying weaknesses in the economy.

The abundance of consumer goods provided growing reassurance of America's productive strength. Automobile sales rose from less than 2 million in 1920 to close to 4.5 million in 1929. The number of registered motor vehicles jumped from 9.2 million to 26.7 million during that same period. The residential use of electricity tripled between 1920 and 1929 as household appliances such as refrigerators and ranges became more readily available. Only 60,000 homes had radios in 1922, but by 1929 that number had leaped to more than 10 million.

The manufacturing labor force that produced this volume of goods consisted of virtually the same number of workers in 1929 as it had in 1920. The remarkable productivity gains flowed in part from more efficient research and development programs and, more important, expanded utilization of electrically driven machinery. The consumption of electricity in manufacturing increased 70 percent between 1923 and 1929. By that year, the United States was producing more electrical power than the rest of the nations of the world combined.

For most Americans, the prosperity of the 1920s was something to be enjoyed rather than critically examined. Prices held remarkably stable, with the Consumer Price Index (1967 = 100) standing at 53.6 in 1921, 51.2 in 1924, and 51.3 in 1929. Profits grew as increased productivity held down labor costs. Wages improved, particularly for skilled workers; wages did not, however, keep pace with expanded productivity. Average weekly wages for manufacturing employees, for example, rose 5 percent between 1923 and 1929 while employee output increased 29 percent over the same period.

Charles Holt's analysis entitled "Who Benefited from the Prosperity of the Twenties?" reveals that per capita real disposable income (in 1929 dollars) rose from $543 in 1920 to $693 in 1929, a 28 percent increase, but this income gain was heavily disproportional in its distribution. Nonfarm income for the top 1 percent jumped 97 percent during these years while the lower 93 percent of the nonfarm population experienced only a 6 percent increase in real disposable income. This imbalanced distribution of income posed obvious problems for sustained prosperity, but its immediate effects were muted by the widespread availability of consumer credit.

Installment buying began in the latter part of the nineteenth century as a strategy for selling more sewing machines, but it did not come into general use until the 1920s. Henry Ford insisted in 1915 that his company was "not interested in promulgating any plan which extends credit for motor cars," but continued expansion of the automobile market required some means of extended purchases. The automobile manufacturers, beginning with the creation of the General Motors Acceptance Corporation in 1919, and personal finance companies acted to expand the availability of consumer credit. By 1926 three-quarters of all car sales were on the installment plan, and a wide range of other goods were purchased in a similar fashion. That same year the National Association of Credit Men warned, "There has been built up in our country a large peak of installment credits, and it is wise for our business people to exercise caution, for undoubtedly in a credit pinch this condition would prove a very disturbing factor." This expression of concern failed to slow down the installment purchase of consumer durables. By 1927, Robert Sobel has estimated, "Over 85 percent of all furniture sales, 80 percent of phonographs, 75 percent of washing machines, and more than half the sales of radios, pianos, sewing machines, vacuum cleaners" consisted of installment contracts.

The structure of American prosperity, imposing as it was to contemporary observers, was marked by numerous fault lines. Agriculture had not fully recovered from its postwar decline. Basic industries such as railroads, textiles, and coal mining experienced economic difficulty in the 1920s. Automobile production and residential housing construction neared the saturation level for their markets by the end of the 1920s. The most significant weaknesses, however, lay in the area that furnished the most dramatic evidence of the nation's surging economy, the stock market.

THE STOCK MARKET IN THE 1920s

The feverish qualities that characterized the roaring twenties were well represented in the stock exchanges of that period. Those marketplaces, subject to their own often lax self-regulation, shaped and reflected the decade's dream of boundless economic opportunity. The headline coverage of the bull market of the late twenties furnished a constant reminder of the abundant possibilities of American life. As John Kenneth Galbraith noted in his study *The Great Crash*, "The striking thing about the stock-market speculation of 1929 wasn't the massiveness of the participation. Rather, it was the way it became central to the culture."

The bull market began to build at the end of 1924 and surged, with periodic setbacks, for the next five years. The Dow-Jones Industrials Averages, whose high was 120.5 in 1924, reached 159.3 in 1925, climbed to 166.6 in 1926, jumped to 202.4 in 1927, soared to 300 in 1928, and peaked at 381 on September 3, 1929. The market had built to its crest and now stood poised before beginning its even more rapid descent.

The tripling of the Dow-Jones Industrials Averages over a five-year period clearly did not reflect comparable development in the larger economy. The market surge drew its strength from an unbridled optimism that fed on easy credit and discounted warning signs.

The volume of sales on the New York Stock Exchange increased 400 percent from 1924 to 1929. This quickening pace was fueled by the expanded volume of brokers' loans, which made possible the record-setting levels of transactions. Margin (the percentage of the stock sale price put up by the buyer) ranged as low as 10 percent in the 1920s, and the remaining cost of the purchase was supplied by a broker's loan, with the stock serving as collateral. The bulk of these loans was provided by banks, but toward the end of the decade corporations became increasingly attracted by the high rate of return.

The ready availability of brokers' loans pumped up stock price inflation. Outstanding loans ran at about $1 billion during the early years of the decade, had risen to $2.5 billion by 1926, $3.5 billion by the end of 1927, $5 billion by November, 1928, $6 billion by January, 1929, and reached $8.5 billion by October, 1929. The demand for such loans forced the interest rate up from 5 percent in early 1928 to 12 percent by the fall of 1929. Corporations, not wishing to leave this lucrative market to the banks, furnished the majority of brokers' loan funds by 1929. Companies such as Bethlehem Steel with $158 million, Standard Oil of New Jersey with $98 million, and Chrysler with $60 million joined the corporate rush into the brokers' loan market in 1929. Many of the major American corporations were now investing their resources in speculation rather than production.

Scattered warnings were voiced about the dangerous buildup, but there was no effective institutional response. The Federal Reserve Board pursued an "easy money" policy for most of the twenties, and when it raised the rediscount rate in 1929 it was a clear case of too little and too late. The Governing Committee of the New York Stock Exchange proved less than effective in policing the transactions of the market. Stock manipulations, pooling arrangements, and fraudulent listings of securities were widespread during the period.

No discouraging words were heard from the White House. President Coolidge, just before leaving office in March, 1929, informed the press that American prosperity was "absolutely sound" and that stocks were "cheap at current prices."

Coolidge's assessment seemed reasonable as the market continued to mount through the spring and summer of 1929. By early September, however, prices had reached their highest level, and the following month the collapse began.

In late October volume on the New York Stock Exchange picked up as prices began to decline. The hope that this was a temporary adjustment before a new rise was quickly shattered. On October 24 a wave of panic selling hit the market, with trading running at a 50 percent higher volume than the previous record. A hastily convened meeting of the heads of the major New York banks, called by Thomas Lamont of the J. P. Morgan house, led to a decision to pool resources and purchase shares of U. S. Steel as a way of bolstering confidence. Lamont then characterized the near chaos on the floor of the exchange as "a little distress selling" that did not reflect any fundamental problems with the market.

Lamont's attempts to stem the growing frenzy on Wall Street proved fruitless. On October 29 panic took command when the bell rang to open trading. In the first half hour, losses ran over $2 billion. By the close of the day, volume of sales had reached 16.4 million shares (a level not to be regained until April, 1969) with losses in excess of $10 billion. The Dow-Jones Industrials Average fell 30 points and stood 150 points below its peak of September 3, 1929.

The New York Times described the turbulence of Black Tuesday: "Stock prices virtually collapsed yesterday, swept downward with gigantic losses in the most disastrous trading day in the stock market's history." Variety, the show business daily, made the same point more succinctly: WALL STREET LAYS AN EGG. John D. Rockefeller, seeking to limit the shock waves, announced that he saw "nothing in the business situation to warrant the destruction of values that has taken place in the past week" and that "my son and I have for some days past been purchasing sound common stocks." Eddie Cantor, the comedian, retorted, "Sure he's buying. Who else has any money left?"

THE SLIDE INTO THE GREAT DEPRESSION

The market crash of October, 1929, signaled the beginning of the largest economic contraction in American history. Despite periodic rallies, the market moved inexorably downward, until by July, 1932, the Dow-Jones Industrials Average stood at 41, nearly 90 percent below its peak of 381 reached in September, 1929. Prices of shares in major corporations marked the frightening downswing: United States Steel fell from 262 to 22, General Motors dropped from 73 to 8, and Montgomery Ward plummeted from 138 to 4.

A glance at the statistics for these years conveys a sense of the constricting economy. The nation's first $100 billion GNP—$103.1 billion in 1929—had shrunk to $90.4 billion in 1930. It dropped further to $75.8 billion in 1931 and then fell to $58 billion in 1932. Disposable personal income suffered a 42 percent decline. Industrial production stood at barely more than half its 1929 level. Over 5,000 banks with total deposits in excess of $3.3 billion failed between 1930 and 1932. The ranks of the unemployed grew to unprecedented size, rising from 1.5 million (3.2 percent of the civilian labor force) in 1929 to 4.3 million (8.9 percent of the labor force) in 1930, then virtually doubling to 8 million (16.3 percent) in 1931 and jumping further to 12 million in 1932 (24.1 percent of the labor force and more than one-third of all nonfarm employees).

The market crash of 1929 triggered America's Great Depression, but only an economy with pre-existing fault lines would have been as vulnerable to the shock waves emanating from Wall Street. The weaknesses on both the international and domestic sides of the economy allowed the crisis to achieve the magnitude it did.

The United States at the close of World War I had the most productive economy and stood as the leading creditor nation. America played a much enlarged role in the international economy of the 1920s, but the policies it pursued operated somewhat at cross purposes. The restrictive tariffs of the period limited imports and ensured a continuing favorable balance of trade. Reciprocal limitations on American imports by other nations helped prevent the volume of American exports from expanding at the rate of increased production. Europe's adverse trading relationship with the United States impeded her ability to repay wartime debts. Debt retirement continued at a scaled-down rate primarily through American loans and capital investment in Germany, which in turn allowed German reparations to the Allies that then supported repayment of debts to the United States. The cutback in American lending at the end of the decade forced defaults of debt repayment, reduced trade, and increased the instabilities of the European economies.

Domestically the "prosperity decade" also had some shaky underpinnings. American agriculture had expanded enormously during the war years, but the postwar reduction of markets created continuing difficulties for the farmer throughout the 1920s. Large-scale investment in new plants and equipment had lifted productivity and industrial output, but by the end of the decade supply outstripped demand in key areas, particularly automobiles, and excess capacity became a problem. Wages had failed to keep abreast of increased productivity in the 1920s, and mass purchasing power, even with greatly extended consumer credit, did not grow apace with output. Secretary of the Treasury Mellon's tax reform program primarily benefited those in the upper brackets and by reducing capital gains taxes encouraged the shift of funds from municipal bonds into the overheating stock market. The Federal Reserve Board exercised no effective restraint on banks' issuance of brokers' loans, and the governing board of the New York Stock Exchange provided only a minimal degree of regulation.

The American economy, which had grown vigorously through the twenties, had developed a number of weak spots by 1929. The market crash, with its enormous losses and shattering of confidence, propelled the troubled economy downward into massive depression. As conditions worsened, the nation looked to Washington for relief and recovery.

GOVERNMENTAL RESPONSE TO THE ECONOMIC CRISIS

Herbert Hoover had been President for seven months when the stock market crashed. During that short period, and for several years previously while he was secretary of commerce, he had warned against excessive stock speculation and loose practices on the exchange. Hoover's concern, after his inauguration in March, was to deflate the speculative bubble without causing it to burst. The raising of the rediscount rate by the Federal Reserve to 6 percent in August failed to tame the bull market, and by October the collapse Hoover feared began.

Hoover's belief that the downturn would be short term proved unfounded, and as the economy slipped deeper into depression, his public image suffered accordingly. Hoover's career before his election to the presidency had earned him widespread admiration. Orphaned before he was ten, Hoover had worked his way through college, studying engineering and geology as a member of Stanford's first graduating class. As a mining engineer he was extraordinarily successful, roaming the globe from China to Nigeria and from India to Peru. By the age of forty he had become a millionaire and, with the outbreak of World War I, devoted himself to public service. During the war, he directed the Commission for Relief in Belgium, which assumed the responsibility for feeding ten million people. President Wilson appointed him to head the Food Administration in 1917 and, at the war's end, he directed American relief activities in Europe, distributing twenty million tons of food to the starving masses. Hoover's war record won him universal acclamation as a humanitarian with exceptional organizational abilities. Hoover became secretary of commerce in 1921 and served until 1928, expanding the department's functions and enhancing his reputation for efficiency.

Hoover's presidential term spanned the market collapse and the slide into the trough of the depression; as conditions worsened, public attitudes hardened against him. The President's initial response to the market break was to meet with business and labor leaders in mid-November and urge that wages not be reduced, that strikes not take place, and that employers seek to provide relief for any workers they laid off. Hoover assured the American public on November 15 that "any lack of confidence in the economic future or the basic strength of business in the United States is foolish." Hoover's attempts to bolster confidence, however, proved increasingly fruitless as the economic indices continued to fall.

By the summer of 1930 all of the industrialized nations were in the grip of the worst depression in modern history. America joined the race toward protectionism by raising tariff barriers. Despite a petition signed by a thousand economists warning against an increased tariff, Hoover signed the Smoot-Hawley bill in June, 1930, adding further constraint to international trade.

Hoover argued in his memoirs that by April, 1931, America was recovering from a "normal recession due to domestic causes" when the effects of a further European collapse pushed the nation into its Great Depression. The United States was clearly in a depression before 1931, but the worsening European situation did intensify America's difficulties. The Austrian bank collapse in the spring of 1931 spread to Germany and Great Britain. In September, 1931, the Bank of England defaulted on gold payments, and Great Britain abandoned the gold standard. The Federal Reserve Board had pursued policies in the wake of the 1929 crash, policies that monetarist Milton Friedman characterized as "passive, defensive, hesitant." It now responded to the British decision by raising the rediscount rate in order to prevent a drain of American gold reserves. The forcing up of interest rates required by this strategy further hampered revival of the nation's economy. Economist Robert A. Gordon summarized the import of what he viewed as the Federal Reserve System's disastrous commitment: "Protection of the gold system was the dominant objective of monetary policy, regardless of what was happening to the domestic economy."

Hoover was not the vigorous proponent of laissez-faire that some of his critics have claimed. He supported increased public works programs and the creation of the Reconstruction Finance Corporation in January, 1932, to extend loans to reinvigorate business and banking and to assist state relief programs. Hoover's range of response to the economic crisis, however, was circumscribed by his commitment to certain values. His biographer, David Burner, speaks of his "tenacious adherence to a philosophy of voluntarism." Hoover regarded individualism as the dynamic element in the development of American economic and social life. He opposed the introduction of welfare and relief programs by the federal government since this, he believed, would erode individual and community responsibility and encourage a dole mentality.

Hoover's refusal to initiate direct federal relief programs was read by many Americans not as a concern for preserving the American character but rather as evidence of a cold, uncaring personality. The President's remark that "No one is actually starving" was quickly challenged with reports of deaths and malnutrition. The toll the Great Depression was taking on the lives of many Americans came to be personally identified with Hoover. The collections of tar-paper shanties housing the homeless came to be known as "Hoovervilles," newspapers covering people sleeping on park benches were called "Hoover blankets," an empty pocket turned inside out was a "Hoover flag." The episode which most discredited Hoover took place in the summer of 1932 when 20,000 veterans of World War I, seeking immediate payment of bonus certificates not due to mature until 1945, gathered in Washington to petition the government. Hoover, fearing disorder, eventually ordered the army to remove them from the nation's capital. The military force, directed with an excess of zeal by General Douglas MacArthur, used tear gas and fixed bayonets to drive the veterans out of the city.

The rout of the Bonus Army was one additional embarrassment to an already beleaguered Hoover reelection campaign. Governor Franklin D. Roosevelt of New York, in accepting the Democratic party's nomination in July, pledged a "new deal" for the American people. Hoover, seeking to evoke support from a nation mired in the worst economic collapse in its history, countered that a Democratic victory would worsen the crisis. He warned that Roosevelt's tariff reduction proposal would ensure that "grass will grow in the streets of a hundred cities, a thousand towns; the weeds will overrun the fields of millions of farms."

Hoover's campaign speeches, in David Burner's words, "were unrelievedly conservative, a defense of the record, not a plan for reconstruction." Voters in November opted overwhelmingly for change, as Roosevelt swept to victory in forty-two states and swamped Hoover in the electoral count, 472 to 59.

TEN

Depression and War:
1933-1945

As the particularly harsh winter of 1932–1933 assailed the nation, the American economy remained locked in the grip of the Great Depression. During the last weeks of the Hoover administration, the economic picture was a dismal mixture of stagnation and regression. Industrial production had ground down, with steel mills operating at less than one-fifth of their capacity. One-quarter of the work force was jobless, and only 25 percent of this beleaguered group received any relief aid. Farm foreclosures continued to mount, and a series of runs on banks led thirty-eight of the governors to declare bank holidays by early March, 1933. The nation awaited with anxious anticipation the inauguration of the new administration on March 4.

Roosevelt had promised a New Deal for the American people during the 1932 campaign, but that pledge lacked specificity. In one key area, federal spending, Roosevelt had actually taken a more conservative position than Hoover, advocating a 25 percent reduction. He had hedged on that commitment to budget cutting, however, by promising to call for "the appropriation of additional funds which would keep the budget out of balance" if required by "starvation and dire need on the part of any of our citizens." Roosevelt's campaign speeches delineated some of the programs his administration would press for: the Civilian Conservation Corps, regulation of utilities, controls on the stock exchanges, and more effective government economic planning. What is striking, however, as New Deal historian William E. Leuchtenburg pointed out, are those economic innovations not mentioned in 1932: "A gigantic federal works program, federal housing and slum clearance, the NRA, the TVA, sharply increased income taxes on the wealthy, massive and imaginative relief programs, a national labor relations board with federal sanctions to enforce collective bargaining—and this does not begin to exhaust the list."

Roosevelt's failure fully to define what the New Deal would consist of reflected in part his unwillingness to raise contentious economic issues during the campaign, but it also reflected the absence of a fully formulated program at that time. Richard Hofstadter has asserted that "at the heart of the New Deal there was not a philosophy but a temperament." That temperament of FDR's, pragmatic and open to experimentation, matched the mood of a country demanding governmental action. A nation caught in a desperate economic situation took heart from a leader who promised boldness: "It is common sense to take a method and try it. If it fails, admit it frankly and try another. But above all, try something."

No American President, with the exception of Abraham Lincoln, took his oath of office in less auspicious conditions than those facing Franklin D. Roosevelt. Delivering his inaugural address on a chilly, overcast day, Roosevelt began on a note of confidence, asserting "my firm belief that the only thing we have to fear is fear itself." He then sketched a number of areas where action by the federal government would be required to revitalize the American economy. Announcing his intention to convene a special session of Congress, Roosevelt warned his listeners that if an effective legislative program to respond to the crisis was not enacted, he would seek broad executive power, "as great as the power that would be given to me if we were in fact invaded by a foreign foe." The *Chicago Tribune*, soon to be an inveterate opponent of the Roosevelt administration, praised the address for its "dominant note of courageous confidence."

The following day, March 5, the President declared a national bank holiday and called Congress into session on March 9. The halt in banking, designed to stanch the flood of withdrawals, allowed the treasury, under emergency legislation, to verify the soundness of individual banks before permitting them to reopen. By March 15 over half of the banks that held 90 percent of all deposits were back in operation. On March 12 President Roosevelt, in a radio "fireside chat," assured the American people that the banking system had now been stabilized. The excess of deposits over withdrawals during the following weeks showed the people's acceptance of the President's statement.

The special session of Congress that commenced on March 9 and adjourned on June 16, the famous Hundred Days, was characterized by constant presidential messages and prodding and feverish legislative activity. The ordinary pace of congressional deliberation quickened under the pressure of enacting a series of major economic reforms. This executive and legislative activism was welcomed by the nation, particularly those ultimate victims of the Great Depression, America's jobless millions.

PROFILE:
The Unemployed

One of the most intimidating aspects of the Great Depression for those living through it was the confusion as to its cause and the consequent uncertainty as to how it would be remedied. Its effects, though, were readily apparent, none more so than the massive unemployment crippling the nation.

One of those who lived through that time of economic collapse recalled it as a "bloodless war." That image captures the heightened sense of threat and anxiety during those years and the diminished ability of Americans to control their own destiny. This war took its toll on the bodies and spirits of most Americans, but its most direct victims were the unemployed and those dependent on them for support.

These grim unemployment figures are the casualty reports of the "bloodless war" of the Great Depression. *Fortune* magazine estimated in September, 1932, that 34 million Americans were without any income. Others were more fortunate in that they still held jobs, but their income had been substantially cut back because of reduced hours and wages.

TABLE 10:1
Unemployment: 1929–1945

Year	Total Unemployed (millions)	% of Civilian Labor Force	% of Nonfarm Employees
1929	1.55	3.2	5.3
1930	4.34	8.9	14.2
1931	8.02	16.3	25.2
1932	12.06	24.1	36.3
1933	12.83	25.2	37.6
1934	11.34	22.0	32.6
1935	10.61	20.3	30.2
1936	9.03	17.0	25.4
1937	7.70	14.3	21.3
1938	10.39	19.1	27.9
1939	9.48	17.2	25.2
1940	8.12	14.6	21.3
1941	5.56	9.9	14.4
1942	2.66	4.7	6.8
1943	1.07	1.9	2.7
1944	.67	1.2	1.7
1945	1.04	1.9	2.7

Source: U.S. Department of Commerce, *Historical Statistics of the United States, Colonial Times to 1970.*

The search for work became for millions a daily exercise in futility, sapping energy and self-confidence. Any employment announcement would attract long lines of applicants. An advertisement for jobs in the Soviet Union elicited responses from 100,000 Americans. Laid-off skilled workers scrambled after openings far below their training and abilities. Caroline Bird, in *The Invisible Scar*, recounts that when the federal government began to inventory job skills for the defense buildup before World War II, a test survey in Kokomo, Indiana, revealed that as a result of the depression "almost half the workers in town were in the wrong jobs: a sheet-metal worker was a shipping clerk; a diemaker was running a sewage plant; a drill-press operator was a janitor...."

The depression afflicting the unemployed was psychological as well as economic. George Orwell, in a study of England's jobless workers, spoke of men "gazing at their destiny with the same sort of dumb amazement as an animal in a trap," being "haunted by a feeling of personal degradation." In America, where individualism and self-reliance were celebrated as preeminent virtues, those feelings were exacerbated. A study of New York families during the depression characterized unemployed breadwinners as suffering from "deep humiliation." Studs Terkel, who captured the mood of this time so well in his evocative oral history, *Hard Times*, described the "internal distress" provoked by the economic crisis: "Everybody, more or less, blamed himself for his delinquency or his lack of talent or bad luck. There was an acceptance that it was your own fault, your own indolence, your own lack of ability. You took it and kept quiet."

Calls for revolution rang out across America in the 1930s, and radicals of various persuasions railed at the passivity they observed. William Saroyan noted with sardonic humor: "Ten million unemployed continue law-abiding. No riots, no trouble, no multimillionaires cooked and served with cranberry sauce, alas."

Franklin D. Roosevelt's pledge to "the forgotten man at the bottom of the economic pyramid" proved more compelling than the cries for social upheaval. The New Deal program of relief and reform effectively defused the growing revolutionary sentiment. Unemployment continued as the least tractable of the problems, with the jobless proportion of the civilian labor force not dropping below 10 percent until the eve of World War II, but even the slower recovery in this area could not dispute the evidence of an economy on the road to revitalization.

LEGISLATION DURING THE HUNDRED DAYS

The plight of the unemployed attracted the immediate attention of the special session. On March 31 Congress created the Civilian Conservation Corps, providing a quarter-million jobs for men between the ages of eighteen and twenty-five in soil conservation and reforestation work. These young men, drawn from families receiving some form of public assistance, were stationed at close to 1,500 camps scattered across the country. The program eventually expanded to a half-million workers, and by 1941 more than two million men had participated.

On May 12 Congress enacted additional legislation to reduce the burdens of the unemployed. The Federal Emergency Relief Act provided $500 million in direct grants to states and municipalities, a step beyond the Hoover administration's policy of furnishing only loans.

The special session took up three New Deal legislative proposals that reflected major advances in government economic planning: the Tennessee Valley Authority bill providing regional energy and flood control development, the National Recovery Administration bill for industrial revitalization, and the Agricultural Adjustment Administration bill to regenerate the weakened farming sector of the economy.

Tennessee Valley Authority

President Roosevelt's program for developing the Tennessee Valley area drew much of its inspiration from the efforts of Senator George Norris. During the first world war, the government had built two nitrogen plants for munitions production and began construction of a large hydroelectric facility on the Tennessee River at Muscle Shoals, Alabama. In the postwar years the government attempted to dispose of these facilities but found no purchasers. Senator Norris championed expansion and government operation of these plants, providing electricity and fertilizer for the region, but bills toward that end were vetoed by President Coolidge in 1931. In Roosevelt, Norris found a President who shared his vision.

On May 18 President Roosevelt signed into law the bill creating the Tennessee Valley Authority. An independent public corporation was empowered to produce electricity and fertilizers and to develop flood control facilities for the seven-state region (Tennessee, North Carolina, Kentucky, Virginia, Mississippi, Georgia, and Alabama). Now that the government was engaged in generating and selling electrical power, it had a yardstick to measure the rates being charged by utility companies. The concept of TVA struck one congressional critic as "an attempt to graft onto our American system the Russian idea." However, most Americans failed to respond to cries of socialism; they marveled instead, in Eric Goldman's words, at this bold attempt to "chain a capricious, destructive river to the development of one of the most depressed areas in the country."

National Recovery Administration

The most ambitious New Deal economic program got under way with Roosevelt's signing of the National Industrial Recovery Act on June

16, 1933. The National Recovery Administration was created to direct a far-reaching program of government planning for the economy. The NRA, modeled upon the War Industries Board of World War I, sought to revive the economy through industrial self-regulation under government supervision. The mechanism for implementing this plan would be fair competition codes, drawn up by representatives of the individual industries, that would regulate production, prices, and wages. Once these codes had been approved by the President, they could be enforced by court injunctions. The restrictive arrangements built into the codes were exempted from anti-trust prosecution. Roosevelt emphasized these new ground rules at the outset of the NRA: "It is a challenge to industry which has long insisted that given the right to act in unison, it could do much for the general good, which has hitherto been unlawful. From today, it has that right."

The NRA, led by the indefatigable Hugh Johnson, got off to a rousing start. Parades were held in many cities, with a quarter-million marching in New York, and the Blue Eagle, the NRA's symbol, appeared all across the land. The hopes for industrial recovery invested in the NRA, however, were not substantially realized before the Supreme Court struck it down in 1935.

The problems the NRA encountered were partially of its own creation. Its extensive public relations campaign created the impression, as Walter Lippmann noted, that "The Blue Eagle was the sole bringer of recovery, and that it was a swiftly moving bird." When the pace of economic recovery did not match the promises, disillusionment set in. The agency suffered as well from its own ambitiousness, attempting to regulate more than 500 industries that produced everything from coal and steel down to broom handles. Complaints against the program began to mount as small producers charged that larger corporations had set codes to enhance their interest, and labor groups protested that wages were slipping in relation to prices.

The NRA, in its two-year existence, did register some gains. Its codes helped eliminate some abysmal working conditions, such as child labor and sweatshops. Its program of industrial coordination applied a brake to the deflationary slide. It failed, however, to induce economic growth. The National Industrial Recovery Act included a provision for $3.3 billion of public works spending, but the administrator of this program, Harold Ickes, expended these funds so slowly that they had a limited effect in stimulating the economy. The NRA, as Otis Graham noted, "without a strong expansionary principle, produced no stunning results." In May, 1935, the Supreme Court, in *Schecter v. United States*, unanimously declared the NRA unconstitutional, citing its illegal transfer of legislative authority to the executive and its improper use of the interstate commerce power.

Agricultural Adjustment Act

The Agricultural Adjustment Act, passed in May, 1933, embodied New Deal planning for the revitalization of the farming sector of the economy. Seeking to restore agricultural purchasing power, which had been depressed since the early 1920s, the act put forward a program to restrict production and raise farm prices. The Agricultural Adjustment Administration countered the perennial problem of farm surpluses by paying rentals for acreage withdrawn from production or by providing subsidies for restricted crops. The funds for this program would be raised by a tax on the processors of these farm products. The AAA's goal lay in raising basic farm commodity prices to gain parity, or equality, with the relative agricultural purchasing power during the years 1909 to 1914, a period when farming had been in a generally healthy economic condition.

The benefits of the AAA program quickly became apparent in farming communities across the land. The farm legislation of the 1920s had suffered from its inability to limit production. The New Deal enactment had met that problem, but part of its implementation generated adverse public reaction. To enable its commodity restrictions to develop properly, the AAA decided at the outset to destroy some existing surpluses. Farmers were paid to plow under ten million acres of the 1933 cotton crop, and over six million pigs were purchased and slaughtered. These stopgap measures unfortunately, according to William E. Leuchtenburg, "fixed the image of the AAA in the minds of millions of Americans, who forever after believed that this was the agency's annual operation."

Nature played a malevolent role during these years in cutting farm output. Beginning in 1930 a drought developed in the East and moved steadily westward to wreak its greatest havoc in the Great Plains states. This drought, described by a weather bureau scientist as "the worst in the climatological history of the country," held large sections of the country in its grip for a full decade. As parched soil crumbled into dust, winds swept over the land, carrying off tons of sere top soil in massive dust storms, or "black blizzards." Donald Worster, in his poignant study, *Dust Bowl*, conveyed the persistent devastation of these storms: "Day after day, year after year, of sand rattling against the window, of fine powder caking one's lips, of springtime turned to despair, of poverty eating into self-confidence."

The federal government responded to this catastrophe with a variety of drought relief programs: loans, soil conservation techniques, tree shelterbelts, and so forth. The long-awaited solution, the return of normal levels of rainfall, did not occur until 1941. By that time thousands of families had been forced off their land and had made painful migrations such as the one immortalized in John Steinbeck's *The Grapes of Wrath*.

In January, 1936, the Agricultural Adjustment Act met the same fate that had befallen the National Industrial Recovery Act, with the Supreme Court deciding in *United States* v. *Butler* that the act was unconstitutional. The Court ruled that the tax on processors of agricultural commodities was in fact a technique for controlling farm production and, as such, fell beyond the limits of the welfare clause. The invalidation of AAA, although a setback, did not undermine the New Deal's farm program. The Soil Conservation and Domestic Allotment Act of 1936 and a second AAA in 1938 that avoided the constitutional objection carried forward the principal elements of the federal government's agricultural planning. These laws, along with legislation limiting farm foreclosures, expanding funds for farm mortgages, and assisting tenant farmers to purchase land, represented a New Deal for the agricultural sector. Widespread prosperity for farmers awaited the wartime economy of the 1940s, but significant gains were already being made. Net income for farm owners stood at less than $2 billion in 1932, but it had risen to $5.1 billion by 1936 and reached $6 billion in 1941.

Bank and Stock Exchange Regulations

The TVA, NRA, and AAA marked the major innovations of the Hundred Days. Roosevelt, in his inaugural address, had promised, as well, "safeguards against a return of the evils of the old order," and he began to press at once for legislation implementing structural economic reforms. Banking became the first target for new federal regulation.

MACHINERY BURIED BY DUST STORM, 1936.
National Archives

CHAPTER TEN

SAN JOAQUIN VALLEY, CALIFORNIA, 1940.
National Archives

On March 9, 1933, five days after FDR's inauguration, Congress passed the Emergency Banking Relief Act. The measure approved the emergency actions already taken by the President and the secretary of the treasury, such as the bank holiday, and gave the President additional discretionary authority over credit, currency, and gold transactions. More substantive banking reform came with the passage in June of the Banking Act of 1933 (Glass-Steagall Act). This law, addressing some of the problems that had undermined confidence in the banking system, separated commercial from investment banking, expanded the Federal Reserve System's stabilizing role, and created the Federal Deposit Insurance Corporation.

Reform of stock exchange practices came through two laws. The Federal Securities Act passed in May, 1933, required that full financial information be made available to investors in new securities. New issues had to be registered with the Federal Trade Commission, and any fraudulent information rendered the company directors vulnerable to civil and criminal charges. More comprehensive regulation of the stock market came in June, 1934, with the passage of the Securities Exchange Act. This law created the Securities and Exchange Commission with wide-ranging authority to oversee securities market practices. It also granted the Federal Reserve Board the power to regulate margin requirements so as to prevent a recurrence of the speculative mania that had preceded the market crash of 1929.

The new SEC took on added responsibilities with the enactment of the Public Utility Holding Company Act in August, 1935. This legislation sought to loosen the control gained by pyramiding holding companies in the electricity and gas utilities area. It eliminated all utility holding companies more than twice removed from the operating facilities, and it empowered the SEC to remove any holding company situated closer to the primary unit if the commission deemed that holding company not to be in the public interest.

Legislation Affecting Farmers

That same year the New Deal addressed the need of the 90 percent of the nation's farmers who were not receiving electricity from central generating stations. President Roosevelt, by executive order, created the Rural Electrification Administration to provide low-interest loans to farmers' cooperatives to run electrical lines into these communities. By 1941 some 40 percent of America's farms had electricity, and by 1950 the figure had risen to 90 percent.

Social Security Legislation

Two of the most disturbing aspects of the Great Depression were the anxiety and sense of powerlessness caused by unemployment and by seeing one's lifetime savings wiped out. Other western industrialized nations, such as Germany, France, and Great Britain, had implemented programs of social insurance by the first decade of the twentieth century. Many had argued, with little success, that the United States should develop a similar program, but now the economic breakdown of the 1930s and the growing enthusiasm for the Townsend Plan made social security politically feasible.

Dr. Francis Townsend, a California physician, devised a scheme in 1933 to provide government benefits for the elderly. Townsend claimed that his plan had been triggered by seeing some older people pawing through garbage cans, "Three haggard, very old women stooped with great age, bending over the barrels, clawing into the contents." The Townsend Plan would provide every retired person over age sixty with $200 a month, provided the recipient spent this money within a month. Townsend defended his program as not merely a pension plan, but as a strategy for revitalizing the economy. Older people would give up jobs to the younger unemployed to qualify for the plan, and their monthly spending would create demand that would further reduce unemployment. Townsend saw the source of funding as a 2 percent sales tax at each stage of transaction from raw product to retail sale. Townsend's proposal attracted a wide and enthusiastic following, but Congress, realizing that the plan would transfer more than half the national income to less than 10 percent of the population, failed to go along. The excitement generated by the Townsend Plan, however, eased the way for passage of a less radical alternative—social security.

The Social Security Act signed by President Roosevelt on August 14, 1935, encompassed a number of benefit programs. It provided for old age and survivors' insurance to be financed by a tax imposed upon employers and employees. The act authorized matching federal grants to the states to provide old age pensions for the destitute, and relief for dependent children and for the blind, crippled, and homeless. The law also created a program of unemployment compensation, funded by a federal payroll tax, which would be administered by the individual states.

Roosevelt, in signing the law, acknowledged the impossibility of providing complete protection from "the hazards and vicissitudes of life." He defended, however, the achievement of social security, explaining that "we have tried to frame a law which will give some measure of protection to the average citizen and to his family against the loss of a job and against poverty-ridden old age." Roosevelt emphasized that the legislation would play a stabilizing role in the economy as well as meeting individual needs. Social security, he said, "represents a cornerstone in a structure that is being built but is by no means complete." This new program "will take care of human needs and at the same time provide for the United States an economic structure of vastly greater soundness."

The social security law had certain weaknesses. It failed to cover large numbers of occupations, excluding workers such as farm laborers and domestics. In addition, its funding mechanism—a tax on employers and employees—had a deflationary impact on an already weakened economy, pulling money out of circulation to build up the system's reserves. The law as passed reflected the Roosevelt administration's assessment of the political limitations on the federal government's assuming expanded social welfare responsibilities. Roosevelt later privately acknowledged the deflationary aspect of the employee contributions but argued that the sense of proprietorship gained through them was worth it: "We put those payroll contributions there so as to give the contributors a legal, moral, and political right to collect their pensions and their unemployment benefits. With those taxes in there, no damn politician can ever scrap my social security program."

ECONOMIC RECOVERY

By the fall of 1936 there was substantial evidence of the economic gains that had been made since Roosevelt assumed office. National income had risen by 50 percent, industrial production had almost doubled, corporate balance sheets had gone from a $2 billion deficit to $5 billion in profits, and net farm income had jumped almost 400 percent. New Deal economic programs had stimulated this expansion in two basic ways. Its monetary policies—abandoning the gold standard, restoring confidence in the banking system and thus encouraging deposits, and devaluating the dollar—played a key role in revitalizing the economy. New Deal fiscal policy, spending for relief, public works, and agricultural supports, had pumped up the economy as well, but Roosevelt had never felt at ease with deficit spending as a matter of policy.

British economist John Maynard Keynes had written to George Bernard Shaw in 1935, informing him that "I believe myself to be writing a book on economic theory which will largely revolutionize—not, I suppose, at once but in the course of the next ten years—the way the world thinks about economic problems." Keynes's The General Theory of Employment, Interest, and Money, published in 1936, challenged the classical position that increasing unemployment would trigger a drop in wages and that companies would then hire additional workers because of the reduced labor cost. Wages, Keynes pointed out, did not fall substantially, and whatever reduction did take place caused a lessening on the demand side of the economy. Keynes's solution to unemployment lay in building demand, with the government accepting final responsibility in this area. The government, faced with a flagging economy, should move toward deficit financing, reducing taxes and interest rates and increasing spending. This "priming of the pump" would swell demand and effectively counter unemployment. For Keynes, an economy plunged into depression and massive unemployment could not rely on a self-correcting process, but required a government willing to deliberately unbalance its budget in order to restore growth. The traditional goal of a balanced budget became appropriate, according to Keynes, only when full employment had been attained.

President Roosevelt, however, drew back from pursuing a government spending policy on the scale the Keynesian theory would have required. For all of the complaints about New Deal spending, the largest annual deficit registered in the 1930s was $3.5 billion in 1936. Even that modest level of deficit financing disturbed Roosevelt, and in 1937 he ordered a cutback in federal spending. This reduction in federal expenditures combined with the drain of the new social security tax helped trigger a sharp recession from mid-1937 to mid-1938. Higher levels of federal spending stimulated recovery, but only with the coming of World War II and its torrent of government spending at ten times the New Deal volume did Keynesian theory find full application.

ORGANIZED LABOR

The New Deal years proved a boom time for unionism, as widespread organizing, particularly in the industrial sector, reversed the declining membership rolls of the 1920s. Labor benefited enormously from the new supportive role played by the federal government. Two key pieces of legislation, the National Industrial Recovery Act in 1933 and the National Labor Relations Act (the Wagner Act) in 1935, encouraged major gains for organized labor.

Section 7(a) of the National Industrial Recovery Act required that every NRA agreement guarantee employees "the right to organize and bargain collectively through representatives of their own choosing," without "interference, restraint, or coercion." The ranks of organized labor had fallen from 5 million in 1920 to 2.7 million in 1933, but Section 7(a) breathed new life into the movement. Organizers for the United Mine Workers fanned out across the coal fields of the country, exhorting the miners with the appeal that President Roosevelt "wanted" them to join the union. Within a year the United Mine Workers' membership more than tripled, while other unions experienced large, although less dramatic, gains.

Although Section 7(a) asserted the rights of employees to organize and bargain collectively, it provided no effective procedure to deal with recalcitrant employers. "After an exhilarating start," labor historian David Brody noted, "section 7a foundered; loopholes developed and enforcement broke down long before the invalidation of the NRA."

When the Supreme Court struck down the NRA on May 27, 1935, Congress was already considering a labor bill that provided more effective organizing protection than Section 7(a). On July 5, President Roosevelt signed the National Labor Relations Act which, as William Leuchtenburg wrote, "threw the weight of government behind the right of labor to bargain collectively." The administrative agency created by the law, the National Labor Relations Board, was empowered to supervise elections held to determine bargaining representatives, and to prevent unfair practices in the area of labor organizing by employers against workers. This new commitment to protect labor's rights fared better than its predecessor, with the Supreme Court in the 1937 decision, NLRB v. Jones & Laughlin Steel Co., declaring it constitutional. By 1941 the National Labor Relations Board had supervised close to six thousand elections affecting two million workers and had received over twenty thousand charges of unfair labor practices.

The passage of the National Labor Relations Act brought to a head a controversy that had been dividing the labor movement. Proponents of industrial unionism, organizing workers on an industry-wide basis, had been challenging the craft union orientation of the American Federation of Labor. At the annual convention of the AFL in October, 1935, John L. Lewis of the United Mine Workers pressed for a full-scale commitment to industrial organization in the mass production areas. Lewis's proposal was voted down, and, with a declaration that the "American Federation of Labor is standing still, with its face toward the dead past," Lewis set out to lead the fight for industrial unionism. The vehicle created by Lewis, Sidney Hillman of the Amalgamated Clothing Workers Union, and others was the Committee for Industrial Organization. Initially a committee of the AFL, the CIO's more militant program led to a formal split with the parent body and to its being renamed the Congress of Industrial Organization. With the CIO in the vanguard, the labor movement entered a tumultuous but extraordinarily successful period. Over the next six years, the basic industries that had resisted unionization—automobiles, steel, rubber, and so forth—were organized. Between 1935 and 1941 union membership almost tripled, jumping from 3.6 million to 10.2 million. The proportion of the nonagricultural labor force belonging to unions more than doubled during this period, rising from 13.2 percent to 27.9 percent.

These labor gains required considerable struggle along with the supportive federal legislation. There were many pitched battles, most notably at the Republic Steel plant in South Chicago, but the most effective tactic proved to be the sit-down strike. In February, 1937, General Motors recognized the United Automobile Workers as bargaining agent after employees sat down for forty-four days at GM factories in Flint, Michigan. During 1936 and 1937 almost a half-million workers took over production facilities using this new type of strike. Thousands of more traditional labor stoppages also took place in 1937, marking that year as the most embattled in the history of labor-management relations to that point. What emerged from this turbulence in the 1930s was a stronger, more broad-based labor movement, extending well beyond the older craft alignments into industrial unionism and prepared to play a more active political and economic role in American society.

PERSPECTIVE ON THE NEW DEAL

The 1938 passage of the Fair Labor Standards Act, which established minimum wages and maximum hours and eliminated child labor in businesses involved in interstate commerce, marked the end of the New Deal legislative program. As the sense of economic crisis had diminished, many had lost their enthusiasm for new federal initiatives, and the commanding congressional majorities began to slip away. After an unprecedented five-year span of government intervention in all areas of the economy, the reform impulse had ebbed and events abroad came to increasingly dominate the nation's attention.

What long-term economic effects did the New Deal produce? Carl Degler points to the emergence and acceptance of the "guarantor state," a government that assumed wide responsibility for the general economic welfare. Degler sees this as a revolutionary shift in attitudes, triggered by the "searing ordeal of the Great Depression," which "purged the American people of their belief in the limited powers of the federal government and convinced them of the necessity of the guarantor state."

New Left historians have proven less enamored of the New Deal's achievements. Howard Zinn saw its attainments as extremely modest: "What the New Deal did was to refurbish middle-class America, which had taken a dizzying fall in the depression, to restore jobs to half the jobless, and to give just enough to the lowest classes (a layer of public housing, a minimum of social security) to create an aura of good will."

Zinn's assessment does less than full justice to the New Deal.

Faced with an economic breakdown of unprecedented proportions, the Roosevelt administration accepted the responsibility of direct public relief programs. It instituted, as well, an extensive range of structural reforms in the American economy, affecting banking, the stock exchange, labor organization, agriculture, and many other segments. These New Deal programs fundamentally altered the relationship of the federal government to the economy. The idea of the economy as a self-correcting mechanism had lost its persuasiveness in the devastated years of the Great Depression. From that time forward, the federal government would play a central role in the economy, monitoring, regulating, and intervening in an attempt to make the system more responsive to human needs.

THE IMPACT OF WAR

World War II freed the American economy from the grip of the Great Depression. The massive volume of government spending stimulated enormous economic growth and resolved that most intractable problem of the 1930s, unemployment.

From September, 1939, when war began in Europe, until the Japanese attack on Pearl Harbor in December, 1941, America gradually built up her defense readiness. Congress passed the first peacetime draft act in September, 1940, and the relatively small American army began to receive large infusions of manpower. In June, 1940, while France was reeling under the onslaught of the *Blitzkrieg*, President Roosevelt, in a speech at the University of Virginia, promised to "extend to the opponents of force the material resources of this nation." Over the next year, Congress appropriated $37 billion, a sum exceeding America's expenditures for World War I, to expand the nation's arsenal and furnish military supplies to those nations fighting Hitler.

America's entry into the war in December, 1941, shifted defense production into even higher gear. The volume of war goods rolling out of the nation's factories ran beyond even the most optimistic projections. Roosevelt's prewar claim that America could produce 50,000 airplanes a year proved an understatement. That figure was almost reached by 1942 and virtually doubled by 1944. Within a year after entering the war, the United States had matched the combined war material output of its enemies and by 1944 was outproducing them by a two-to-one margin.

GIANT GEARS FOR AMERICAN WARSHIPS.
National Archives

CHAPTER TEN

WOMEN WORKERS AT CALIFORNIA AIRCRAFT PLANT.
National Archives

The wartime economy spawned a host of government agencies that sought to coordinate and direct production, control prices, and allocate manpower. The ranks of the unemployed, which still stood at over 8 million in 1940, were depleted by the demands of defense production and the armed services. By 1945 America's military services had over 12 million men and women in uniform. Labor shortages replaced labor surplus as a pressing national problem. During the war, 5 million women entered the work force, often taking positions that had not been previously open to them. By war's end, women constituted one-third of the labor force.

Workers benefited from the booming economy. Paychecks for manufacturing employees, increased by overtime, jumped 50 percent between 1941 and 1945, while the Consumer Price Index rose only 23 percent. Organized labor gained as well, winning greater acceptance as a key element in the production race and expanding its membership from 10.2 million in 1941 to 14.3 million by 1945.

For the nation's farmers, the focus on controlled production during the New Deal gave way to an all-out drive to meet agricultural needs both domestically and abroad. Despite a reduced work force, farmers increased their total output 11 percent between 1941 and 1945, with food production increasing even more rapidly. Net farm income doubled during these years.

Government expenditures fueled the surging economy, as federal spending increased almost tenfold between 1940 and 1945. Frederick Lewis Allen noted that "The New Dealers had been conscientiously trying to 'prime the pump' by government expenditures of a few billions a year; what they had done with a teaspoon was now being done with a ladle." The gross national product more than doubled during these years.

The $316 billion expended by the federal government from 1941 to 1945 marked a stunning acceleration of spending. The dollar amount, not taking inflation into account, was twice as high as all federal spending since George Washington's presidency.

The Roosevelt administration had hoped to pay for 50 percent of the cost of the war by increased taxation. New tax legislation helped raise internal revenue receipts from $7.4 billion in 1941 to $43.8 billion in 1945. Wider-ranging tax laws, and the new policy of withholding taxes from paychecks led to a doubling of individual returns filed during these years. An excess-profits tax restrained business gains during the war. Net corporate profits after taxes, which stood at $6.9 billion in 1940, rose to $12.2 billion by 1943 and had fallen back to $10.5 billion by 1945. The goal of meeting 50 percent of the war's cost by taxation was not attained. Approximately 43 percent was raised through taxes, a decided improvement over the World War I experience when approximately one-third of the cost was met by tax revenues. Government borrowing during the second world war was facilitated by individual purchases of some $40 billion worth of savings bonds.

The World War II years saw a return of prosperity to the American economy. Income rose significantly, and many households received two paychecks. Price controls and rationing curbed inflation, limiting its rise to an annual rate of 5 percent. As victory approached, however, a persistent underlying concern came to be increasingly expressed. Would the economy continue its high level of performance into the postwar period, or did the war years simply mark a temporary departure from the weakened economy of the 1930s?

TABLE 10:2
Gross National Product, Federal Government Expenditures,
and National Debt: 1940–1945
(In billions of dollars)

Year	GNP	Federal Govt. Expenditures	National Debt
1940	99.7	9.6	43
1941	124.5	14	49
1942	157.9	34.5	72.4
1943	191.6	78.9	136.7
1944	210.1	94	201
1945	211.9	95.1	258.7

Source: U.S. Department of Commerce. *Historical Statistics of the United States, Colonial Times to 1970.*

ELEVEN

Reconversion and the Rise of a Consumer Culture:
1945–1960

POSTWAR AMERICA

The end of World War II in the summer of 1945 brought both elation and anxiety to the American people. The collective sigh of relief at victory masked an underlying concern: would the nation's economy tumble back to the 17.2 percent unemployment rate of 1939, when close to 9½ million persons were out of work?

This fear took on added substance as defense production phased down. The Pentagon quickly canceled $35 billion in war-related contracts. The rapidly filling pool of unemployed defense workers might soon be further expanded with the demobilization of the twelve million men and women in the armed forces. The planning that had been done for the paring down of military troop levels had assumed that the war in the Pacific would continue through 1946. The unanticipated resolution of the fighting in mid-1945 rendered the existing demobilization schedules almost worthless. Intense public pressure developed almost immediately to bring the troops home.

Those who viewed the underlying cause of the Great Depression as excessive productive capacity now were faced with a more serious dilemma. This "excessive" capacity had been brought into use during the war and had been further expanded. Were we now facing a new depression with an even greater idle productive capacity pulling down the nation's economy?

This fear proved largely groundless. The most pressing economic issue over the next several years involved curbing inflationary pressures rather than preventing a slide back into the economic doldrums of the 1930s. The pent-up demand for consumer products created by a wartime economy, fueled with large savings held by many two-income families, pressured American industry to reconvert as quickly as possible to profit from this enormous market.

Depression followed by war had rendered the material dimensions of the American dream elusive for most. Now that peace was at hand, many sought to transform their postponed hopes—for new housing, automobiles, electrical appliances, and so forth—into practical shopping lists.

Housing

Housing stood at the top of most of these lists and proved the most difficult demand to meet. Residential housing construction had boomed in the 1920s before becoming one of the most severely depressed sectors of the economy. Some 937,000 housing units had been built in 1925; eight years later the annual figure had declined to 93,000. The housing market, after years of underproduction, faced an unprecedented demand from millions of returning veterans.

The construction industry, limited only by the availability of supplies, strove to catch up. One builder, William Levitt, drew upon his wartime experience of hastily constructing housing for defense workers. Buying up large tracts of farmland thirty miles from New York City, Levitt seemingly built developments overnight. His secret was to adapt aspects of the assembly line to mass-produce housing. A three-bedroom home on a 75-by-100 lot sold for under $10,000. Other entrepreneurs provided models selling for less than $5,000. Veterans with their GI loans and others who had been shut out of the housing market eagerly snapped them up. Housing starts rose from 326,000 in 1945 to 1.9 million in 1950. The backlog of demand had largely been met by then, and starts would not approach the 2 million mark until the 1970s when the baby boom produced by these postwar families entered the housing market.

Automobiles

The creation of Levittowns and similar suburbs outside metropolitan centers across the country depended upon the increasing availability of automobiles. With proliferating suburbs and long distances between home, places of employment, shopping malls, churches, and so forth, multi-car ownership became commonplace.

Passenger automobile production had been suspended during the war years, and Detroit rushed to reconvert its plants. The nation's auto producers in the postwar years included not only General Motors, Ford, and Chrysler, but a half-dozen smaller firms: Studebaker, Packard, Nash, Hudson, Kaiser-Frazer, and Crosley. Their haste to resume civilian production reflected not only a desire for immediate profits but also a concern for reestablishing buyer loyalty.

Problems of supply and strikes, including a 113-day walkout beginning in November, 1945, at General Motors, delayed the gearing up of automobile production. Although 2.1 million cars were sold in 1946 and 3.5 million in 1947, the demand still ran high. In April, 1948, Ford had back orders for 1½ million vehicles. In 1949 auto production passed the 5 million mark for the first time in the nation's history, and supply had finally caught up with demand.

The growing stream of products flowing out of America's factories found an avid army of buyers. The consumer culture that had emerged in the 1920s and then been thwarted by the depression now appeared full-blown. Hollywood producer Samuel Goldwyn, prior to releasing the film *The Best Years of Our Lives* in 1946, commissioned pollster George Gallup to ascertain if the potential audience shared the title's sentiments. Gallup's research persuaded Goldwyn that for most Americans these were, indeed, the best years.

RECONVERSION

Those years, however, had their troubling aspects. Harry S. Truman assumed the presidency in April, 1945, amidst the winding down of a hot war and the emergence of a cold one. On the domestic economic

---

front, he faced less dangerous but still adamant encounters. As the process of reconversion began, organized labor sought to break out of the wage restraints of the war years. No longer bound by "no strike" pledges, coal miners, auto and steel workers, meat-packing employees and hundreds of thousands of others walked off their jobs in contract disputes. In fact, 8.2 percent of all workers were involved in strikes in 1945 resulting in 38 million idle man-days. The following year, 1946, proved the most strife-torn in American labor history, with close to 5 million workers, 10.5 percent of the labor force, being idle 116 million man-days.

A similar conflict of interest antagonized producers and consumers. Producers sought the lifting of wartime price ceilings, and consumers pressed to retain them as a hedge against inflation. As constraints were removed, prices shot up rapidly, rising 34 percent between 1945 and 1948. When Gallup asked Americans in October, 1946, whether they were finding it more difficult to make ends meet than they had the previous year, 71 percent replied affirmatively.

ECONOMY AND THE GOVERNMENT

A wide-ranging debate soon developed on what role the federal government should play in stabilizing an erratic postwar economy. President Truman had assumed office at the end of a period during which the government's intervention in the economy had increased enormously. Most Americans knew little about the man now occupying the White House. Would he press New Deal initiatives further in the direction of a managed economy? Would he be able to deflect the conservative call for a return to a free market economy?

Truman's economic policy reflected his judgment that the American people wanted "a rest from experiments." Those New Dealers who wished to extend further the government's intervention would be largely disappointed with the Fair Deal. During Truman's administration, the Social Security System would become more inclusive and its benefits would increase, the minimum hourly wage would rise from forty to seventy-five cents, and a public housing program would begin. The Truman years reflected a consolidation rather than a pressing forward of the governmental economic initiatives of the 1930s. Clearly by the late 1940s the "mixed economy" that had developed during the New Deal years had firmly rooted itself in American life. Challenges would be raised then and later to various aspects of governmental intervention in the economy, but a political consensus (on its legitimacy) had already been achieved.

One piece of economic legislation is symptomatic of the transition from the New Deal to the Fair Deal. In January, 1945, congressional liberals introduced a full employment bill. The proposed legislation would have mandated Keynesian economic policy by its requirement that when "full employment cannot otherwise be achieved" the federal government must "provide such volume of federal investment and expenditure as may be needed to assure continuing full employment."

The bill committed the government to an unprecedented level of systematic economic planning. Each year the President would submit a forecast of the economy's performance and the steps he planned to guarantee full employment. He would have a council of economic advisers and a joint congressional economic committee would be created to act upon his annual report.

The Truman administration viewed the proposal as too far-reaching and did not contest the modifications that congressional opponents forced upon it. The bill that the President signed in February, 1946, had lost its Keynesian fervor. It no longer spoke of full employment but rather obligated the government to use "all practicable means . . . in a manner calculated to foster and promote free competitive enterprise . . . to promote maximum employment, production, and purchasing power." The act did create the congressional Joint Economic Committee and the President's Council of Economic Advisers.

Truman spoke of the law as "a commitment by the government to the people . . . to take any and all of the measures necessary for a healthy economy." The Council of Economic Advisers, assessing the law's impact from the vantage point of the 1970s, noted that unemployment had averaged 4.6 percent in the quarter-century since the act went into effect. The unemployment rate for the twenty-five-year-period ending in 1940 had been 10.9 percent, but that figure reflected the unemployment surge of the depression. Going back to the 1904–1929 period the rate was 4.7 percent, virtually identical with that of the postwar years. The council concluded that although "small departures from maximum employment" had not been reduced, there had been success in checking large increases in unemployment. Historian Harvard Sitkoff judged the legislation more harshly, complaining that its "weaknesses and the halfhearted attempts to administer it have left us with a permanent body of unemployed and underemployed."

TAFT-HARTLEY ACT

Organized labor disliked Truman's acceptance of a weakened full-employment bill, but it soon faced a more potent threat. The Eightieth Congress, elected in November, 1946, marked the return of Republican control of both houses for the first time since 1931. At the top of that party's legislative agenda was a determination to reduce the economic and political power of organized labor. At the opening of the January session, the new chairman of the Senate Labor and Public Welfare Committee, Robert Taft of Ohio, and the new chairman of the House Committee on Labor and Education, Fred Hartley of New Jersey, introduced bills designed to roll back the gains labor had made since the passage of the Wagner Act in 1935. The bills passed their respective houses by sizable majorities, and the Taft-Hartley bill that emerged from the conference committee contained the following provisions: closed shops—where union membership was a precondition of being hired—were prohibited; union shops—where workers would have to join a union after being hired—were permitted unless state right-to-work laws barred them; unions could not make political contributions in federal elections; union officials had to sign affidavits that they were not Communists; the President was given authority, when he believed that the national interest was being threatened, to seek a federal court injunction requiring an eighty-day cooling off period prior to a strike; secondary boycotts and jurisdictional strikes were forbidden; businesses could call upon the National Labor Relations Board to prevent unfair labor practices. Truman, labeling it "a shocking piece of legislation," vetoed the bill. Congress overrode the veto by 3–1 margins in both houses, and the Labor Management Relations Act, 1947 (its formal title), became law.

DEFENSE SPENDING

The partisan struggles that marked domestic policy diminished considerably in the area of foreign affairs. The Truman administration found broad-based public and congressional acceptance of its hardening cold war position. The deteriorating relationship with the Soviet Union and anxieties about internal subversion won support for the Truman Doctrine, the Marshall Plan, and the creation of NATO. It was not, however, until the outbreak of fighting in Korea that military spending rapidly escalated.

TABLE 11:1
National Defense and Veterans Benefit Outlays as Percentages of Total Federal Spending and GNP: 1945–1960

Year	Total Federal Spending (year ending June 30) (in billions of dollars)	National Defense (in billions of dollars)	% of Total Federal Spending	% of Annual GNP	National Defense plus Veterans Benefits (in billions of dollars)	% of Total Federal Spending	% of Annual GNP
1945	95.2	81.6	85.7	38.5	82.7	86.9	39.0
1946	61.7	44.7	72.4	21.4	48.1	78.0	23.0
1947	36.9	13.1	35.5	5.7	20.0	54.2	8.6
1948	36.5	13.0	35.6	5.0	19.4	53.2	7.5
1949	40.6	13.1	32.3	5.1	19.7	48.5	7.7
1950	43.1	13.1	30.4	4.6	21.9	50.8	7.7
1951	45.8	22.5	49.1	6.9	28.0	61.1	8.5
1952	68.0	44.0	64.7	12.7	49.4	72.6	14.3
1953	76.8	50.4	65.6	13.8	54.9	71.4	15.1
1954	70.9	46.6	65.7	12.8	50.9	71.8	14.0
1955	68.5	40.2	58.7	10.1	44.7	65.3	11.2
1956	70.5	40.3	57.1	9.6	45.1	64.0	10.8
1957	76.7	42.8	55.8	9.7	47.7	62.2	10.8
1958	82.6	44.4	53.8	9.9	49.6	60.0	11.1
1959	92.1	46.6	50.6	9.6	52.0	56.5	10.8
1960	92.2	45.9	49.8	9.1	51.3	55.6	10.2

Source: Data from U.S. Department of Commerce,
Historical Statistics of the United States, Colonial Times to 1970

The roots of what came to be known as the military-industrial complex were established during the second world war. The imperatives of unprecedented production and technological innovation brought the military, big business, and the scientific community into a new working relationship. Charles E. Wilson, president of General Electric, made the case for maintaining this connection into peacetime in a 1944 speech to the Army Ordnance Association. Arguing that "the tendency to war is inevitable," Wilson warned that postwar America should opt for "full preparedness according to a continuing plan." General Dwight Eisenhower, in a memorandum circulated to the army command in 1946 while he was chief of staff, insisted that the principle of integrating national resources learned in World War II be applied to peacetime: "The future security of the nation demands that all those civilian resources which by conversion or redirection constitute our main support in time of emergency be associated closely with the activities of the army in time of peace."

However, the end of World War II witnessed a speedy reconversion by industry to civilian economic pursuits. Manufacturers, many of whose expanded production facilities were built with government funds and transferred to them at great savings, rushed to stake their claims in the civilian markets. The armed forces, which stood at 12 million when Japan surrendered, were reduced to 3 million by the following summer, and to 1½ million by the summer of 1947. Spending for national defense fell apace, dropping 45 percent from fiscal year 1945 to 1946 and 71 percent from fiscal year 1946 to 1947. The military budget hovered at $13 billion a year until the United States entered the Korean conflict. Military expenditures then jumped to $22.5 billion in fiscal year 1951, virtually doubled the following year, and then continued above the $40 billion mark for the rest of the decade.

THE CONSUMER CULTURE

The American economy in the 1950s produced an unprecedented level of goods, what Max Lerner described as a "wilderness of commodities." Most Americans were gladly swept up in the quest to accumulate more and more of the products that had come to define the good life. The editors of *Fortune* applauded America for having institutionalized in her economy "a permanent revolution," one capable of moving the nation to an ever higher standard of living. This era of abundance attracted the attention of social analysts, who attempted to assess its impact on the American character. David Riesman in his *The Lonely Crowd* (1950), William H. Whyte, Jr., in *The Organization Man* (1956), and David Potter in *People of Plenty* (1954) examined the social and psychological dimensions of an economy of abundance. Max Lerner, in *America as a Civilization* (1957), voiced a reservation that would eventually come to trouble more and more Americans. A nation moving out of an extended depression, he argued, saw expansion as an undiluted blessing. The economic system had made enormous progress in generating goods and services but had failed to develop a sense of direction. Where, he asked, does it go from prosperity?

The advertising industry played the role of midwife in the birth of a consumer culture. Madison Avenue and the man in the gray flannel suit became popular symbols of an increasingly sophisticated process for transforming the flood of new products from luxuries into necessities. Advertising revenues, which stood at $2.9 billion in 1945, jumped to $11.9 billion by 1960. Price competition increasingly yielded to advertising campaigns as the primary strategy for expanding market penetration. These campaigns, drawing heavily upon behavioral and motivational research, had an ideal medium for focusing desires: television.

The Gallup poll asked Americans in May, 1949, if they had ever seen a program on television, and 56 percent had not. Less than one million families owned sets at this time, but that number would soon dramatically swell. In 1949, some 3 million television sets would be produced; in 1950 the figure was 7.5 million. By 1956 over three-quarters of all American homes would have a television set.

THE TECHNETRONIC ERA

Television was simply the first manifestation of a postwar wave of products and processes that created what Zbigniew Brzezinski called the technetronic era. Innovations in technology and electronics profoundly altered American life, creating what has been termed a "second industrial revolution."

Large-scale research and development in electronics conducted during World War II very shortly reshaped major sectors of the civilian economy. UNIVAC, the first commercial computer, came on the market in 1950. The pace of high-technology innovation was such that the second-generation computer, which replaced vacuum tubes with transistors, appeared within a few years.

The most impressive potential application of electronic technology lay in the automation of the productive process. Electronic mechanisms, which provided feedback control from one phase of production to another, created an automatically self-regulated manufacturing system. *The New York Times*, in an April 8, 1955, article headlined "Automation Puts Industry on the Eve of Fantastic Robot Era," marveled at a process that allowed automated machines to "adjust to variable productive conditions, correct their own mistakes, inspect the finished product and even change their own parts when parts break or wear out." This new technology, the report continued, was already being used "to refine oil, make artillery shells, put together television sets, bake cakes, process chemicals, generate electrical power, mail out insurance bills, put through transcontinental telephone calls and build automobile engines." The robot era the *Times* heralded developed rather slowly. Sales of industrial control and processing equipment amounted to less than $90 million in 1954. Five years later they reached $175 million.

THE WORK FORCE

Labor viewed these impending changes in the work environment as a mixed blessing. Automation reduced many physically tedious tasks but posed the larger danger of eliminating jobs. The argument that automation would eventually create more and better jobs did little to reassure the worker who felt threatened by its immediate impact. The new electronic technology in the productive sector, in fact, merely accelerated the trend toward an increasing proportion of the work force in service occupations. By the mid 1950s white-collar workers outnumbered blue-collar workers for the first time. Daniel Bell, in an essay on the "information society," analyzed the shifting composition of the labor force more specifically: "From 1860 to about 1906, the largest single group in the work force was in agriculture. In the next period, until about 1954, the predominant group was industrial. Currently, the predominant group consists of information workers."

Organized labor lost much of its fervor in the 1950s. A movement that had enrolled over 10 million workers between 1937 and 1945 failed to significantly expand that base in the postwar period. The proportion of union members in the labor force began to decline after the mid-1950s.

TABLE 11:2
Labor Union Membership as Percentage of Total Labor Force and Non-agricultural Employment: 1945–1960

Year	Union Membership	% of Total Labor Force	% of Nonagricultural Employment
1945	14.3 million	21.9	35.5
1950	14.3 million	22.0	31.5
1955	16.8 million	24.4	33.2
1960	17.0 million	23.6	31.4

Source: U.S. Department of Commerce, *Statistical Abstract of the United States, 1979.*

In December, 1955, the American Federation of Labor, directed by George Meany, and the Congress of Industrial Organizations, presided over by Walter Reuther, merged. The AFL-CIO, headed by Meany for the next quarter-century, proved unable to use its combined strength to reinvigorate the labor movement. In 1957 a Senate select committee chaired by John McClellan (D., Ark.) held hearings on labor corruption, particularly in the Teamsters' Union. The AFL-CIO expelled the 1.4-million-member union from the federation, but that did not satisfy those members of Congress who still saw the need for legislation to curb corrupt labor practices. The Landrum-Griffin Act of 1959 sought to guarantee democratic procedures in unions, barred individuals convicted of serious crimes from holding union offices, and regulated financial practices.

A Gallup poll taken after the McClellan hearings asked Americans whether corruption and racketeering were pretty widespread in unions, limited to just a few unions, or didn't exist. Results showed that 43 percent saw corruption as a widespread problem, 34 percent saw it as limited, 2 percent thought there was none, and 21 percent had no opinion on the question. A Roper poll also taken in 1957 asked which group was doing the least good for the country. Of the respondents 44 percent named labor leaders, while only 12 percent singled out business leaders.

By the end of the 1950s organized labor was in the ironic position of being criticized as "big labor" at the very time it represented a shrinking portion of the labor force. Many of the leaders of the AFL-

CIO had been part of the labor insurgency of the late 1930s and early 1940s when entire industries had been organized. They now led a movement that had lost much of the fervor and public support of those earlier years.

The American labor force by the end of the 1940s consisted of close to 70 million workers, one-third of whom were female. The number of workers had risen by 7.4 million from 1950 to 1960, and 65 percent of that gain were women. This emerging postindustrial labor force, with a declining proportion of production workers, differed considerably from the work force of the 1930s. The labor movement now faced the problem of adapting the strategies used to organize predominantly blue-collar workers in the depression years to unionizing white-collar workers in more prosperous times.

ENERGY

The consumer culture that developed in the United States in the postwar era was made possible in large part by the availability of abundant, cheap energy. The production and utilization of millions of automobiles, television sets, freezers, and other goods made enormous energy demands. A study by Joel Darmstadter and S. H. Schurr of global energy use estimated that in 1950 the United States, with 6.1 percent of the world's population, consumed 44.5 percent of the energy expended. Ten years later, despite the rapid pace of industrialization around the world, the United States still consumed over one-third of all energy.

America's energy consumption in 1950 had risen 40 percent over the 1940 level. By 1960 it stood 30 percent higher. The mix of fuel resources had changed significantly during these years. Coal utilization sharply declined while petroleum and natural gas grew to provide three-quarters of the energy consumed.

During the 1950s America's production of energy-generating fuels grew at an annual rate of 1.9 percent while the consumption of those fuels expanded at a 2.8 percent annual rate. In 1955, the nation's fuel consumption surpassed fuel production for the first time, 39.2 quadrillion BTUs to 39.1 quadrillion BTUs. By 1960, that gap had widened to 2.3 quadrillion BTUs.

CHAPTER ELEVEN

TABLE 11:3
Energy Consumption by Major Source: 1940–1960

			% of Consumption		
Year	Total Consumption (Quadrillion BTUs)	Coal	Crude Petroleum	Natural Gas	Other
1940	23.9	52.4	31.4	11.4	3.8
1950	33.6	38.1	39.8	18.1	4.0
1955	39.2	29.1	44.2	23.3	3.5
1960	44.1	22.8	45.1	28.5	3.6

Source: U.S. Department of Commerce, *Statistical Abstract of the United States, 1979.*

The soaring use of energy is most dramatically evidenced in the American love affair with the automobile. From 1945 to 1960, the nation's population grew 30 percent while the number of motor vehicles on the road increased by almost 140 percent, from 31 million to 73.9 million. Automotive horsepower rose from 4.4 billion in 1950 to 10.4 billion in 1960.

PROFILE:

The Automobile Industry in the 1950s

The automobile industry, according to economic analyst Peter Drucker, "stands for modern industry all over the globe. It is to the twentieth century what the Lancashire cotton mills were to the early nineteenth century: the industry of industries."

In the 1950s this American "industry of industries" was at the crest of its power and acceptance. In the years shortly ahead it would be confronted by critics of the safety and efficiency of its products, by foreign competitors, by an environmental awareness that singled out the automobile as a prime polluter, and by an energy crisis producing long gas lines waiting for an ever more expensive fill-up. But those problems, although anticipated by some, failed to cloud most Americans' infatuation with the automobile.

The auto industry in the 1950s was the pacesetter of the economy.

Close to one-sixth of all workers were tied, directly or indirectly, into the production of cars. When Detroit was booming, the ripples were felt in the steel, rubber, and glass industries and beyond them in the larger economy.

Auto sales soared in the 1950s. The cars coming off the assembly lines were heavy, over-powered, and stressed comfort over safety. The standard American car had become, in the words of one critic, "the dinosaur in the driveway." In 1955, the peak sales year of the decade, 7.9 million automobiles were sold. They averaged 12.7 miles per gallon. Passenger vehicles had consumed 25 billion gallons of fuel in 1950. By 1960 the demand had risen to 42 billion gallons.

TABLE 11:4
Passenger Car Factory Sales and Wholesale Value: 1950–1960

Year	Motor Vehicle Factory Sales (in millions)	Wholesale Value (in billions of dollars)
1950	6.7	8.5
1951	5.3	7.2
1952	4.3	6.5
1953	6.1	9.0
1954	5.6	8.2
1955	7.9	12.5
1956	5.8	9.8
1957	6.1	11.2
1958	4.3	8.0
1959	5.6	10.5
1960	6.7	12.2

Source: U.S. Department of Commerce, *Historical Statistics of the United States, Colonial Times to 1970.*

Detroit's big-car philosophy left a market opening into which American Motors and foreign producers moved. American introduced the compact Rambler in 1956, and within three years it had a 6 percent share of the market, 360,000 units. Foreign car sales jumped even more dramatically. In 1955 total foreign car sales in the United States were approximately 50,000, less than 1 percent of the market. By 1957 they passed the 200,000 mark, and two years later 600,000 foreign cars, primarily Volkswagens, were sold in America, over 10 percent of the market. The Big Three responded to this challenge by introducing their line of compacts in the fall of 1959. General Motors' Corvair, Ford's Falcon, and Chrysler's Valiant soon recaptured most of the small car market. By 1962 foreign import sales had fallen below 5 percent. Detroit had gained a temporary victory. It would not be long, however, before import sales began edging up again.

The capping of the auto age came with the enactment of the federal interstate highway program in 1956. President Eisenhower had urged its passage in a special message to Congress, citing the need for an upgraded, safer network of roads that would meet the growing demands of automobile and truck traffic. The message contained a cold war note, stressing the system's value for mobilization and evacuation in the event of an atomic attack. The program had other champions, the automotive industry lobby, construction firms, and city planners who envisioned urban renewal programs developing around the 7,000 miles of roadway scheduled for metropolitan areas.

The building of this interstate system quickly became the largest public works project in history. The initial planning called for a 41,000-mile network to be completed by 1972 at a cost of approximately $26 billion. The federal government would provide 90 percent of the cost, drawing upon a highway trust fund created from gasoline taxes. Secretary of the Treasury George Humphrey, a man who prided himself on keeping a close eye on the federal purse strings, embraced the program: "America lives on wheels, and we have to provide the highways to keep America living on wheels and keep the kind and form of life we want." President Eisenhower offered a more succinct assessment in his memoirs: "More than any single action by the government since the end of the war, this one would change the face of America." That pouring of concrete roadways, changing America's face, would still be in progress two decades after Eisenhower left the White House. The system, with additional mileage tacked on, would still be years from completion, and its eventual cost would approach $100 billion.

AGRICULTURE

The postwar decade and a half witnessed a decline in the farm population and the number of farms, but agricultural production soared. In 1910 one out of three Americans lived on a farm. By the late 1940s it was one in six, and by 1960, one in twelve. The number of farms fell from six million in 1945 to four million by 1960. The total value of farm output, measured in constant (1958) dollars, however, rose from $29.8 billion in 1945 to $39.2 billion in 1960.

The American farmer's ability to expand production rapidly despite the declining number of farms and workers has several explanations. Although there were two million fewer farms in 1960 than there had been in 1945, this decrease was offset by an increase in average acreage from 191 to 297. The farms that were disappearing were predominantly smaller ones, and American farming was increasingly becoming agribusiness. The rising production of these years, however, can be more directly attributed to mechanization and advances in biochemistry and genetics.

The postwar mechanization of the American farm constituted an acceleration of an earlier trend. From 1945 to 1960 the number of tractors doubled, and the number of grain combines tripled. Mechanical horsepower in use on farms rose 400 percent from 1950 to 1960. This continuing transition from work animals to motorized equipment increased production in ways that might escape immediate attention. Dale Hathaway, in his *Government and Agriculture*, has pointed out that approximately 90 million acres of cropland, one-quarter of the total, were used in 1920 to produce feed for horses and mules. By 1960 less than 10 million acres were required for this purpose.

The most dramatic impetus for increased production came from advances in biochemistry and genetics. Research and development in these areas now rivaled mechanization as a stimulus to agricultural output. Farming by the 1950s had become increasingly sophisticated, relying heavily upon synthetic fertilizers, herbicides, and insecticides. Plant genetic engineering had moved beyond experimentation with existing seed strains toward creating entirely new strains. This newer research meshed with the continuing mechanization trend in seeking to develop plants that were suited for harvesting by that process. Plants, in Nathan Rosenberg's description, were "being 'redesigned,' as were guns and cutlery in the nineteenth century, so that they can be produced more effectively by machinery."

Challenges were eventually voiced at some of the changes that had reshaped postwar agriculture. Critics warned of the dangers of heavy applications of insecticides and herbicides; consumers complained that the "new" fruits and vegetables had lost their distinctive taste. In the 1950s, however, most Americans marveled at the farmers' success story. Between 1945 and 1960 man-hours of farm labor were cut in half. The farmer who provided food for 14.6 people in 1945 fed 25.8 by 1960.

When Soviet Premier Nikita Khrushchev visited the United States in 1959 and government leaders wished to impress him with America's productive capacity, they chose an ideal illustration—a huge Iowa corn farm.

THE PERFORMANCE OF THE AMERICAN ECONOMY: 1945–1960

For those Americans in 1945 who feared a plunge back into depression, the postwar economy provided almost immediate reassurance. Inflationary, not deflationary, pressures posed the immediate threat to the economy. Real GNP growth began in 1948 and by 1951 had regained the level of wartime 1945.

TABLE 11:5
GNP in Current and Constant Dollars and Real Growth Rate: 1945–1960

Year	GNP in Current Dollars (billions)	GNP in Constant (1972) Dollars (billions)	Real GNP Growth Rate (% change from previous year)
1945	212.3	560.0	−1.5
1946	209.6	476.9	−14.8
1947	232.8	468.3	−1.8
1948	259.1	487.7	4.1
1949	258.0	490.7	.6
1950	286.2	533.5	8.7
1951	330.2	576.5	8.1
1952	347.2	598.5	3.8
1953	366.1	621.8	3.9
1954	366.3	613.7	−1.3
1955	399.3	654.8	6.7
1956	420.7	668.8	2.1
1957	442.8	680.9	1.8
1958	448.9	679.5	−.2
1959	486.5	720.4	6.0
1960	506.0	736.8	2.3

Source: *Economic Report of the President*, 1980.

The economy in the 1950s grew at an annual average rate of 3.2 percent, marked by a surge in the early years induced by the Korean conflict, followed by a recession in 1953–54, a vigorous recovery and expansion through mid-1957, a new recession until early 1958, followed by renewed growth through 1960.

Disposable personal income in current dollars rose from $149 billion in 1945 to $349.4 billion in 1960. The per capita rise in disposable personal income from $1,065 to $1,934 was less dramatic because of the strong rate of population growth. The baby boom, ordinarily thought of as an immediate postwar phenomenon, continued well into the 1950s, peaking in 1957 with slightly more than 4.3 million births.

The most striking change between the pre-depression American economy and that of the 1950s lay in the increased level of involvement by the federal government. Governmental economic intervention had grown to curb a depression, had expanded further to win a world war, and continued to extend itself into an era of prosperity. By the postwar years the federal government, under both Democratic and Republican administrations, increasingly implemented Keynesian principles. It had accepted the role, in Robert Heilbroner's term, of "guarantor" of the economy. Federal spending in the 1950s grew to accommodate that policy and to meet the defense needs of the cold war.

Massive federal expenditures served as one prod to the economy. The "knowledge revolution" served as another source of stimulation. This revolution encompassed the tremendous expansion of higher education during these years, the increased commitment by government and business to research and development, and the technological breakthroughs in electronics and communications that made knowledge more accessible.

In the decade of the 1950s the number of degree-seeking students rose from 2.3 to 3.5 million. The institutions housing these students increased their budgets even more sharply, going from $2.25 billion to $5.6 billion.

Science and engineering specializations attracted many of these students. By 1960 there were over one million scientists and engineers, twice the number of a decade before. The level of total support for basic research and development more than kept pace, increasing from $5.2 billion in 1953 to $13 billion by 1960.

TABLE 11:6
Federal Budget Receipts and Outlays, Fiscal Years 1950–1960
(in billions of dollars)

Fiscal Year	Receipts	Outlays	Surplus or Deficit (−)
1950	39.485	42.597	−3.112
1951	51.646	45.546	6.1
1952	66.204	67.721	−1.517
1953	69.574	76.107	−6.533
1954	69.719	70.890	−1.170
1955	65.469	68.509	−3.041
1956	74.547	70.460	4.087
1957	79.990	76.741	3.249
1958	79.636	82.575	−2.939
1959	79.249	92.104	−12.855
1960	92.492	92.223	.269

Source: *Economic Report of the President*, 1980.

By the end of the 1950s the American economy seemed to possess all of the strengths of maturity. The danger that it might pass along into senility appeared averted by the constant reinvigoration afforded by technological innovation. Economist John Kenneth Galbraith published *The Affluent Society* in 1958, and its title soon became part of the popular vocabulary. Galbraith stressed the importance of understanding the new post-scarcity condition of the American economy, warning that the "affluent country which conducts its affairs in accordance with rules of another and poorer age also foregoes opportunities." The opportunities Galbraith foresaw included greater attention to public need rather than private consumption, and the eradication of persistent poverty. For Galbraith and many liberals, planning and social commitment joined to the abundance an affluent society had at its disposal gave promise of a more humane society. Rising prosperity had become, in Peter Clecak's phrase, "welfare capitalism's secular equivalent of grace."

That vision would animate much of the next two decades but its energy would ebb as the nation discovered "stagflation" and a new sense of economic constraints.

TWELVE

From Affluence to Constraint:
1960–1980s

The 1960s began with a President pledging to get America moving again, to lead the nation vigorously into a new frontier. That vision was partially realized before the decade ended when astronaut Neil Armstrong set foot on the moon. That dramatic achievement, a tribute to American will and technology, evoked a sense of pride at a time when the nation's spirit was deeply troubled. The optimism and sense of renewed possibility that had marked the beginning of the 1960s had been strained again and again by assassins' bullets. America was mired in a war in Southeast Asia, a conflict that spurred massive demonstrations in this country and soured the political environment. A further legacy of that unpopular effort was the rampant inflation that would resist control throughout the 1970s.

The history of the American economy from 1960 to 1980 is in many respects an account of progress and strength. The greatly expanded production of goods and services, the growth of a labor force that increasingly reflected the diversity of the population, the development of a range of programs to assist the economically disadvantaged—these are substantial achievements. And yet, there was much in American economic life during these years that made them, in William Leuchtenburg's phrase, a "troubled feast."

This period witnessed the emergence of an ecological awareness that was increasingly sensitive to the environmental costs of uncontrolled industrial development. The use of the GNP as a barometer of social well-being was challenged by proponents of limited growth and the philosophy that "small is beautiful."

Those who dismissed such concerns and looked to continued American economic supremacy had much to be concerned about by the latter part of the 1970s. On all sides there lay evidence of a loss of thrust in the economy. Declining productivity, increasingly outmoded production facilities, unfavorable trade balances, a shrinking dollar, an energy crisis, stagflation (high inflation with high unemployment)—these were some of the deep fissures undermining the American economy as the 1970s ended.

The mood of the nation had darkened considerably from the euphoria of the early 1960s. President Carter, in a speech on energy in July, 1979, acknowledged this erosion of confidence. For the first time in the nation's history, he pointed out, "a majority of our people believe that the next five years will be worse than the past five years."

POPULATION

In 1960 there were 180.7 million Americans. By the end of the 1970s that number had increased by 22.9 percent to 221.9 million. The larger portion of this 41.2 million gain had occurred in the 1960s, a decade that witnessed a net gain of 24.2 million. Population growth in the 1970s measured 17 million.

These demographic changes, when analyzed more carefully, reveal patterns that are economically significant. The rate of population increase for the 1960s was 13 percent, and this dropped to less than 9 percent for the 1970s. Between 1970 and 1979 the number of persons under the age of eighteen declined by 10 percent, falling from 70 million to 63 million. At the other end of the age spectrum, the number of Americans age sixty-five or older increased at approximately three times the rate of overall population growth in the 1970s, rising from 20 million to 25 million. The aging of the American population places an increasing strain on the funding formula for social security. In 1950 the ratio of contributors to all beneficiaries of the system was 14 to 1. By 1960 the ratio had fallen to 5 to 1, by 1970 it had dropped further to 3.5 to 1, and by 1980 it had reached 3 to 1. The payroll tax to fund social security jumped sharply in the 1970s, creating a growing insistence that the program be supported by general federal revenues.

ECONOMIC GROWTH

The nation's output of goods and services in 1960 stood at $506 billion, five times the 1929 figure, in current dollars. In slightly more than a decade, the gross national product doubled, creating a trillion dollar economy by 1971. By the end of the 1970s it would double again, reaching $2.37 trillion in 1979. This quadrupling of the GNP in two decades was abetted, in considerable measure, by the developing inflationary trend. If we correct for inflation and examine real GNP growth, we find significant, but far less dramatic, improvement. In constant 1972 dollars, GNP rose from $737 billion in 1960 to $1.4 trillion in 1979.

MANAGING THE ECONOMY

The central theme of John F. Kennedy's 1960 presidential campaign had been his commitment to get the nation moving again. The policy makers Kennedy appointed to develop this strategy of economic growth came from the ranks of the new economists. These planners, led by Walter Heller, chairman of the Council of Economic Advisers, sought to manage the economy on Keynesian principles, directing fiscal and monetary policies to assure high performance. President Kennedy, in a speech at Yale University in June, 1962, defended his administration's willingness to intervene more actively in the economy, insisting that "myths" about federal fiscal policy and public indebtedness must yield to a more realistic understanding of modern economic planning. Former President Eisenhower, in an article published early the following year entitled "Spending into Trouble," spoke for many made uneasy by the new economics: "I say that the time-tested rules of financial policy still apply. . . . No family, no business, no nation can spend itself into prosperity. . . . But all of us would feel more comfortable and secure if our national leadership exercised the foresight and self-discipline to balance its budget and to begin paying back something on the national debt."

The Kennedy administration, however, chose to spur economic growth by pressing for a large tax reduction and adding to the budgetary deficit. The tax cut bill, amounting to $14 billion, was passed in February, 1964, after Lyndon Johnson had assumed the presidency. It marked, for Walter Heller, "the most overt and dramatic expression of the new approach to economic policy." By the following year the new economics seemed to have delivered all that it had promised: a growing economy with low unemployment and stable prices.

TABLE 12:1
Consumer Price Index: 1967–1979

1967	100.0
1968	104.2
1969	109.8
1970	116.3
1971	121.3
1972	125.3
1973	133.1
1974	147.7
1975	161.2
1976	170.5
1977	181.5
1978	195.4
1979	217.4

Source: *Economic Report of the President, 1980.*

Unfortunately, new disruptive pressures would soon develop that proved less amenable to solution. The Keynesian strategy, as John Kenneth Galbraith noted, has a "fatal inelasticity." Under ordinary political conditions, expenditures can be increased but not as readily reduced, whereas taxes can be cut but not as easily raised. Fiscal policy, with these constraints, has limited applicability. "It will work," according to Galbraith, "wonderfully against deflation and depression but not very well against inflation."

In 1965 the United States intensified its military involvement in

Vietnam. From the middle of that year through 1968, defense spending increased 60 percent. President Johnson rejected his economic advisers' recommendation in December, 1965, that he seek a tax increase to stave off inflation. Johnson was less fearful of inflationary pressures at this time than of provoking a full-scale congressional debate on the war. Eventually, in June, 1968, a 10 percent income surtax was passed, but this proved insufficient to curb mounting inflation.

Inflation had been a minor problem during the early 1960s, increasing at an annual rate of 1.8 percent from 1960 to 1967. It now emerged as a more persistent difficulty and came to bedevil the American economy in the 1970s.

By the early 1970s a new term—*stagflation*—had been coined to characterize the condition of the American economy. Spending for the Vietnam War during the Johnson years, coming on top of a large base of defense and Great Society expenditures, had been fueled by expanding the money supply. The inflation that emerged during these years intensified at the beginning of the 1970s, despite an economic slowdown and high unemployment. This simultaneous inflation along with a sluggish economy and high unemployment—stagflation—posed an obvious dilemma for economic planners. The strategy for dealing with either one of these problems would tend to exacerbate the other. The Nixon administration gave priority to curbing inflation.

In August, 1971, President Nixon initiated the nation's first peacetime program of wage and price controls, beginning with a ninety-day freeze on wages, prices, and rents. Nixon's economic program also addressed the nation's unfavorable balance-of-payments position and the weakening of the dollar. The convertibility of dollars into gold was now terminated, a prelude to the devaluation of the dollar later that year. The primacy of the dollar in the international monetary system that had developed since World War II was coming to an end, to be replaced by floating exchange rates.

The Nixon wage and price control program moved from Phase One, the ninety-day freeze, to Phase Two, which involved a complicated set of regulations governing permissible pay increases and price rises, and which lasted until January, 1973. Phase Three consisted largely of voluntary guidelines, and this relaxation of controls triggered a new inflationary surge. In June, 1973, the President imposed a sixty-day price freeze, followed by a lifting of regulations until the authority to impose controls expired in April, 1974.

Phase One and Phase Two of the Nixon controls had been moderately successful, keeping inflation below 4 percent in 1972. With the easing of controls in 1973, inflation began to reassert itself. It received a major boost in October when the Organization of Petroleum Exporting Countries announced a 70 percent increase in the price of oil, with the cost per barrel going from $3 to $5.11. Less than three months later, on January 1, 1974, OPEC raised prices even more sharply, with the cost per barrel jumping to $11.65. Imported oil prices had now risen almost 400 percent in a span of three months.

When Gerald Ford took over the presidency after Richard Nixon's resignation in August, 1974, the economy was moving into the most severe recession it had experienced since the Great Depression. This year-long contraction marked an intensification of the earlier aspects of stagflation, double-digit inflation and high unemployment, along with new pressure from soaring energy costs. Real GNP dropped 1.4 percent in 1974 and fell a further 1.3 percent in 1975. The Ford administration initially followed a restrictive fiscal and monetary policy, with the President vetoing a large number of spending bills. As inflation began to moderate, fiscal policy shifted to stimulate the lagging economy. Increased federal expenditures and a $22 billion tax cut triggered economic recovery, but helped create the largest budgetary deficit in history, $66 billion in fiscal year 1976.

The Carter presidency began in 1977 with his pledge to have a balanced budget by the end of four years. That goal became increasingly elusive in an economy that continued to be plagued by inflation, high unemployment, and rising energy costs. Inflation had been squeezed down by the recession to 5 percent in 1976, but soon began to mount again, rising to 6.6 percent in 1977, jumping to 9 percent in 1978, and soaring to 12.7 percent by the end of 1979. Declining productivity growth, reduced level of savings, and inadequate capital investment all hampered the economy, but President Carter singled out inflation as "the most intractable and corrosive problem of them all." Inflationary pressures were fed further by increasing oil costs, with the official OPEC price standing at $24 a barrel in December, 1979; that was 800 percent above its level only slightly more than six years earlier.

One of the victims of the economic turmoil of the 1970s was a sense of belief in the ability of the government to manage the economy effectively. The *Economic Report of the President, 1968* clearly conveyed the attitude of the economic advisers of the Kennedy-Johnson years toward the federal government's role in assuring a high-performance economy in the early 1960s. "During these seven years of achievement," they noted, "fiscal and monetary policy had been actively and consciously employed to promote prosperity." They stressed the continuous analysis and intervention that promoted maximum economic performance: "No longer does federal economic policy rely primarily on the 'automatic stabilizers' built into our system, or wait for a recession or serious inflation to occur before measures are taken."

TABLE 12:2
Federal Spending and Surpluses or Deficits: 1960–1979
(in billions of dollars)

Fiscal Year	Federal Spending	Surplus or Deficit (−)
1960	92.2	.269
1961	97.8	−3.4
1962	106.8	−7.1
1963	111.3	−4.8
1964	118.6	−5.9
1965	118.4	−1.6
1966	134.7	−3.8
1967	158.3	−8.7
1968	178.8	−25.2
1969	184.5	3.2
1970	196.6	−2.8
1971	211.4	−23.0
1972	232.0	−23.4
1973	247.1	−14.9
1974	269.6	−4.7
1975	326.2	−45.2
1976	366.4	−66.4
Transition quarter*	94.7	−13.0
1977	402.7	−45.0
1978	450.8	−48.8
1979	493.7	−27.7

Source: *Economic Report of the President, 1980.*

*From 1960 to 1976 the fiscal year ran from July 1 to June 30. Beginning in October, 1976, the fiscal year shifted to October 1 to September 30. The period from July 1 to September 30, 1976, when the changeover took place is a separate fiscal period called the transition quarter.

That confidence in the ability to manage the economy soon encountered increasing public skepticism. Economic planners in the late 1960s and throughout the 1970s faced conflicting problems. The inflation unleashed by the Vietnam War scourged the economy over the next decade. However, the traditional formulas for curbing inflation proved politically difficult to administer during a period of sluggish growth and high unemployment. These difficulties were heightened by structural problems in the economy and by the growing leverage possessed by the OPEC cartel.

President Jimmy Carter's letter to Congress accompanying his

TABLE 12:3
National Defense Expenditures as Percentages
of Total Federal Spending and GNP: 1960–1979

Fiscal Year	Total Federal Spending (billions of dollars)	National Defense Expenditures (billions of dollars) Current Dollars	Constant (1972) Dollars	% of Total Federal Spending	% of GNP
1960	92.2	45.2	73.8	49.0	9.1
1961	97.8	47.4	77.4	48.5	9.1
1962	106.8	49.0	77.2	45.9	9.0
1963	111.3	50.1	76.8	45.0	8.7
1964	118.6	51.5	77.0	43.4	8.4
1965	118.4	47.5	69.3	40.1	7.2
1966	134.7	54.9	76.3	40.8	7.6
1967	158.3	68.2	92.0	43.1	8.8
1968	178.8	78.8	101.4	44.1	9.5
1969	184.5	79.4	97.9	43.0	8.8
1970	196.6	78.6	90.3	40.0	8.2
1971	211.4	75.8	81.2	35.9	7.4
1972	232.0	76.6	76.6	33.0	6.9
1973	247.1	74.5	70.0	30.1	6.0
1974	269.6	77.8	67.9	28.9	5.7
1975	326.2	85.6	67.1	26.2	5.9
1976	366.4	89.4	65.6	24.4	5.5
Transition quarter	94.7	22.3	16.0	23.5	(NA)
1977	402.7	97.5	66.7	24.2	5.3
1978	450.8	105.2	67.3	23.3	4.8
1979	493.7	117.7	71.1	23.8	5.0

Sources: U.S. Department of Commerce. *Statistical Abstract of the United States, 1979,* and *Economic Report of the President, 1980.*

Economic Report of the President, 1980 reflected a much more constrained sense of the limits of economic management than the report twelve years earlier. "We are," he informed Congress, "making the adjustment to the realities of the economic world the 1970s brought into being. It is in many ways a more difficult world than the one that preceded it. Yet the problems it poses are not insuperable."

In contrast with the earlier report's celebration of planning abilities that promoted prosperity, Carter offered a more modest perspective: "There are no economic miracles waiting to be performed. But with patience and self-discipline, combined with some ingenuity and care, we can deal successfully with the new world. The 1980s can be a decade of lessened inflation and healthy growth."

FEDERAL SPENDING

Federal expenditures in current dollars rose more than 500 percent from 1960 to 1979, increasing from $92.2 billion to $494 billion. In constant 1972 dollars, federal spending during these years almost doubled, going from $150.8 billion to $284.1 billion. Federal outlays as a percentage of GNP moved up slightly, rising from 18.5 percent in 1960 to 21.6 percent in 1979.

DEFENSE SPENDING

Although defense spending in the period from 1960 to 1980, measured as a percentage of gross national product, never attained the level that it had in the 1950s, it nonetheless became the target of sustained criticism. An unlikely source initially helped focus public attention on military expenditures. Dwight Eisenhower, in a televised farewell address on January 17, 1961, as he left the presidency, described for his audience the recent emergence of "an immense military establishment and a large arms industry." Although he accepted the necessity for these developments, Eisenhower cautioned the American people about their "grave implications." "Our toil, resources, and livelihood are all involved," he noted; "so is the very structure of our society." In a passage that soon became as famous as George Washington's earlier farewell warning about entangling alliances, Eisenhower insisted that in "the councils of government, we must guard against the acquisition of unwarranted influence, whether sought or unsought, by the military-industrial complex. The potential for the disastrous rise of misplaced power exists and will persist."

By the middle of the 1960s a wide-ranging body of criticism directed against military spending had appeared, criticism that went far beyond Eisenhower's concern about the potential dangers of the military-industrial complex. It argued that the defense sector had already absorbed too large a portion of the nation's resources and constituted a drain on the vitality of the larger economy. The increasingly unpopular Vietnam War, which added a total of $110 billion in incremental costs to regular defense spending, intensified complaints about the Pentagon budget. As America's military involvement in Southeast Asia wound down, defense spending in constant dollars declined, with 1976 expenditures at two-thirds of the 1968 level. However, with growing concern over arms buildup in the Soviet Union and with a movement away from detente, American military spending began to rise again by the end of the 1970s.

Proponents of a high level of defense spending have argued that the maintenance of national security stands as the government's primary responsibility. Whatever proportion of America's resources is needed to defend the nation's interests should be assigned to that purpose. As the definition of national security expanded to take on global responsibilities and as the technology of weaponry became more sophisticated and expensive, the economics of national defense grew accordingly. The enlarged defense budgets were justified not only as a necessity in a threatening world, but also as a stimulus to the American economy, guaranteeing production and jobs.

Those claims have evoked many challenges. The strongest case against large-scale military spending, in both its comprehensiveness and its specificity, has been put forward by Seymour Melman, a professor of industrial engineering. In *Our Depleted Society*, Melman examined the impact of channeling hundreds of billions of dollars and a large proportion of the nation's scientists and engineers into the defense sector. Melman contended that "an unprecedented concentration of America's technical talent and fresh capital on military production" had eroded the nation's industrial base. "Entire industries are falling into technical disrepair," he warned, "and there is massive loss of productive employment because of inability to hold even domestic markets against foreign competition."

In two subsequent studies, *Pentagon Capitalism* and *The Per-*

manent War Economy, Melman broadened his critique, exploring structural changes that had emerged in the American economy as a result of a generation of heavy military expenditures. By the early 1960s, Melman noted, the Department of Defense had become the central management for an extensive military-industrial system. Firms operating within this system were freed of the competitive constraints of the marketplace. They became "failure-proof," protected against the normal consequences of poor design or bad management. The growth of this "war economy," rather than providing the stimulation so often claimed, represents for Melman a "parasitic" development, draining the larger host economy.

Melman's research embodies the most systematic criticism of the economics of national defense. In addition to the studies already mentioned, he has prepared a scaled-down version of the military budget that he contends would allow for adequate defense, and he has directed a series of studies that provide detailed analyses of how specific industries might convert from military to civilian production.

Regardless of the persuasiveness of Melman's argument that a generation of massive military spending has weakened America's economic position, and despite the numbers who may shake their heads in dismay at reading about the latest weapons cost overruns in the morning headlines, the question of what is the appropriate level of commitment to national defense remains a contentious issue. Is parity with the nation's potential enemies adequate, or must there be superiority? Should "worst case analysis" be employed, positing the maximum conceivable threat, or should a more restrained standard be used? In the past, claims of a bomber gap, and then a missile gap, encouraged increased defense expenditures. In the latter part of the 1970s, a renewed sense of threat evoked by a Soviet arms buildup led to an expansion of defense appropriations. Multibillion dollar weapons systems, such as the MX missile, the Trident submarine, and the air-launched cruise missile, are being added to the nation's arsenal, and projections for the defense budget from 1981 to 1985 run as high as one trillion dollars.

SOCIAL WELFARE EXPENDITURES

Franklin D. Roosevelt, in his second inaugural address delivered in January, 1937, noted the progress that had already been made in stemming the ravages of the Great Depression. He pointed as well, however, to the immense task that lay ahead. "I see," Roosevelt told the American people, "one-third of a nation ill-housed, ill-clad, ill-nourished." Roosevelt assured his audience that he spoke in hope, not despair, because the nation, understanding the injustice of these conditions, proposed to eliminate them. The standard that American social achievement must be measured by, the President insisted, "is not whether we add more to the abundance of those who have much; it is whether we provide enough for those who have too little."

Over the next quarter-century the American economy surged up from the depressed level of the mid-1930s, with national production and income rising at a sharp rate. This outpouring of goods, which more and more Americans had the means to accumulate, led, by the end of the 1950s, to the characterization of the United States as the "affluent society." Yet poverty, less extensive and visible than it had been during the Great Depression, still persisted in the land. In the early 1960s poverty was "rediscovered" and restored to a leading position on the public agenda, as a President once again pledged to eliminate it from this society.

The publication in 1962 of Michael Harrington's *The Other America* served as a catalyst for the renewed attention to poverty in American society. Harrington challenged the assumption that "the nation's problems were no longer a matter of basic human needs, of food, shelter, and clothing." The reality was that "tens of millions of Americans are, at this very moment, maimed in body and spirit, existing at levels beneath those necessary for human decency." In a moving portrayal, Harrington recounted the deprivation of the rural poor of Appalachia, the unemployed of the urban ghetto, and the impoverished elderly of the nation. Harrington's indictment of a society that averted its face from these conditions helped stir a public response. One of those affected by Harrington's account was Walter Heller, chairman of the Council of Economic Advisers, who gave his copy of the book to President Kennedy. Heller began holding planning meetings in the summer of 1963 to formulate a strategy for a concerted government attack on poverty that President Kennedy planned to make part of his 1964 legislative program. After Kennedy's death, President Johnson committed himself to legislative enactment of this campaign against poverty, seeing it as a cornerstone of what came to be called the Great Society program. In January, 1964, in his first State of the Union address, Johnson told the assembled congressmen that his new administration "today, here and now, declares unconditional war on poverty in America."

Congress responded to the President's call to arms, and in August Johnson signed the Economic Opportunity Act of 1964. It contained a variety of tactics for attacking poverty: federal funding for local community action groups that would devise neighborhood and city-wide campaigns, the Job Corps to develop vocational skills, VISTA (Volunteers in Service to America)—a domestic version of the Peace Corps—and a number of other programs. Appropriations for the first stage of this assault on poverty came to $800 million, and in 1965 more programs were added, including Medicare, which provided financial assistance through Social Security for medical care of the elderly.

As the war against poverty built momentum in its first years, America's commitment to another war, in Southeast Asia, began to place increasing demands on the nation's resources. The enthusiasm with which the President had declared an all-out assault on poverty began to give way to more limited expectations. In 1966 President Johnson, noting that "even a prosperous nation cannot meet all its goals all at once," announced that "the rate of advance of the new programs has been held below what might have been proposed in less troubled times."

The war in Vietnam proved only one of several constraints on the original commitment to eliminate poverty. Some of the community action groups, which the enacting legislation had required to reflect "maximum feasible participation" of the poor, had antagonized political leaders with their programs, and had been accused of mismanagement and fraud. The providing of a wide range of services for the poor evoked resentment from many Americans who were barely beyond the threshold of poverty themselves. The major restraint, however, on sustaining a long-term commitment to eradicating poverty lay in its original underlying economic assumptions. The belief that the American economy, with proper fiscal and monetary management, would continue to expand, and thus provide sufficient revenues to overcome the challenge of poverty, began to erode as the economy faltered in the 1970s. A decade after the war against poverty began, the Office of Economic Opportunity, which had led the campaign, was phased out and its remaining programs parceled out to other federal agencies.

Making an assessment of the gains realized during these years is a complicated matter. Federal social welfare expenditures rose enormously, climbing from $25 billion in 1960 to $220 billion in 1977. As a proportion of total federal spending, they doubled, going from 28 percent in 1960 to 56 percent in 1977. All of these funds, which included Social Security payments, were not, however, allocated to alleviate poverty.

To what extent did the war on poverty succeed? It clearly did not achieve the ambitious goal originally set by President Johnson. Determining specifically how much poverty was eliminated during these years poses certain difficulties. The government's definition of the poverty line came from a 1964 Social Security statistical study that took the cost of an "economy food basket" and, determining that food expenditures constituted one-third of an average family budget, multiplied by three. That figure, $3,165 for a family of four, was annually upgraded based on the Consumer Price Index.

Bureau of the Census data show that 28.5 million Americans (14.7 percent of the nation's population) lived below the poverty line in 1966. By 1977 that number had been reduced to 24.7 million—11.6 percent of the population. A January, 1977, study by the Congressional Budget Office, however, challenged the existing standard for assessing poverty. It contended that, because the data included only monetary and not "in-kind" income, the number of the impoverished had been vastly increased. By adding in-kind benefits, Medicaid, rental subsidies, food stamps, and so forth, to income, the CBO study argued, the poverty ranks would decline by two-thirds. The CBO approach of adding benefits to income has certain problems. It allows, as a number of critics have pointed out, the irony of medical payments for a major illness moving a person beyond the poverty level line. It does, however, for all its shortcomings, offer some assessment of the impact of the war on poverty programs in alleviating economic deprivation in America. These in-kind expenditures, which grew from $2.3 billion in 1965 to $40 billion in 1976, fell short of the "unconditional" war President Johnson promised to wage, but served, in areas of basic needs, to reduce the plight of the nation's least fortunate.

ENERGY

For a quarter-century after World War II the American economy drew upon cheap and abundant energy for extraordinary expansion. By the mid-1950s the nation's consumption of fuel resources began to edge past production, but that posed no immediate problem because of the availability of inexpensive fuel imports. Indeed, when inflation is taken into account, energy costs were lower in the 1960s than they had been in the 1950s. From 1960 to 1970 total energy consumption rose 51 percent, going from 44.1 quads (quadrillion British thermal units) to 66.8. In the 1970s this sense of abundance yielded to the harsher reality of long gas lines and skyrocketing energy costs. Total energy consumption in the 1970s rose at only one-third the rate it had in the previous decade, moving from 66.8 quads in 1970 to 78 in 1979.

Oil

Petroleum constitutes the main component of the nation's mix of energy sources. As imported oil came to provide for an increasing proportion of America's needs, the vulnerability to cutbacks in supply or sharp price hikes rose accordingly. In 1960 the United States imported 1.8 million barrels of oil a day, 19 percent of its consumption. By 1970 it was importing 3.4 million barrels a day, 24 percent of its needs. By 1977 imports had jumped to 8.5 million barrels a day, 47.5 percent of consumption. Although 1977 marked the peak in volume of oil imports for the decade, a new round of OPEC price increases in 1979 sharply raised the bill for imported petroleum.

Between 1970 and 1979 import costs for oil climbed 2,000 percent. In 1970 petroleum imports cost $2.9 billion. By 1972 they had risen to $4.6 billion. OPEC's price hikes beginning in the fall of 1973 increased that year's bill to $8.4 billion, and in 1974 it shot up to $26.6 billion. By 1977 it stood at $45 billion, fell back because of reduced imports in 1978 to $42.3 billion, but, with a $10-a-barrel OPEC increase in 1979, soared to $60 billion.

On November 7, 1973, responding to the oil embargo and OPEC price increase, President Nixon in a televised address urged the American people to "set as our national goal . . . that by the end of this decade we will have developed the potential to meet our own energy needs without depending on any foreign sources." Nixon labeled this commitment Project Independence, comparing it in importance to the Manhattan Project, which developed the atomic bomb, and the Apollo Project, which placed men on the moon. This venture, however, proved more difficult to accomplish than those earlier programs. In this case, there were conflicting policies being urged on Congress by energy producers, environmentalists, and consumers' groups. In addition, the American public, reading of record profits by the oil companies, expressed widespread doubt about the legitimacy of the crisis. This skepticism persisted throughout the decade. A *New York Times* opinion poll in November, 1979, a month before the deadline President Nixon had set for completing Project Independence, asked, "Do you think the energy shortage we hear about is real, or are we just

TABLE 12:4
Energy Consumption by Major Source: 1960–1977

Year	Total Consumption (quadrillion BTUs)	Percent of Consumption			
		Crude petroleum	Coal	Natural gas	Other
1960	44.1	45.1	22.8	28.5	3.6
1965	53.0	43.6	22.3	30.2	3.9
1970	66.8	44.0	18.9	32.8	4.3
1971	68.3	44.7	17.6	32.9	4.7
1972	71.6	46.0	17.3	31.7	4.9
1973	74.6	46.7	17.8	30.2	5.2
1974	72.4	46.1	17.7	29.9	6.3
1975	70.7	46.4	18.2	28.3	7.2
1976	74.2	47.0	18.5	27.4	7.1
1977	76.6	48.6	18.5	26.0	6.9

Source: U.S. Department of Commerce. *Statistical Abstract of the United States, 1979.*

being told there are shortages?" Only 37 percent thought the shortage real, with 54 percent believing that they were "just being told." Those whose doubts had been evoked by the success of the oil companies in the 1970s found confirmation for their belief with *Fortune* magazine's publication of its ranking of the 500 largest industrial corporations in 1979. Exxon headed the list, and nine of the top fifteen positions were held by oil companies.

By the beginning of the 1980s energy independence still lay well in the future, with oil imports running at slightly more than 8 million barrels a day. In the latter part of the 1970s government programs to reduce dependence on foreign energy sources sought to increase domestic production by decontrolling prices on oil and natural gas, to cut wastefulness through incentives and requirements for energy efficiency and conservation, and to develop a Strategic Petroleum Reserve to limit the impact of a cutoff in supply. Increased attention, as well, began to be paid to expanding the role of other energy sources in meeting the nation's requirements.

Coal

Coal would seem the most obvious choice to play an expanded role in America's mix of energy sources. The United States possesses one-quarter of the world's reserves, making it "the Saudi Arabia of coal." Although in 1940 coal provided over one-half of all the energy America consumed, by the 1970s it supplied less than one-fifth. The energy crisis led to calls for a reversal of that trend, with President Carter setting a goal of an 80 percent increase in coal production by 1985. The major difficulty, however, in enlarging coal's contribution to the nation's energy requirements lay not in production, since much idle production capacity already exists, but in limited demand.

A number of restraints inhibit rapid acceleration of coal utilization. Electrical utilities offer the primary market for coal, but the growth rate for consumption of electricity is dropping sharply. Until the 1970s the use of electricity expanded at an annual rate of 7 percent, but by 1979 it had fallen below 3 percent. Reserve generating capacity almost doubled between 1970 and 1979. Coal is providing a larger share of energy for the generation of electricity with the number of kilowatt-hours made from coal rising 10 percent in 1979, but the reduced projections for future electricity consumption limit coal's potential growth in this area.

Environmental considerations pose additional constraints. Studies warn that with the increased burning of coal, carbon dioxide levels in the atmosphere would create the "greenhouse effect." Infrared energy, prevented from escaping the earth's atmosphere by the carbon dioxide, would warm the climate and could have a disastrous impact on global agricultural productivity. In addition, the air pollutants released by burning coal—particularly sulfur dioxide, which produces "acid rain"—would threaten air quality standards. Technological devices, such as soot precipitators and "scrubbing" equipment, can reduce this problem, but they are expensive, and utilities have been hesitant to make the large capital investment. Increasingly, the call has been made for "environmental detente," a relaxation of air quality standards to encourage conversion to coal.

At a time of increased awareness of shrinking energy resources, the abundance of coal lends it a particular attractiveness. Greater utilization of coal can reduce dependence on oil imports. By the end of 1979, some 29 oil-burning plants had been converted to coal, with a savings of 125,000 barrels of oil a day. A stepped-up pace of conversions will be encouraged in the 1980s by government subsidies. Although the gains to be made from substituting coal for oil are apparent, the larger costs, both environmental and economic, are still unclear. The conflict between those insisting on high environmental quality standards and others pressing for fewer restraints on utilizing available energy resources promises to be a continuing battle throughout the 1980s. The environmental questions go beyond the concern about the greenhouse effect and air pollutants, involving also the destruction caused by strip mining and the development of coal slurry pipelines in western areas already experiencing water shortages.

The long-term economic costs of a national commitment to expanded coal use are difficult to project. The price of coal has risen considerably in the 1970s, but not as sharply as that of oil. A major upswing in coal utilization will require not only large capital investment in pollution-control technology, but a significant upgrading of rail and water transportation facilities.

Leaders of the major non-Communist energy-consuming nations, at their summit meeting in Venice in June, 1980, committed their countries to, as *The New York Times* described it, "break out of the oil noose that is strangling Western economies." The primary weapon they singled out for achieving this liberation was expanded coal utilization. President Carter, in joining this declaration, was affirming on a broader plane the strategy he had insisted the United States must pursue to alleviate its energy problems. Coal, for all its liabilities, offers the nation abundant energy, and that opportunity would be used, at the very least, to provide a transition period for developing alternative energy resources.

Nuclear Energy

Although coal received renewed attention as an energy resource in the 1970s, nuclear power, long championed as the energy of the future, found its prospects clouded. Proponents of nuclear power in the 1950s had encouraged its development as a clean, safe, and inexpensive energy source; however, those claims came under serious challenge in the 1970s, raising doubts as to its ability to meet the nation's energy needs over a long period.

The first nuclear reactor used for the commercial generation of electricity went into operation in Shippingport, Pennsylvania, in 1957. By 1960 five reactors were operating, and by 1970 that number had risen to nineteen, producing 1.4 percent of the nation's electricity. In 1975 fifty-one nuclear power plants provided 9 percent of the electricity output, and President Ford called in that year for the addition of 135 new nuclear plants over the next decade.

The growth of the nuclear industry, however, had begun to encounter obstacles. A group of scientists, including five Nobel laureates, presented a statement to the President and Congress in August, 1975, warning that "it now appears imprudent to move forward with a rapidly expanding nuclear power plant construction program." They urged a phasing down of the commitment to nuclear energy until research resolves the "present controversies about safety, waste disposal, and plutonium safeguards." Their concern was mirrored in a growing public protest movement against nuclear energy development.

THREE MILE ISLAND NUCLEAR POWER PLANT.
U.S. Department of Energy

PRESIDENT JIMMY CARTER EXAMINING
THREE MILE ISLAND CONTROL ROOM, APRIL 1, 1979.
U.S. Department of Energy

Nuclear power had run into economic problems as well by the mid-1970s. The declining growth of electricity demand, sharply increased costs for building a nuclear plant, and a tighter money market reduced orders for reactors from thirty-four in 1973 to four in 1974, and three in 1975. Indeed, from 1974 until the end of the decade, each year saw more cancellations of reactor orders for the American market than new orders.

On March 28, 1979, the nuclear power industry suffered an even greater setback. A combination of mechanical malfunction and operator errors at the Three Mile Island plant near Middletown, Pennsylvania, caused the most serious accident in the twenty-two-year history of commercial nuclear energy production. For a week the nation's attention was focused on the damaged plant, where an unsettling drama was being played out. The loss of coolant for the reactor had resulted in the formation of a large and, it was feared, potentially explosive hydrogen bubble. Governor Thornburgh advised that pregnant women and small children move away from the area of the plant while attempts went on to reduce the bubble. The threat of a bubble explosion proved groundless, the most serious of a number of misleading and contradictory statements issued to the public by the Nuclear Regulatory Commission and the utility operator during the crisis.

Within a week after the accident, life began to return to normal in the community surrounding the plant, but the repercussions would continue well into the future. The anxiety and outrage felt by the residents of the Middletown area who experienced this trauma came to be shared by many other Americans who now joined the ranks of those opposing nuclear power development. For the operators of the Three Mile Island plant, the accident proved a long-term economic disaster. Decontaminating and repairing the shut-down reactor and containment facilities would take years and cost hundreds of millions of dollars. When the cost of purchasing replacement electricity is added, overall cost estimates run as high as $2 billion.

The accident at Three Mile Island led to calls for a permanent moratorium on nuclear power development. The presidential commission that studied the accident held back from that judgment, concluding instead that "if the country wishes, for larger reasons, to confront the risks that are inherently associated with nuclear power, fundamental changes are necessary if those risks are to be kept within tolerable limits."

CHAPTER TWELVE

President Carter in December, 1979, insisted, "We cannot shut the door on nuclear energy. We do not have the luxury of abandoning nuclear power or imposing a lengthy moratorium on its further use." Two months later the Nuclear Regulatory Commission, which had been conducting safety checks and establishing new standards, lifted its eleven-month moratorium on licensing new nuclear facilities, allowing a plant twenty miles outside of Chattanooga, Tennessee, to begin reactor testing.

Although nuclear energy production is developing rapidly in Western Europe, its future in the United States is more doubtful. The early promise of cheap, safe energy has dimmed considerably. Construction costs of nuclear power plants have risen enormously, and new safety standards will add to that expense. The problem of nuclear waste disposal has eluded any fully satisfactory solution. Industry claims of essentially risk-free operation were badly undermined at Three Mile Island, and future development of nuclear energy will confront a much more skeptical American public.

Early estimates of a thousand nuclear power plants operating by the turn of the century have been drastically scaled down. At the beginning of 1980 there were seventy-two operating reactors producing about 13 percent of the nation's electricity. An additional ninety-two reactors were at various stages of construction, but a number of these may not be completed because of financial pressures. For the foreseeable future, nuclear power will prove unable to play its promised role of reversing the nation's energy shortage.

Other Energy Sources

The crisis of the 1970s hastened research and development aimed at bringing new sources into the nation's energy mix. A wide range of alternative energy possibilities is being explored, with solar power and synthetic fuels (synfuels) attracting the largest interest.

The sun's energy is increasingly being tapped through solar water heaters and energy-conscious home design. A major breakthrough in utilizing solar energy will come with the production of low-cost photovoltaic cells, which convert sunlight into electricity. Department of Energy projections indicate that solar electricity costs can be made competitive by the mid-1980s. Solar energy stored in plants is being used for gasohol, and varied technologies for converting organic matter into gases and liquid fuels are emerging. Solar energy research, long under-funded, is now receiving large-scale government and private support in an attempt to make fuller use of the primary renewable resource.

In June, 1980, President Carter signed into law legislation creating the United States Synthetic Fuels Corporation. This government-owned company received a five-year appropriation of $20 billion to develop production of oil and gas from coal, and oil from shale. The legislation also committed, subject to congressional appropriation, an additional $68 billion for the following seven years to enable the program to arrive at its goals of 500,000 barrels of oil a day by 1987 and 2 million barrels a day by 1992. The corporation would encourage the growth of a synthetic fuels industry by loans, price and purchase guarantees, and—if these proved insufficient to induce private development—government production of these alternative sources. Although major obstacles lay in front of this ambitious program, particularly in the environmental area, after prolonged discussion a full-scale attempt is finally being mounted to draw upon these large reserves.

A more readily available strategy for curbing the impact of the energy crisis lay in conservation. As cheap, abundant energy gave way to shortages and spiraling prices, more Americans searched for ways to limit their energy consumption. Wasteful and inefficient energy usages that had been accepted without much questioning now came in for critical examination. The move to smaller horsepower cars, better insulated homes, more energy-efficient appliances, as well as industrial and business energy-conservation programs cut into the nation's energy consumption. Total energy consumption in the United States for 1979 was 78 quadrillion BTUs, a slight drop from the previous year, and the first decline in a nonrecession year since 1952. Estimates for the 1980s project a slight annual increase in energy consumption, around 1 percent, a marked reduction from the 4.3 percent of the 1960s and the 2 percent of the 1970s.

THE AUTOMOBILE INDUSTRY

The energy crunch of the 1970s had a profoundly unsettling effect on the American automobile industry. Automobile production, which for over a half-century had epitomized American industrial skill, fell victim in the 1970s to rising gasoline costs and increased market penetration by imports. As the decade drew to a close, one of Detroit's "Big Three," Chrysler, teetered on the verge of bankruptcy, and the American auto industry was about to lose its leadership position in total production to the Japanese.

The problems that befell Detroit in the 1970s had been developing for some time. The industry, relying on increasingly outmoded facilities, remained largely committed to a big-car philosophy into the 1970s. Gasoline shortages and sharp price increases, stricter government safety and fuel-efficiency requirements, and severe competition from imports exerted enormous pressure and eventually forced a fundamental redirection of the American automobile industry.

In 1960 Detroit sold 6.7 million new cars, which averaged 12.4 miles per gallon. Ten years later the American automobile industry sold 6.5 million cars, now averaging 12.1 miles per gallon. Japanese imports, which accounted for 26,000 sales in 1965, had risen to 381,000 by 1970. Detroit's output climbed to 9.7 million cars in 1973, but the first wave of gasoline shortages and price hikes dropped sales to 7.3 million in 1974 and 6.7 million in 1975. Sales moved back up to 8.5 million in 1976 and 9.2 million in 1977, but Detroit faced some pressing difficulties. The Automotive Fuel Economy Program mandated by the government required that, beginning with the 1978 model year, annual increments in fuel efficiency be incorporated to arrive at an average 27.5 mile-per-gallon standard by 1985, twice the 1975 average. Meeting these goals required massive capital investment to redesign and retool "down-sized" cars and improve engine performance. Japanese imports, already surpassing American fuel-efficiency standards, captured a larger share of the market. Close to 700,000 Japanese automobiles were sold in the United States in 1975 and, buoyed by a new wave of gasoline price increases, that figure rose to 1.6 million in 1979. Imports, overall, had secured 23.5 percent of the American market, placing them well ahead of Ford and Chrysler.

By the end of the 1970s the American automobile industry was in a beleaguered condition. Chrysler had suffered losses in 1979 of over $1 billion and was saved from bankruptcy only by a $1.5 billion government loan guarantee. Ford finished the year in the black, but only because overseas profits made up for substantial losses in its North American operations. Leaders of this formerly dominant industry found themselves in the embarrassing position of having to petition Washington for protection in their home markets.

Detroit has already begun its campaign to improve these gloomy conditions. The auto industry, led by General Motors, is making an $80 billion capital investment between 1978 and 1985, upgrading production facilities and automating many manufacturing procedures. Each of the Big Three companies has begun to challenge Japanese market penetration by turning out smaller, lighter weight, more fuel-efficient four-cylinder automobiles. Detroit is clearly moving onto a more competitive footing in the 1980s, but it will be a smaller industry, employing fewer workers and playing a less dominant role in the American economy than it did in the past.

THE STEEL INDUSTRY

The American steel industry, whose fortune is usually closely linked with the economic health of the automobile business, was plagued in the 1970s by many of the problems afflicting Detroit: outmoded production facilities, more demanding environmental standards, and a rising tide of imports. Up through the 1960s American steel companies, aided by relatively inexpensive energy costs and no serious challenges from imports, made do with aging, inefficient plants. Upgrading those facilities in the 1970s proved difficult for an industry now facing soaring energy costs, federal requirements for installing expensive pollution-control devices, and aggressive market competition from foreign producers. Sales of Japanese iron and steel went from $900 million in 1970 to $2.3 billion in 1977. By 1977 imported steel had gained 21 percent of the American market.

The steel industry looked to Washington for relief, both for a relaxation of environmental standards and for limitations on imports. Although no concessions were made on the environmental front, the Carter administration in January, 1978, established a "trigger price" program to reduce steel imports. It established minimum prices for various types of imported steel, and any pricing below that level would initiate an investigation by the Treasury Department and possible fine for "dumping." The steel industry would have preferred an import quota, but the Carter administration felt that that degree of protectionism would undermine its position of supporting free trade and might fuel inflation by enabling the steel companies to press for price increases. The trigger price program reduced import pressure, particularly from the Japanese, but the American steel industry still faced deep-seated problems as the 1970s ended. Capital investment will have to increase enormously to create the efficient, environmentally sound steel mills the Japanese have already developed. United States Steel at the end of 1979 cut back drastically on its older production facilities, permanently shutting down fifteen plants and firing 12,500 employees. Whether this pruning will lead to significant upgrading of its other facilities is unclear, since the corporation has been channeling much of its capital investment into its nonsteel holdings. The steel industry moves into the 1980s, as well, aware that its production planning must take into account the reduced orders that will be coming from a leading customer, the automobile industry. Changes adopted by Detroit to regain its competitive position—down-sizing and lighter weight cars—will be helpful to the aluminum and plastics industries, but will add another weight to steel's burden.

GOVERNMENT REGULATION

Although the automobile and steel industries have looked to Washington to bail them out of their predicaments, they and other businesses often cite the government as the source of their difficulties. A particular target of their criticism is the regulatory agencies, at whose doorstep they lay much of the responsibility for flagging productivity and higher prices. Mobil, in an advertisement, lashed out at an "overgrown and virtually insatiable regulatory bureaucracy" that it claimed "has done vastly more harm than good."

The bulk of such attacks is focused on the newer "social" regulatory agencies: the Equal Employment Opportunity Commission (1965), the Occupational Safety and Health Administration (1970), the Environmental Protection Agency (1970), and the National Highway Traffic Safety Administration (1970). Opposition to these agencies ranges from those who believe they should be dissolved because market forces could better handle the issues they are involved in to those who accept the necessity for such regulation but protest the manner in which the agencies carry out their responsibilities. A study commissioned by the Business Round Table showed that in 1977 regulations imposed by six federal agencies on forty-eight major corporations added $2.5 billion to the cost of their business operations. A number of such studies, usually showing much larger costs, have been made public as the attack on the regulatory agencies has been stepped up. What they ordinarily do not show, in part because they are not easily quantified, are the benefits that have accrued to the nation because of these programs: cleaner air and water, safer work places, fewer discriminatory employment practices, and so forth.

The 1980 report of the President's Council of Economic Advisers gave evidence of some responsiveness to business complaints against the regulatory agencies. In a lengthy section entitled "Striking the Proper Balance in Regulation," the council pointed to progress in deregulating the airline and trucking industries, as well as moving, in the social regulatory agencies, toward "more flexible and more cost-effective" policies. As evidence of this new orientation, the council cited President Carter's executive order of March 23, 1978, requiring that agencies prepare an analysis that would "examine the costs and other burdens imposed by the proposed regulatory action and compare them with those of alternative actions differing in approach, timing, degree of stringency, or scope." Lest critics of these agencies take too much heart from this more accommodating spirit, the council concluded this section of its report by noting that although "some regulation can be largely or wholly eliminated, most of the government's regulatory activities are here to stay."

PRODUCTIVITY

The rate of productivity growth serves as a basic measure of an economy's health. Productivity—the output of goods and services per hour of work—underwent a serious erosion of its rate of growth during the past quarter-century. From 1955 to 1965 American productivity increased at an annual rate of 3.1 percent; from 1965 to 1973 it rose at a 2.3 percent annual rate; from 1973 to 1978 it grew at a 1.1 percent annual rate; and in 1979 it suffered a decline of .9 percent. If we compare American productivity growth to that of other leading industrialized nations, we find that from 1972 to 1978, while productivity was rising 1 percent a year in the United States, it climbed 4 percent annually in West Germany, and surged at a 7 percent annual rate in Japan.

America's loss of productivity has been ascribed to a variety of causes, such as the decline in research-and-development spending, the energy crunch, and the growing proportion of service workers in the labor force. A major drag, however, on productivity performance has been the condition of the nation's industrial plants and equipment. The average age of the physical components of America's industrial base is close to eighteen years, whereas West Germany's is twelve, and Japan's is ten. The upgrading and technological refurbishing of the nation's productive facilities will require large-scale capital investment. The rate of capital formation (corporate and personal savings) will have to be stepped up. Personal saving (measured as percentage of disposable income) had fallen by the end of 1979 to less than 4 percent, its lowest mark since the Korean War. Throughout the 1970s it stood around 6 percent—less than one-half of the West German rate and less than one-third of the Japanese.

The Japanese and West German economies benefited not only from this capital formation, which they could channel into productive facilities, but also from their nations' limited military expenditures. West German military spending in the 1970s came to approximately one-sixth of the American level, and Japanese military expenditures were only one-twentieth. The ability of the Japanese to invest 20 percent of their GNP in plants and equipment, along with the West Germans' 15 percent, goes far to explain their surpassing in productivity growth an American economy that committed 10 percent of its GNP to such investment.

AGRICULTURE

American agriculture in the 1960s and 1970s managed to escape the productivity problem that came to trouble other sectors of the economy. From 1960 to 1970 agricultural productivity, measured in output per hour of work, rose 77 percent, and from 1970 to 1979 it increased 60 percent.

The trend that had begun in the 1930s toward fewer farms with larger acreage continued throughout this period. The number of farms declined from 4 million in 1960 to 2.6 million in 1979, while average acreage rose from 300 to 450. Large corporate agricultural operations, agribusiness, accounted for an increasing share of farm output. Cattle-raising provided dramatic evidence of this trend, with half the nation's production centered in some 400 industrialized feed lots. The value of farm equipment more than tripled during this period, while farm employment dropped sharply from 7 million in 1960 to less than 4 million in 1979. Government subsidies to agriculture increased substantially, climbing from $700 million in 1960 to $3 billion in 1978. Net income from farming went from $11.5 billion in 1960 to $33 billion in 1979.

Agricultural exports developed significantly during these years and proved particularly important in reducing the worsening trade deficits of the 1970s. In 1960 the United States exported agricultural products valued at $4.8 billion, $1 billion more than its agricultural imports for that year. In 1978 American agricultural exports had grown to $29.4 billion, $14.8 billion more than the value of farm products coming into this country.

LABOR

The American labor force passed the 100 million mark during these years, increasing by almost half as it grew from 69.6 million in 1960 to 102.9 million in 1979. This rapid expansion was fed not only by the post–World War II baby boom now moving into the work force, but by the increasing proportion of American women entering the job market.

PROFILE:

WOMEN WORKERS

Throughout American history women have been engaged in productive activity, making significant contributions to the nation's economic development. Because most of these women did not receive wages for this work, however, it has not counted as "gainful" employment and they were not included as part of the labor force. While that productive work continues, an increasing proportion of women have entered the labor force. In 1900 one out of five American women of working age held a job, but by the end of the 1970s that ratio had risen to one in two.

Not only were women entering the labor force in sharply increasing numbers, but many were obtaining jobs in occupations that had been traditionally closed to them. Their success in crossing these barriers and in challenging prejudicial treatment in other areas of employment was facilitated by the 1964 Civil Rights Act, which prohibited sexual and racial discrimination in hiring and job advancement. The federal agency created to ensure compliance with the act, the Equal Employment Opportunity Commission, faced a number of early obstacles in pursuing its responsibility. Its advocacy of affirmative action programs for women and minorities was often challenged as support for reverse discrimination. Although it negotiated a number of sizable settlements with companies accused of discriminatory practices, the agency lacked the staff to cope with the flood of individual complaints that poured in. By 1977 the backlog of cases had reached 130,000, and the new chairperson, Eleanor Holmes Norton, targeted "systemic discrimination," in a corporation or a whole industry, as an EEOC priority.

TABLE 12:5
Women in the Civilian Labor Force: 1960–1979

Year	Number of Women in Civilian Labor Force (millions)	Women as Percentage of Civilian Labor Force	Women Workers as Percentage of Female Working Age Population
1960	23.2	33.4	37.7
1965	26.2	35.2	39.3
1970	31.5	38.1	43.3
1975	37.0	39.9	46.3
1979	43.4	42.2	51.0

Source: Economic Report of the President, 1980.

Although federal legislation in 1963 mandated equal pay for equal work, median wages for full-time female workers have remained at approximately 60 percent of men's wages for the past four decades. In 1939 they came to 58 percent of men's earnings; in 1963 they were 59.6 percent; in 1978 they had dropped to 59 percent when the median earnings for full-time male workers were $15,730, compared with $9,350 for full-time female workers. The persistence of this pay gap, despite the expansion of employment opportunities for women, is attributed by economist Frances Hutner to the continuing movement into low-paying, predominantly female jobs. One-half of all women workers are in jobs that are 70 percent female, and one-quarter hold jobs that are 95 percent female. "'Equal pay' is ineffective," Hutner asserts, "when it means equal pay for equal work and most women are not doing the same work as men." One strategy advocated for shrinking the male-female wage differential is to press for equal pay for work of "comparable worth." A group of Denver nurses sued that city on grounds of sex discrimination because municipal tree trimmers and parking meter repairmen received more pay then they did. U.S. District Court Judge Fred Winner, in a 1978 decision rejecting the nurses' argument, remarked that their premise held "the possibility of disrupting the entire economic system of the United States of America. . . . I'm not going to restructure the entire economy of the United States." Eleanor Holmes Norton of EEOC sees "comparable worth" as a viable principle: "For the average woman who works— who is increasingly the average woman—I do believe this is the issue of the 1980s."

In addition to seeking to secure equal employment opportunity, the federal government during this period acted to improve the safety of the workplace. In 1969, in the wake of a West Virginia mining disaster that took seventy-eight lives, Congress enacted the Coal Mine Health and Safety Act. The following year it created the Occupational Safety and Health Administration to attempt to reduce the number of deaths from industrial accidents (14,000 annually) and the estimated yearly loss of 100,000 lives from occupationally caused illnesses. The agency faced an uphill battle from the outset, encountering widespread resistance from employers. In addition, OSHA was pitifully understaffed, with fewer than three thousand inspectors for five million workplaces across the country. The agency discovered, as well, that new hazardous industrial chemicals were being introduced at a far more rapid rate than OSHA was able to establish safety levels for existing toxic substances. A new director, Dr. Eula Bingham, appointed in 1977, drastically cut back on the agency's lesser enforcement responsibilities and focused attention on high-hazard work areas and chemical carcinogens. Opponents of OSHA have continued to argue that the economic costs of moving toward virtually risk-free work environments are prohibitive, but proponents of safety regulation counter that it is inappropriate to set a dollar limit on basic health protection and that the overall impact of such regulation is cost-effective because of reduced medical expenses and fewer injury-related absences.

Concern about the quality of the work experience during this period went beyond health and safety considerations. The Department of Health, Education and Welfare published a study in 1972 entitled *Work in America*, which described the "blue-collar blues" and "white-collar woes" of workers faced with dull, repetitive, and unsatisfying jobs. A variety of experiments, involving flexible work schedules, restructuring of jobs, and expanding worker initiative, attempted to reduce dissatisfaction. But as the decade progressed, the problems of inflation and unemployment proved more troubling to workers.

The American economy in the 1970s suffered from persistently high unemployment. During the mid-1970s, the unemployment rate—8.5 percent in 1975, then 7.7 percent in 1976, and 7 percent in 1977—ran at its highest level since before the second world war.

Those holding jobs found their earnings eroded by inflation. Department of Labor statistics show that from 1960 to 1969 wages for workers in manufacturing, construction, and wholesale and retail trade rose 44 percent in current dollars and 16.7 percent after inflation. From 1970 to 1979 earnings for that same group of workers increased 90 percent, but the after-inflation gain was only 1.7 percent.

Organized labor experienced a steady proportional decline during the 1960s and 1970s. In 1955, at the time of the merger of the American Federation of Labor and the Congress of Industrial Organizations, one out of every three nonagricultural workers belonged to a union. Over the next quarter-century, 37 million new jobs were added to the American economy, but the ranks of unionized labor failed to keep pace with this growth. Organizing drives were often sporadic, and much of the labor force expansion occurred in occupations that had no tradition of unionism. In addition, many industrial unions suffered membership losses as jobs were exported by multinational corporations to cheaper labor markets and as companies relocated in sun-belt states that had right-to-work laws. Organized labor made some sizable gains among white-collar workers, particularly government employees and teachers. Nonetheless, when George Meany retired in 1980 after heading the AFL-CIO for twenty-five years, membership in unions had slipped from one in three nonagricultural employees to less than one in four.

OVERVIEW

In 1954 historian David M. Potter, in his study *People of Plenty*, insightfully analyzed how the American character had been shaped by economic abundance. In 1979 the chairman of the Federal Reserve Board, Paul Volcker, after testifying before a congressional committee on the drain on the nation's wealth caused by oil-price hikes, concluded, "The standard of living of the average American has to decline. I don't think you can escape that."

The quarter-century separating Potter's exploration of American abundance and Volcker's anticipation of decline had brought fundamental changes in the nation's economic position. The remarkable surge of prosperity that began in the post–World War II period had started to sputter by the 1970s. An economy that had seemed invulnerable suffered a series of heavy blows: oil shortages and skyrocketing prices, widening trade deficits and an unstable dollar, slipping productivity, and that debilitating combination of high unemployment and rampant inflation, stagflation. It appeared to many that there had been a gradual, at first imperceptible, hardening of the economic arteries. Like an aging top athlete whose loss of skill had suddenly become apparent, the American economy found itself surrounded by younger, more vigorous challengers.

This slowing down of economic growth came at a time when many had begun to question using the gross national product as a standard of the nation's well-being. An ecological awareness had emerged which perceived the rapid expansion of goods and services as bringing in its wake a host of bads and disservices to the environment. President Nixon, in signing the National Environmental Policy Act on January 1, 1970, had promised that "the 1970s absolutely must be the years when America pays its debt to the past by reclaiming the purity of its air, its waters, and our living environment." A body of environmental legislation was enacted during the decade, legislation that brought significant progress toward those goals, although it evoked much criticism from those who claimed it diverted too much capital from productive enterprise.

Although many environmentalists had long advocated a slow-growth economy, the winding down of the American economy in the late 1970s came not from an adoption of that strategy but because of structural weaknesses. A conference sponsored by the U.S. Senate Subcommittee on International Trade, the New York Stock Exchange, and Harvard University in July, 1980, published a statement decrying the erosion of the American economy, which the participants maintained was "losing its competitive edge." They insisted that the nation "must confront the reality that we are not Number 1 in economic performance and will suffer continued decline unless we undertake very basic changes in our attitude and policies."

Many of the changes advocated by the Harvard conference fall within the framework of what Amitai Etzioni, a former White House adviser, has labeled "reindustrialization." Etzioni argues that sustained overconsumption and underinvestment in productive facilities has sapped America's economic strength. To reverse that development, Etzioni insists, will take "a decade of public and private belt-tightening" while reindustrialization, the rebuilding of the infrastructure and capital goods sectors of the American economy, takes place. The financing of this reindustrialization will be encouraged, in Etzioni's plan, "by broad-stroke economic incentives" involving accelerated depreciation, tax-structure inducements for savings and investment, and subsidies for research and development, particularly in the energy area. "Most Americans," Etzioni believes, "if presented with a realistic program of reindustrialization, would be willing to make the needed sacrifices."

Etzioni's assumption that most Americans would willingly accept at least a decade-long drop in their standard of living while the nation's industrial base was being rebuilt raises certain questions. The economic formulation for reindustrialization is much easier to draft than the political. Which groups are to be particularly burdened during this rebuilding period, and which groups will not be disadvantaged? MIT economist Lester Thurow, whose study *The Zero-Sum*

Society perceptively examines the troublesome political aspects of moving into a slow-growth condition, has noted, "Nations have little trouble uniting on issues like war and space exploration, but domestic issues of income distribution are tough for a democracy. It is not we versus them, but us versus us."

For most of American history, and particularly since the second world war, economic abundance offered the promise of alleviating whatever distressed the nation. An ever expanding economy would provide the resources to eliminate social inequities gradually. The American economy, for the immediate future, can no longer sustain the expectation of constant material improvement in living standards. Acknowledgment of that reality can lead to bitterness at the paring down of the American dream or to an acceptance of the challenge posed by these new economic constraints. As the economy whose abundance allowed a sense of being able to do everything slows down, American society must now answer the difficult question of how most equitably to distribute its more limited resources. This poses a disturbing challenge to the nation's economic and political systems, but it may well be that a national character so shaped by abundance will draw additional strength from this encounter with constraint.

REFERENCES AND SUGGESTED READINGS

CHAPTER ONE

Bridenbaugh, Carl. *The Colonial Craftsman*. Chicago: University of Chicago Press, 1961.

Bruchey, Stuart, ed. *The Colonial Merchant*. New York: Harcourt Brace & World, 1966.

Bruchey, Stuart. *The Roots of American Economic Growth*. New York: Harper & Row, 1968.

Curtin, Philip. *The Atlantic Slave Trade: A Census*. Madison, Wis.: University of Wisconsin Press, 1969.

Fite, Gilbert C., and Reese, Jim E. *An Economic History of the United States*. Boston: Houghton Mifflin, 1973.

Hofstadter, Richard. *America at 1750*. New York: Knopf, 1971.

Jordan, Winthrop. *White over Black: American Attitudes toward the Negro*. Chapel Hill, N.C.: University of North Carolina Press, 1968.

Josephy, Alvin M. *The Indian Heritage of America*. New York: Knopf, 1968.

Morris, Richard B., ed. *Encyclopedia of American History*. New York: Harper & Row, 1961.

Morris, Richard B. *Government and Labor in Early America*. New York: Columbia University Press, 1966.

Nettles, Curtis P. *The Roots of American Civilization*. New York: Appleton-Century-Crofts, 1938.

Ver Steeg, Clarence. *The Formative Years, 1607–1763*. New York: Hill & Wang, 1964.

CHAPTER TWO

Degler, Carl N. *Out of Our Past: The Forces That Shaped Modern America.* New York: Harper & Row, 1970.

Gipson, Lawrence H. *The Coming of the Revolution, 1763–1775.* New York: Harper & Row, 1954.

Harper, Lawrence A. *The English Navigation Laws: A Seventeenth Century Experiment in Social Engineering.* New York: Columbia University Press, 1939.

Heilbroner, Robert L. *The Worldly Philosophers.* New York: Simon & Schuster, 1953.

Hofstadter, Richard. *America at 1750.* New York: Knopf, 1971.

Nettles, Curtis P. "British Mercantilism and the Economic Development of the Thirteen Colonies." *Journal of Economic History* 12 (Spring 1952), 105–14.

North, Douglass C. *Growth and Welfare in the American Past.* Englewood Cliffs, N.J.: Prentice-Hall, 1974.

Thomas, Robert P. "A Quantitative Approach to the Study of the Effects of British Imperial Policy upon Colonial Welfare: Some Preliminary Findings." *Journal of Economic History* 25 (December 1965), 615–38.

Rossiter, Clinton. *Seedtime of the Republic.* New York: Harcourt Brace & World, 1953.

Samuelson, Paul A. *Economics.* New York: McGraw-Hill, 1973.

Ver Steeg, Clarence L. "The American Revolution Considered as an Economic Movement." *Huntington Library Quarterly* 20 (August 1957), 361–72.

CHAPTER THREE

Beard, Charles A. *An Economic Interpretation of the Constitution of the United States.* New York: Macmillan, 1913.

Bjork, Gordon. "Weaning of the American Economy: Independence, Market Changes, and Economic Development." *Journal of Economic History* 24 (December 1964), 541–60.

Brown, Robert E. *Charles Beard and the Constitution.* Princeton, N. J.: Princeton University Press, 1956.

Giedion, Siegfried. *Mechanization Takes Command.* New York: Oxford University Press, 1948.

Jensen, Merrill. *The New Nation.* New York: Knopf, 1950.

McDonald, Forrest. *We the People: The Economic Origins of the Constitution.* Chicago: University of Chicago Press, 1958.

Miller, J. C. *Alexander Hamilton, Portrait in Paradox.* New York: Harper & Row, 1959.

Nettles, Curtis P. *The Emergence of a National Economy, 1775–1815.* New York: Holt, Rinehart & Winston, 1962.

North, Douglass C. *The Economic Growth of the United States, 1790–1860.* Englewood Cliffs, N. J.: Prentice-Hall, 1961.

Woodbury, Robert S. "The Legend of Eli Whitney and Interchangeable Parts." *Technology and Culture* 1:3, 235–54.

CHAPTER FOUR

Bruchey, Stuart. *The Roots of American Economic Growth, 1607–1861: An Essay in Social Causation.* New York: Harper & Row, 1968.

Fite, Gilbert C., and Reese, Jim E. *An Economic History of the United States.* Boston: Houghton Mifflin, 1973.

Gates, Paul W. *The Farmer's Age: Agriculture, 1815–1860.* New York: Holt, Rinehart & Winston, 1960.

Giedion, Siegfried. *Mechanization Takes Command.* New York: Oxford University Press, 1948.

Goodrich, Carter, ed. *Canals and American Economic Development.* New York: Columbia University Press, 1961.

Hammond, Bray. *Banks and Politics in America from the Revolution to the Civil War.* Princeton, N. J.: Princeton University Press, 1957.

Hession, Charles H., and Sardy, Hyman. *Ascent to Affluence.* Boston: Allyn & Bacon, 1969.

Hunter, Louis C. *Steamboats on the Western Rivers.* Cambridge, Mass.: Harvard University Press, 1949.

Kranzberg, Melvin, and Pursell, Carroll W., Jr., eds. *Technology in Western Civilization.* Vol. 1. New York: Oxford University Press, 1967.

Malin, James C. *The Contriving Brain and the Skillful Hand in the United States.* Lawrence, Kansas.: Coronado Press, 1955.

North, Douglass C. *The Economic Growth of the United States, 1790–1860.* Englewood Cliffs, N. J.: Prentice-Hall, 1961.

Rostow, W. W. *The Stages of Economic Growth: A Non-Communist Manifesto.* Cambridge, Mass.: Harvard University Press, 1961.

Taylor, George Rogers. *The Transportation Revolution, 1815–1860.* New York: Holt, Rinehart & Winston, 1966.

Wade, Richard C. *The Urban Frontier: Pioneer Life in Early Pittsburgh, Cincinnati, Lexington, Louisville, and St. Louis.* Chicago: University of Chicago Press, 1964.

CHAPTER FIVE

Andreano, Ralph, ed. *The Economic Impact of the American Civil War.* Cambridge, Mass.: Schenckman, 1967.

Chandler, Alfred D., Jr., ed. *The Railroads: The Nation's First Big Business.* New York: Harcourt Brace & World, 1965.

Cochran, Thomas C. "Did the Civil War Retard Industrialization?" *Mississippi Valley Historical Review* 48 (September 1961), 197–210.

David, Paul A., Gutman, Herbert, Sutch, Richard, and Wright, Gavin. *Reckoning with Slavery.* New York: Oxford University Press, 1976.

Fishlow, Albert. *American Railroads and the Transformation of the Ante-Bellum Economy.* Cambridge, Mass.: Harvard University Press, 1965.

Fogel, Robert W., and Engerman, Stanley L. *Time on the Cross: The Economics of American Negro Slavery.* Boston: Little, Brown, 1974.

Gates, Paul W. *Agriculture and the Civil War.* New York: Knopf, 1965.

Giedion, Siegfried. *Mechanization Takes Command.* New York: Oxford University Press, 1948.

Hacker, Louis M. *Triumph of American Capitalism.* New York: Columbia University Press, 1940.

Luraghi, Raimondo. *The Rise and Fall of the Plantation South.* New York: New Viewpoints, A Division of Franklin Watts, 1978.

Niemi, Albert W., Jr. *United States Economic History.* Second Edition. Chicago: Rand McNally, 1980.

Phillips, Ulrich Bonnell. *American Negro Slavery.* New York: D. Appleton & Company, 1918.

Robbins, Roy M. *Our Landed Heritage: The Public Domain, 1776–1936.* Princeton, N. J.: Princeton University Press, 1942.

Rogin, Leo. *The Introduction of Farm Machinery in Its Relation to the Productivity of Labor in the Agriculture of the United States During the Nineteenth Century.* Berkeley, Cal.: University of California Press, 1931.

Rostow, W. W. *The Stages of Economic Growth: A Non-Communist Manifesto.* Cambridge, Mass.: Harvard University Press, 1961.

Woodman, Harold D., ed. *Slavery and the Southern Economy.* New York: Harcourt Brace & World, 1966.

CHAPTER SIX

Chandler, Alfred D., Jr. "The Beginnings of 'Big Business' in American Industry." *Business History Review* 32 (Spring 1959), 1–31.

Degler, Carl N. *Out of Our Past: The Forces That Shaped Modern America.* New York: Harper & Row, 1970.

Hidy, Ralph, and Hidy, Muriel *Pioneering in Big Business: A History of the Standard Oil Company of New Jersey, 1882–1911.* New York: Harper & Row, 1955.

Josephson, Matthew. *The Robber Barons, The Great American Capitalists, 1861–1901.* New York: Harcourt Brace & World, 1934.

Kirkland, Edward. *Industry Comes of Age: Business, Labor, and Public Policy.* New York: Holt, Rinehart & Winston, 1961.

Kolko, Gabriel. *Railroads and Regulation, 1877–1916.* Princeton, N. J.: Princeton University Press, 1965.

Lloyd, Henry Demarest. *Wealth Against Commonwealth.* New York: Harper Brothers, 1894.

Nevins, Allan. *Study in Power: John D. Rockefeller, Industrialist and Philanthropist.* Two vols. New York: Scribner's, 1953.

North, Douglass C. *Growth and Welfare in the American Past*. Englewood Cliffs, N. J.: Prentice-Hall, 1974.

Porter, Glenn. *The Rise of Big Business, 1860–1910*. New York: Crowell, 1973.

Shannon, Fred A. *The Farmer's Last Frontier: Agriculture, 1860–1897*. New York: Holt, Rinehart & Winston, 1945.

Thernstrom, Stephan. *The Other Bostonians: Poverty and Progress in the American Metropolis, 1880–1970*. Cambridge, Mass.: Harvard University Press, 1973.

Unger, Irwin. *The Greenback Era: A Social and Political History of American Finance, 1865–1879*. Princeton, N. J.: Princeton University Press, 1968.

Wall, Joseph F. *Andrew Carnegie*. New York: Oxford University Press, 1970.

CHAPTER SEVEN

Chandler, Alfred D. *The Visible Hand: The Managerial Revolution in American Business*. Cambridge, Mass.: Harvard University Press, 1977.

Cochran, Thomas C., and Miller, William. *The Age of Enterprise: A Social History of Industrial America*. New York: Harper & Row, 1961.

Dubofsky, Melvyn. *Industrialism and the American Worker*. New York: Crowell, 1975.

Ginger, Ray. *Age of Excess*. New York: Macmillan, 1975.

Hays, Samuel P. *The Response to Industrialism*. Chicago: University of Chicago Press, 1957.

Heilbroner, Robert L. *The Economic Transformation of America*. New York: Harcourt Brace Jovanovich, 1977.

Hofstadter, Richard, ed. *The Progressive Movement*. Englewood Cliffs, N. J.: Prentice-Hall, 1963.

Klein, Maury, and Kantor, Harvey A. *Prisoners of Progress, American Industrial Cities, 1850–1920*. New York: Macmillan, 1976.

Kolko, Gabriel. *The Triumph of Conservatism*. New York: Free Press, 1963.

Nelson, Daniel. *Managers and Workers, Origins of the New Factory System in the United States, 1880–1920*. Madison, Wis. University of Wisconsin Press, 1975.

Noble, David F. *America by Design: Science, Technology and the Rise of Corporate Capitalism*. New York: Knopf, 1977.

Ostrander, Gilman M. *American Civilization in the First Machine Age, 1890–1940*. New York: Harper & Row, 1970.

Stearn, Gerald Emanuel, ed. *Gompers*. Englewood Cliffs, N. J.: Prentice-Hall, 1971.

Tarbell, Ida M. *The History of the Standard Oil Company*. David M. Chalmers, ed. New York: Norton, 1966.

Taylor, Frederick W. *The Principles of Scientific Management*. New York: Harper, 1911.

Vatter, Harold G. *The Drive to Industrial Maturity*. Westport, Conn.: Greenwood Press, 1975.

Wiebe, Robert H. *Businessmen and Reform*. Cambridge, Mass.: Harvard University Press, 1962.

CHAPTER EIGHT

Brody, David. *Labor in Crisis, The Steel Strike of 1919*. Philadelphia: Lippincott, 1965.

Clark, John M. *The Costs of the World War to the American People*. New Haven, Conn.: Yale University Press, 1931.

Cuff, Robert D. *The War Industries Board*. Baltimore: Johns Hopkins University Press, 1973.

Dubofsky, Melvyn. *Industrialism and the American Worker*. New York: Crowell, 1975.

Gilbert, Charles. *American Financing of World War I*. Westport, Conn.: Greenwood, 1970.

Graham, Otis L., Jr. *The Great Campaigns*. Englewood Cliffs, N. J.: Prentice-Hall, 1971.

Leuchtenburg, William, E. "The New Deal and the Analogue of War" in Braeman, John, Bremner, Robert H., and Walters, Everett, eds. *Change and Continuity in Twentieth-Century America*. Columbus: Ohio State University Press, 1964.

Link, Arthur S. *Woodrow Wilson and the Progressive Era: 1910 1917*. New York: Harper, 1954.

Morris, Richard, ed. *Labor and Management*. New York: Arno Press, 1973.

Murray, Robert K. *Red Scare*. Minneapolis: University of Minnesota Press, 1955.

Nevins, Allan, and Hill, Frank E. *Ford: Expansion and Challenge, 1915–1933*. New York: Scribner's, 1957.

Rae, John B., ed. *Henry Ford*. Englewood Cliffs, N. J.: Prentice-Hall, 1969.

Riesman, David. *Abundance for What? and Other Essays*. Garden City, N. Y.: Doubleday, 1964.

Rostow, W. W. *The World Economy: History and Prospect*. Austin: University of Texas Press, 1978.

Sloan, Alfred P., Jr. *My Years with General Motors*. Garden City, N. Y.: Doubleday, 1963.

CHAPTER NINE

Bernstein, Irving. *The Lean Years: A History of the American Worker, 1920–1933*. Boston: Houghton Mifflin, 1966.

Burner, David. *Herbert Hoover: A Public Life*. New York: Knopf, 1979.

Friedman, Milton, and Schwartz, Anna J. *The Great Contraction, 1929–1933*. Princeton, N. J.: Princeton University Press, 1965.

Galbraith, John Kenneth. *The Great Crash*. Boston: Houghton Mifflin, 1961.

Gordon, Robert Aaron. *Economic Instability and Growth: The American Record*. New York: Harper & Row, 1974.

Holt, Charles. "Who Benefited from the Prosperity of the 1920s?" *Explorations in Economic History* 14 (July 1977).

Hoover, Herbert. *The Memoirs of Herbert Hoover: The Great Depression, 1929–1941.* New York: Macmillan, 1952.

Kindleberger, Charles. *The World in Depression, 1929–1939.* Berkeley, Calif.: University of California Press, 1973.

Leuchtenburg, William E. *The Perils of Prosperity, 1914–1932.* Chicago: University of Chicago Press, 1958.

McCoy, Donald R. *Coming of Age: The United States During the 1920's and 1930's.* Baltimore: Penguin, 1973.

Romasco, Albert U. *The Poverty of Abundance: Hoover, the Nation, the Depression.* New York: Oxford University Press, 1965.

Schlesinger, Arthur M., Jr. *The Age of Roosevelt: The Crisis of the Old Order.* Boston: Houghton Mifflin, 1957.

Sobel, Robert. *The Great Bull Market: Wall Street in the 1920s.* New York: Norton, 1968.

Temin, Peter. *Did Monetary Forces Cause the Great Depression?* New York: Norton, 1976.

CHAPTER TEN

Allen, Frederick Lewis. *The Big Change, 1900–1950.* New York: Harper & Row, 1952.

Bernstein, Irving. *Turbulent Years: A History of the American Worker, 1933–1941.* Boston: Houghton Mifflin, 1970.

Bird, Caroline. *The Invisible Scar.* New York: David McKay, 1966.

Brody, David. "The Emergence of Mass-Production Unionism" in Braeman, John, Bremner, Robert H., and Walters, Everett, eds. *Change and Continuity in Twentieth-Century America.* Columbus: Ohio State University Press, 1964.

Degler, Carl. *Out of Our Past: The Forces That Shaped Modern America.* New York: Harper & Row, 1970.

Fine, Sidney. *Sit-Down: The General Motors Strike of 1936–1937.* Ann Arbor, Michigan: University of Michigan Press, 1969.

Garraty, John A. *Unemployment in History: Economic Thought and Public Policy.* New York: Harper & Row, 1978.

Goldman, Eric F. *Rendezvous with Destiny: A History of Modern American Reform.* New York: Vintage, 1977.

Graham, Otis L., Jr. *Toward a Planned Society: From Roosevelt to Nixon.* New York: Oxford University Press, 1976.

Hawley, Ellis A. *The New Deal and the Problem of Monopoly: A Study in Economic Ambivalence.* Princeton, N. J.: Princeton University Press, 1966.

Hofstadter, Richard. *The American Political Tradition and the Men Who Made It.* New York: Vintage, 1974.

Janeway, Eliot. *The Struggle for Survival.* New Haven, Conn.: Yale University Press, 1951.

Leuchtenburg, William E. *Franklin D. Roosevelt and the New Deal.* New York: Harper & Row, 1963.

Nelson, Donald. *Arsenal of Democracy: The Story of War Production.* New York: Harcourt Brace Jovanovich, 1946.

Polenberg, Richard. *War and Society.* Philadelphia: Lippincott, 1972.

Terkel, Studs. *Hard Times: An Oral History of the Great Depression.* New York: Pantheon, 1970.

Worster, Donald. *Dust Bowl: The Southern Plains in the 1930s.* New York: Oxford University Press, 1979.

Zinn, Howard, ed. *New Deal Thought.* Indianapolis, Ind. Bobbs-Merrill, 1966.

CHAPTER ELEVEN

Bell, Daniel. *The End of Ideology: On the Exhaustion of Political Ideas in the Fifties.* New York: Collier, 1961.

Clayton, James, ed. *The Economic Impact of the Cold War.* New York: Harcourt Brace & World, 1970.

Clecak, Peter. *Crooked Paths: Reflections on Socialism, Conservatism, and the Welfare State.* New York: Harper & Row, 1977.

Davies, Richard O. *The Age of Asphalt.* Philadelphia: Lippincott, 1975.

Drucker, Peter. *The Concept of the Corporation.* New York: John Day, 1946.

Editors of *Fortune. U.S.A.—The Permanent Revolution.* Englewood Cliffs, N. J.: Prentice-Hall, 1951.

Galbraith, John Kenneth. *The Affluent Society.* Boston: Houghton Mifflin, 1958.

Graham, Otis L., Jr. *Toward a Planned Society.* New York: Oxford University Press, 1976.

Hathaway, Dale E. *Government and Agriculture: Public Policy in a Democratic Society.* New York: Macmillan, 1963.

Hodgson, Godfrey. *America in Our Time.* Garden City, N. Y.: Doubleday, 1976.

Lekachman, Robert. *The Age of Keynes.* New York: Random House, 1966.

Lerner, Max. *America As a Civilization.* New York: Simon & Schuster, 1957.

Potter, David M. *People of Plenty: Economic Abundance and the American Character.* Chicago: University of Chicago Press, 1954.

Riesman, David. *Abundance for What? and Other Essays.* Garden City, N. Y.: Doubleday, 1964.

Rosenberg, Nathan. *Technology and American Economic Growth.* New York: Harper & Row, 1972.

Rostow, W. W. *The World Economy: History and Prospect.* Austin: University of Texas Press, 1978.

Sitkoff, Harvard. "Years of the Locust: Interpretations of the Truman Presidency Since 1965" in Kirkendall, Richard S., ed. *The Truman Period As a Research Field.* Columbia: University of Missouri Press, 1974.

Vatter, Harold G. *The American Economy in the 1950s.* New York: Norton, 1963.

White, Lawrence J. *The Automobile Industry since 1945.* Cambridge, Mass.: Harvard University Press, 1971.

Whyte, William H., Jr. *The Organization Man.* New York: Simon & Schuster, 1956.

CHAPTER TWELVE

Blair, John M. *The Control of Oil.* New York: Pantheon, 1977.

Clecak, Peter. *Crooked Paths: Reflections on Socialism, Conservatism, and the Welfare State.* New York: Harper & Row, 1977.

Economic Report of the President, 1980. Washington, D.C.: U. S. Government Printing Office, 1980.

Eisenhower, Dwight D. "Spending Into Trouble," *Saturday Evening Post,* 236 (May 18, 1963), 15–16.

Harrington, Michael. *The Other America: Poverty in the United States.* New York: Macmillan, 1963.

Leuchtenburg, William E. *A Troubled Feast: American Society Since 1945.* Boston: Little, Brown, 1979.

Melman, Seymour. *Our Depleted Society.* New York: Dell, 1965.

———Pentagon Capitalism: The Political Economy of War. New York: McGraw-Hill, 1970.

——— *The Permanent War Economy.* New York: Simon & Schuster, 1974.

Potter, David M. *People of Plenty: Economic Abundance and the American Character.* Chicago: University of Chicago Press, 1954.

Pursell, Carroll W., Jr. *The Military-Industrial Complex.* New York: Harper & Row, 1972.

Scott, Rachel. *Muscle and Blood.* New York: E. P. Dutton, 1974.

Stevens, Robert Warren. *Vain Hopes, Grim Realities: The Economic Consequences of the Vietnam War.* New York: New Viewpoints, A Division of Franklin Watts, 1976.

Stobaugh, Robert, and Yergin, Daniel, eds. *Energy Future.* New York: Random House, 1979.

Thurow, Lester C. *The Zero-Sum Society: Distribution and the Possibilities for Economic Change.* New York: Basic Books, 1980.

U. S. Department of Education, Health, and Welfare. *Work in America.* Cambridge, Mass.: MIT Press, 1973.

Index

Adams, Henry, 121
Adams, John, 20
Affirmative Action Programs,
247
Agricultural Adjustment Act,
180–181
Agricultural Marketing Act,
158
Agriculture: Civil War, 88–90;
colonial, 2–4, 9–10, 12–15;
environmental concern,
212; farmers' discontent,
102–107; Food Adminis-
tration, 146; New Deal,
180–181, 184; post Civil
War, 72–74; post World
War I, 157–159; post World
War II, 211–213; recent
changes, 245–246; share-
cropping and tenancy,
101–102; regional
specialization, 51–53,
75–76, 88–89, 98–101;
technological change,
42–45, 72–75; value of
exports, 135
Allen, Frederick Lewis, 194
American Federation of Labor,
118–119, 131–134, 162, 189
AFL-CIO, 207–208, 249, 251
Anti-trust: Clayton Act,
143–144; Federal Trade
Commission, 143; Sherman
Act, 120; Theodore

Roosevelt and, 127–128;
Woodrow Wilson and,
143–144
Articles of Confederation,
33–35
Automation, 205–206
Automobile industry: during
the 1950's, 209–211; Henry
Ford, 148–150; post World
War II boom, 199; recent
changes, 240–241; role in
the economy, 134, 136–137,
163–165, 168

Baltimore and Ohio Railroad,
63
Baltimore, Lord, 32
Bank of the United States,
41–42, 66–68
Banking: agrarian opposition,
106; American Revolution,
30–31; Civil War, 91–92;
depression of the 1930's,
170–171; Federal Reserve
Act, 141–142; Andrew
Jackson and, 66–68;
National Banking Act,
91–92; regulation, 141–142,
181–184
Beard, Charles A., economic
interpretation of the
Constitution, 39–41
Bernstein, Irving, 163
Bessemer process, 81–82
Boone, Daniel, 36
Borden, Gail, 87
Brandeis, Louis, 141
Brown, Robert, 39
Bryan, William Jennings, 107

Brzezinski, Zbigniew,
technetronic era, 205–206
Burner, David, 171–172
Business consolidation,
108–109, 134–137,
143–144
Business Round Table,
243–244

Calhoun, John C., on tariffs,
58–59
California, agriculture, 99
Canning industry, 99
Capitalism, colonial, 17
Carnegie, Andrew, 114–115
Carnegie Corporation, 115
Carter, Jimmy: economic
policies, 222, 224–225; on
nuclear energy, 239; on
synthetic fuels, 240
Cattle industry, 99–101
Central Pacific Railroad,
83–84
Chandler, Alfred D., Jr., 79,
134
Civil War and the economy,
87–93
Clayton Anti-trust Act,
142–144, 162
Coal consumption
(1960–1977), 232
Coal industry: concern over
shortages, 96–97; pre Civil
War, 80–81; post Civil War,
114; recent trends, 232–235
Cochran, Thomas C., 92–93
Colonies, English, 7
Colonization, European, 3–5
Commons, John R., 116

Congress of Industrial
    Organization (CIO), 189
Constitution, Charles A.
    Beard's economic
    interpretation, 39–41
Consumer culture, 204–205
Consumer price index
    (1967–1979), 220
Coolidge, Calvin, analysis, 166
Cotton: and the Civil War,
    88–89; gin, 43–45; and
    southern agriculture, 53,
    76; textile industry, 55–56

David, Paul A., 72
Deere, John, 73
Defense spending, post World
    War II, 224–227
Degler, Carl, 19
Depressions: (1819), 65;
    (1857), 88; (1873), 114, 117;
    (1893), 106–107; (1921),
    155; Great Depression,
    167–188
Dubofsky, Melvyn, 151

Economic growth: colonial,
    19; pre Civil War, 71–72;
    pre World War I, 134–135;
    pre World War II, 183–185;
    recent, 213–216, 219; zero,
    251–252
Economic Report of the
    President 1980, 225
Edison, Thomas Alva,
    135–136
Eisenhower, Dwight D.,

economic policies, 204,
    211, 225–226
Energy: coal, 233–235;
    colonial, 10; consumption
    (1940–1960), 208–209,
    (1960–1977), 232; late
    nineteenth century, 96,
    nuclear, 235–239; 120, oil,
    231–233; other sources,
    239–240
Erie Canal, 60–62
Etzioni, Amitai, 251
Evans, Oliver, 42–43

Fair Deal, 200–201
Fair Labor Standards Act, 190
Farmers' Alliance, 105–106
Federal Emergency Relief Act,
    177
Federal Reserve System,
    141–143
Federal Securities Act, 184
Federal spending (1960–1979),
    224–225
Federal Trade Commission,
    143
Federalist economic program,
    40–42
Fogel, Robert W., 77–78
Ford, Gerald R.: economic
    policies, 222; on energy,
    235
Ford, Henry, 135–136,
    148–150
Foreign relations, influence on
    the economy (1783–1815),
    49–50

Franklin, Benjamin, 38
Friedman, Milton, 170
Frontier thesis, 96

Galbraith, John Kenneth, 215, 220
Gates, Paul W., 51
Georgia, colony, 7
Giedion, Siegfried, 43
Gompers, Samuel, 131–134, 151–153
Government: aid to canal development, 60–62; aid to Chrysler Corporation, 243; aid to manufacturing, 42, 57–59; aid to railroad development, 80, 82–83; aid to turnpike development, 62; and banking, 66–68; and business (1920's), 159; and the economy (1865), 119–121, (1945–1960), 200–202, (1960–1980), 219–225; federal budget (1950–1960), 215; finances (1916–1919), 147; land policies, 64–66; regulation, 243–244
Graduation Act, 65
Graham, Otis, 153
Grange, 104
Greenbackers, 104–105
Greenbacks, 91
Great Society, 221

Hacker, Louis M., 92

Hamilton, Alexander: 38, economic program, 40–42; economic views, 45–46, 106
Hammond, Bray, 68
Hammond, James, 88
Harper, Lawrence, A., 28
Harrington, Michael, 228
Hat Act, 21
Haymarket Affair, 118
Heilbroner, Robert, 26, 214
Hilgard, E.W., 72
Hofstadter, Richard, 19, 123–124, 174
Holt, Charles, 164
Homestead Act, 65–66
Hoover, Herbert C.,: 158, response to depression, 160, 169–172
Housing, post World War II, 198–199

Immigration: colonial, 6–8, 11–12; pre Civil War, 85–86; post Civil War, 97, 115–116, 124
Income tax: Civil War, 91; (1920's), 160; and Populism, 106; World War I, 146
Indentured servant system, 11
Industrial Workers of the World (IWW), 151
Inflation: American Revolution, 30–31; Civil War, 91; Post World War I, 148, 150; post World War II, 200; recent, 221–224

Interstate Commerce Act, 119
Iron Acts, 21
Iron industry and railroads,
79, 81

Jamestown, 8
Jefferson, Thomas: economic
views, 45–46; embargo,
49–50; ideology, 46, 97
Johnson, Lyndon B., economic
policies, 221, 229
Joint-stock company, 5

Kansas, agriculture, 99
Kelly, William, 81–82
Kennedy, John F., economic
policies, 219–220, 223, 228
Keynes, John Maynard, 187
Keynesian economics, 187,
201, 219–220
Knights of Labor, 118
Kolko, Gabriel, 129
Korean War, 204

Labor: colonial, 10–12; early
textile industry, 55–56;
early trade unions, 68–69,
84–85; early twentieth
century, 131–134, 151–153;
organized, and the New
Deal, 188–190; organized
(1920's), 161–162; post
Civil War, 117–119; post
World War II, 202, 206–
208; slave, 11–12, 76–78;
unemployment in the Great
Depression, 175–177;
women, 55–56, 246–250
Land Act of 1820, 65

Land grants, railroad, 83
Land Ordinance of 1785, 37
Land policy: American Revo-
lution, 32; (1783–1815),
36–38; (1815–1840), 64–66;
post Civil War, 97
Land reform, American
Revolution, 32
Land speculation, 23, 32,
36–37, 65
Landrum-Griffin Act, 207
Lerner, Max, 204–205
Leuchtenburg, William, 146,
174, 180, 218
Levittown, 198–199
Lowell, Francis Cabot, 55
Lowell system, 55–56

MaCormick, Cyrus Hall,
74–75
McCoy, Donald, 158
McKinley, William, 107
McNary-Haugen Act, 158–159
Management, scientific,
129–130
Manufacturing: agricultural
machinery, 44, 73–75, 98;
colonial, 15–16; (1815–
1840), 53–56; (1840–1865),
74–75, 78, 86–87, 89–90;
(1865–1900), 109–115;
Hamilton and, 42;
(1900–1920), 134–137,
148–150, 152; (1920–1945),
163–164, 178–179, 191;
(1945–1980), 199, 204–206,
209–211, 226; scientific
management in, 129–130

Marketing: post Civil War, 110; Madison Avenue and the consumer culture, 204–205
Marshall, John, 47–49, 67
Marshall Plan, 203
Massachusetts: colonial, 25; Shays' Rebellion, 35
Massachusetts Bay Company, 9
Meat-packing industry, 99–101
Mellon, Andrew, 159–161
Melman, Seymour, 226–227
Mercantilism: economic philosophy, 4, 6; effect upon the American Revolution, 20–23, 28–29; role of colonies, 6–7
Merchant, colonial, 5
Mid Atlantic States, colonial, 13–14
Middle Colonies, agriculture, 13
Miller, J. C., 41
Molasses Act, 21, 23
Money: American Revolution, 30–31; Civil War, 91–92; effect of the Second Bank of the U. S., 66–68; and free silver, 106–107
Moody, John, 127
Morrill Tariff, 89, 92
Mortgages, farm, 102
MX missile, 227

National Association of Manufacturers, 161
National Banking Act, 91–92

National Labor Relations Act (Wagner Act), 189–190
National Labor Union, 117
National Monetary Commission, 141–142
National Recovery Administration, 178–180
National Road, 62
National Trades Union, 69
National War Labor Board, 151
Natural gas consumption (1960–1977), 232
Nettles, Curtis P., 20, 29
New Deal, 173–175, 177–186
New England: colonial agriculture, 13; tariff support, 58; textile manufacturing, 54–56
New Frontier, 217
New York, canals, 60–61
Niemi, Albert W., 93
Nixon, Richard M.: economic policies, 221–223; on energy, 231–232; environmental concern, 250–251
North, Douglass C., 28, 103
Northeast: agriculture, 73–74; industry, 78, 89–90
Northern Securities Company, 127
Northwest Ordinance, 37
Nuclear energy, 235–239

Occupational Safety and Health Administration (OSHA), 248–249
Ocean transportation, 63–64

Office of Economic Opportunity (OEO), 230–231
Ohio: anti-trust, 112; canals, 61–62; public domain, 37
Ohio and Erie Canal, 61–62
Oil: consumption (1960–1977), 232; recent trends, 231–232
OPEC, 231–232
Orwell, George, 176–177

Pacific Railway Act, 83, 92
Penn, William, 32
Pennsylvania: coal, 80–81; milling, 43; turnpikes, 62–63
Phillips, Ulrich B., 76
Plymouth Company, 7
Population: colonial America, 11, 19; early settlements, 8–9; European, 4; and immigration (1820–1859), 85–86, (1865–1914), 116; in 1900, 123–124; (1960–1980), 218: and poverty, 230; urban, 115
Populism, 106
Potter, David M., 95, 250
Prices, consumer index, 150, 230
Proclamation of 1763, 23
Progressive Movement, 124–127, 139–144
Pullman Strike, 151
Pure Food and Drugs Act of 1906, 128

Quit rents, 32

Railroads: and the coal industry, 80; competition with canals, 79; during the Civil War, 87; impact upon agriculture, 97–98; network in 1900, 134; transcontinental, 82–85
Regulation: Interstate Commerce Act, 119; New Deal, 178–184; Progressive Movement, 128–129, 139–144; recent, 243–244
Reindustrialization, 251
Rhodes, James Ford, 118
Rockefeller, John D., 111–114
Roosevelt, Franklin D.: economic philosophy, 174; economic policies, 177–186, 190–191; and Keynesian economics, 187; on poverty, 228; on unemployment, 177; and World War II, 194–195
Roosevelt, Theodore: and the muckrakers, 124; on trusts, 127–128
Rossiter, Clinton, 29
Rostow, W. W., "take-off" thesis, 71–72

Samuelson, Paul A., 27
Securities and Exchange Commission, 184
Share-cropping and tenancy, 101–102
Shays' Rebellion, 35
Sherman Anti-trust Act, 127–128
Silver controversy, 106–107

Slater, Samuel, 54–55
Slavery: colonial, 11;
  profitability, 76–78
Smith, Adam, 26–28
Smith, John, 7–8
Social Security, 185–186
Social welfare, 227–230
Solar energy, 239
South: agriculture, 52–53, 76;
  colonial, 14–15; opposition
  to tariffs, 58
South Carolina, railroads, 63
South Chicago, labor violence,
  189
Stagflation, 218, 221
Stamp Act, 23–24
Standard Oil Company,
  111–113, 126–128
Steel industry: early, 81–82;
  and organized labor,
  152–153; recent, 242–243
Stockmarket (1920's), 165–167
Supreme Court, influence on
  economic issues 47–49, 162
Swift, Gustavus F., meat
  refrigeration, 100–101

Taft, William Howard, 162
Taft-Hartley Act, 202
Tarbell, Ida M., 126
Tariffs: Civil War, 89–90;
  early, 57–59; promoted by
  Hamilton, 42; Progressive
  era, 140–141
Taylor, Frederick W., 129–130
Technology: agricultural,
  72–73, 97–101, 212; and
  American life, 135–137,
  215; American system, 45;

Bessemer process, 81–82;
  energy, 231–240; housing,
  198–199; mechanization,
  42–45, 86–87, 109–110;
  military, 226; technetronic
  era, 205–206; textiles,
  54–56
Tennessee Valley Authority, 178
Texas: cattle industry, 100;
  farmers' alliance, 105–106
Textile industry, 54–56
Three Mile Island, 238
Tocqueville, Alexis de, 56–57
Transportation: canals, 60–62;
  ocean, 63–64, 98; railroads,
  79–80, 82–87, 97–98, 134;
  rivers, 59–60; turnpikes,
  62–63
Truman, Harry S., economic
  policies, 200–202
Turner, Frederick Jackson,
  frontier thesis, 96–97

Underwood-Simmons Tariff,
  140–141
Union Pacific Railroad, 83–84
Union shop, 202
Unions: early trade, 68–69,
  84–85; late nineteenth
  century, 117–119; twentieth
  century, 131–134, 151–153,
  161–162, 189–190, 202,
  206–208
United Mine Workers (UMW),
  162, 189
UNIVAC, 205
Urban development, 122–124
U. S. Steel Corporation,
  114–115, 131, 153

Ver Steeg, Clarence L., 31–32
Vietnam War, 229–230
Virginia Company, 7–8
VISTA, 229

War: American Revolution,
  29–32; of 1812, 48–49;
  Civil, 87–91; First World,
  144–148; Korean, 204;
  Second World, 191–195;
  Vietnam, 229–230
Wealth of Nations, 26–28
West, agricultural expansion,
  75–76

Wheat, 98
White, William Allen,
  129
Whitney, Asa, 82
Whitney, Eli, 43–45
Winthrop, John, 8–9
Women, workers, 55–56,
  246–250
Wool Act, 21
World War I, 144–148
World War II, 191–195

Zero-Sum Society, 251–252
Zinn, Howard, 190